Crete

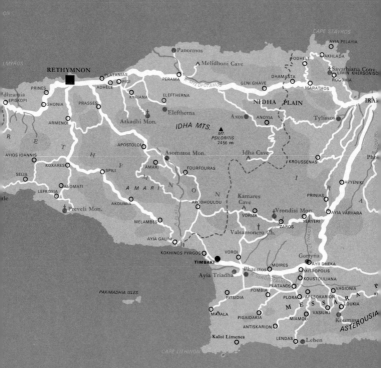

Travelers' Guide

Crete

by John Bowman

with 16 photographs by Herbert Spencer

THE BOBBS-MERRILL COMPANY, INC.
Indianapolis and New York

By the same author:
Robert Louis Stevenson

The Bobbs-Merrill Company, Inc.
A Subsidiary of Howard W. Sams & Co., Inc.
Publishers/Indianapolis Kansas City New York

Text © Copyright Helga Greene 1962
Revised and expanded edition © Copyright Helga Greene 1969
Photographs © Copyright Herbert Spencer 1962, 1969
Maps by Janet Landau
General Editor: Judith Greene

Library of Congress catalog card number 69-20310

Printed in Great Britain

CONTENTS

CONTENTS

MAPS AND CHARTS

Acknowledgments

The author wishes to take this opportunity to acknowledge the many sources and people who inevitably contribute to a book such as this. In particular, I should like to single out Mr Andreas Vlahakis of the Greek National Tourist Organization, Iraklion, Crete. Without his prompting, this guide would never have been begun; without his help, it could never have been completed.

Special thanks are also due to Katy Antonogiannaki, Anestis Makridakis and Eva Mazonaki.

Mount Iouktas seen through the sacred horns that
crown the walls of the Palace of Knossos

This charging bull, one of many frescoes reproduced in their original locations at Knossos, conjures up visions of the Labyrinth and the Minotaur

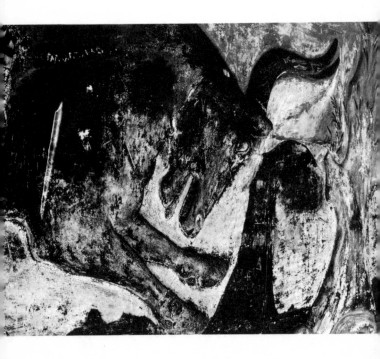

The original stone throne of the Priest-King in the
Throne Room at Knossos

Windmills help to irrigate the coastal plain near Mallia, just above some of the finest beaches on Crete. The climate here is such that even bananas flourish

The remains of the Palace of Phaestos, silhouetted in
the dramatic light of dawn

Central Courtyard, Phaestos, looking across the
Messara Plain with the Idha range in the distance

In the shadow of the near-by mountains, this ceremonial altar has survived at the Palace of Mallia. Seeds or crops were probably consecrated in the hollows, with prayers for continuing fertility

Cretans perform most of their daily activities out of doors; this woman is doing her laundry by the roadside in the village of Potamies

This roadside chapel is typical of the hundreds
scattered over Crete; some hold services only a few
times a year, but they are always open to wayfarers,
and many have fine old frescoes

Cretans have always preferred to express their devotion in modest and non-monumental ways, as is testified by this icon enshrined in a wall near Knossos

Little simulacra crowd the altar in the Chapel of
Ayios Georgios of Selinaris. These modern votive
offerings represent people and parts of the body that
the petitioner wants cured or protected

Giant reeds – both as natural growth and as man-made fences – serve as wind-breakers for the farm plots along the coast near Ierapetra

The forbidding bluffs of Sfakia, dropping sheer to the sea, characterize the rugged, primeval features of Crete's southern regions

Fishermen's boats and nets spread out on the beach near Ierapetra, the largest town on the south coast. Less than two hundred miles from here, across the Libyan Sea, lies Africa

In the harbour of Rethymnon, two fishermen go about their work early in the morning; some Cretans fish off shore at night, using lanterns

The road leading down to the remote village of
Khora Sfakia on the south coast

Chart of Excursions

Centre	Town sights Major	Minor	Major excursions Half day	Full day	Minor excursions Half day	Full day	Overnight excursions
Iraklion (2 days)	Archaeological Museum Harbour, Venetian Castle and Wall Fountain Square Market Cathedral of Ayios Menas	Historical and Ethnographic Museum Basilica of St Mark Church of Ayios Titos Venetian Armoury Liberty Square Church of St Katherine	Knossos (5 km.) p. 140 Mallia (39 km.) p. 241 Tylissos (14 km.) p. 198	Gortyna, Phaestos and Ayia Triadha (65 km.) p. 172 Mallia, Ayios Nikolaos and Gournia (90 km.) pp. 241 & 258 Lasithi Plain and Dhiktaion Cave, (69 km.) p. 161 Arkadhi Monastery and Rethymnon (112 km.) p. 198	Arkhanes, Mount Iouktas and Vathypetro (21 km.) p. 156 Fodhele (34 km.) p. 159 Eileithyia Cave, Amnisos, Nirou Khani and Limin Khersonisou (31 km.) p. 242 Kastelli-Pedhiados (37 km.) p. 166 Melidhoni Cave (60 km.) p. 199	Ano Viannos and Arvi (85 km.) p. 165	Gortyna, Phaestos, Ayia Triadha and Matala (80 km.) p. 188 or Leben (111 km.) p. 190 or Tombs of the Messara (89 km.) p. 193 Rethymnon and Khania (150 km.) pp. 198 & 206 Ierapetra via Ayios Nikolaos (109 km.) pp. 241 & 256 or Ano Viannos (105 km.) p. 165 Kamares for Mt Idha Summit and Caves (57 km.) p. 168
Rethymnon (1 day)	Loggia and Museum Venetian Fort	Arimondi Fountain Churches Minarets	Arkadhi Monastery (22 km.) p. 204	Iraklion and Knossos (83 km.) pp. 198 & 140 Khania (72 km.) p. 206	Preveli Monastery (38 km.) p. 197 Melidhoni Cave (30 km.) p. 199	Fourfouras for Amari Province (43 km.) p. 196 Ayia Galini (64 km.) p. 196 Khora Sfakion (80 km.) p. 207	Phaestos, Ayia Triadha and Gortyna via Iraklion (143 km.) pp. 198 & 172 or Spili (105 km.) p. 195 Anoyia for Mt Idha Summit and Caves (54 km.) p. 168
Khania (2 days)	Archaeological Museum (Church of St Francis) Janissaries' Mosque Church of St Nicholas Church of Ayii Anargyri Minaret Harbour	Historical Museum Inner and Outer Walls Other Venetian buildings and churches Cathedral of Our Lady Arsenals Khalepa Quarter	The Akrotiri including Ayia Triadha Monastery (17 km.) p. 219	Rethymnon and Arkadhi Monastery (94 km.) pp. 206 & 204	Aptera (15 km.) p. 208 Ghonia Monastery (24 km.) p. 237 Theriso (17 km.) p. 222 Mournies (5 km.) p. 222	Khora Sfakion (74 km.) p. 222 Kastelli-Kissamou for North-west Crete (42 km.) p. 236 Palaiokhora for Selinou Province (77 km.) p. 233	Gorge of Samaria (44 km.) p. 228 Rethymnon and Iraklion (150 km.) pp. 206 & 198 Gavdhos Island (by boat from Palaiokhora, 77 km.) p. 235
Ayios Nikolaos (1 day)		Museum 'Bottomless Pool' Almyros	Gournia (19 km.) p. 258 Mallia (33 km.) p. 244 Kritsa and Lato (16 km.) p. 252 Gournia and Ierapetra (38 km.) p. 256	Mallia, Knossos and Iraklion (76 km.) pp. 241 & 140 Gournia and Sitia (74 km.) p. 258 Lasithi Plain and Dhiktaion Cave (48 km.) p. 161	Elounda and Spinalonga (11 km.) p. 254	Psira and Mokhlos Islands (by boat) p. 255	Sitia and Eastern Crete including Kato Zakros (122 km.) pp. 258 & 263 Arvi via Ierapetra (86 km.) p. 256

INTRODUCTION

Mention Crete to most people and they will retort with something such as '... one of those Greek islands ... with the Minoans, isn't it?' Although it is obvious why people should think this, the fact is that Crete is not just another Greek island. Its independent history goes back a very long way – Crete did not even join the Greek nation officially until 1913 – and the islanders often think of themselves as Cretans first and Greeks second. This is nothing to worry about, but the visitor might at least be aware of it. Beyond this, the casual tourist should also be warned that all who have come to know Crete really well – lured though they may have been by the Minoan sites – end by becoming involved with another Crete, an island with many other layers of culture, a realm of nature, a living people.

Moreover, because of the island's intense variety, with its rich archaeological sites, dramatic landscapes and proud traditions, we can understand the self-sufficiency of its inhabitants and their feeling that Crete has everything to offer the visitor. One of the biggest islands in the Mediterranean, it appears still larger, owing to the configuration of mountains and valleys which can make a journey of even a few miles into an exciting expedition – an effect, it must be admitted, sometimes reinforced by the condition of certain minor roads.

Statistics show that most tourists arrive during July, August and September, with another slight rise around April owing to Easter festivities. But, as yet, Crete is never overrun with tourists; Knossos and Iraklion may occasionally give the impression that organized tourism has taken over, but these are only cruise parties ashore for the day. Apart from this, any real traveller can feel pretty much as though he has the island to himself.

This guide is designed for just such a traveller, whether he comes to spend one day or one year on Crete, and is generally organized into three sections: the travel data and practical information necessary for planning a trip; essays on the background of the island; and the actual sights and itineraries, fanning out from the main centres. To help each visitor in planning his own holiday, we

B

have included the Chart of Excursions facing p. 29, showing the various major and secondary sights that can be visited from each of the main centres. All the principal archaeological sites, incidentally, are accessible throughout the year, though some of the caves, mountain peaks or remote villages and chapels might be cut off by winter storms.

The natural centre for visiting the major archaeological sites – Knossos, Gortyna, Phaestos, Mallia and Gournia – is Iraklion, the commercial hub of the island and also the home of the world's greatest collection of Minoan art. While Iraklion is a pleasant, bustling town with varied facilities and popular beaches, it does not have the nostalgic elegance of the Venetian and Turkish remains of the former administrative capital, Khania. This town, which can also be reached directly by ship or air from the mainland, provides a good base for visiting some of the wilder and lesser-known parts of Crete – Sfakia Province and the Gorge of Samaria in the south, and the extreme western regions. At the other end of the island, lazing on the beaches of the attractive little towns of Ayios Nikolaos or Sitia can be combined with visiting such sites as Gournia or the recently excavated palace at Kato Zakros. And Rethymnon – on the north coast, halfway between Iraklion and Khania – offers its own attractions, from historical buildings to a sandy beach.

Apart from the trip across the island to Phaestos and the interesting sights of the Messara Plain, the whole interior provides endless inducements to explore: spectacular mountains to be climbed or just looked at, according to your inclination, ancient myth-haunted caves, isolated monasteries and villages where the life of the people has changed little over the centuries. Visitors with more time will have the opportunity of discovering lesser-known sites and fragmentary ruins as well as remote villages and deserted beaches in every corner of the island.

A final word about discovering Crete. On the one hand, Crete appears to yield easily to the curiosity of the foreigner; the people seem open and spontaneous and their hospitality encourages everyone to feel that he has broken through the surface. But Crete has hidden depths. It has not turned itself into a tourist-centred society, and there are many things about it which provoke strong reactions. Life on Crete is still hard for many and can appear unrefined, to say the least. But it is a rich, unique, intense way of life, and the longer a person stays the more this comes to be appreciated.

For the discerning even the shortest visit to Crete cannot fail to be a stimulating and rewarding adventure.

Note on Pronunciation

Although there are a number of dialect differences between the Greek spoken on Crete and on the mainland (see p. 104), the main challenge to foreigners who attempt to use Greek is to place the stress on the right syllable. Native Greek speakers must hear the correct stress before they recognize the word. To help with this, the Index lists all Greek names and words with an acute accent to mark the stress.

GETTING TO CRETE

AIR

The only scheduled commercial flights to Crete are from Athens and Rhodes, the former being served by most of the major international airlines. Internal air traffic in Greece is a monopoly of Olympic Airways, which has an excellent safety record. For flights within Greece, travellers are limited to 34 pounds of luggage free of charge.

Flights from Athens Airport connect with Iraklion or Khania. There are two to three flights daily in each direction between Athens and Iraklion, with a flight time of 55 minutes. Between Athens and Khania there are one to two flights daily in each direction, with a flight time of 50 minutes.

Between Rhodes and Iraklion there is an air service from April to October with four flights weekly in each direction. The flight time is 60 minutes.

SEA

Some of the shipping lines that run regular car ferries to Greece during the spring, summer and autumn months from Italian and Yugoslav ports call in at Iraklion on the way to or back from Rhodes, Cyprus and Israel, and occasionally other Eastern Mediterranean ports. If you wish to travel from any of these ports direct to Crete inquire about the schedules of the following shipping lines:

Epirotiki Lines, 91 Regent Street, London w1; 608 Fifth Avenue, New York.

Kavounides Shipping Co. Ltd, 23 Haymarket, London sw1; U.S. agent: Cruise and Coach Corporation, 680 Fifth Avenue, Suite 1801, New York.

Adriatica Steamship Line, 35 St James's Street, London sw1; U.S. agent: Italian Line, One Whitehall Street, New York.

Alternatively, there are services from various Mediterranean ports to Piraeus, the port of Athens, run by these and several other shipping lines. From Piraeus there are regular car ferries to Iraklion and Khania run by the Efthymiadis Lines, Akti Kondyli 10, Piraeus, Greece (London agent: Mann & Son Ltd, 67 Grosvenor Street, London w1). There are normally daily sailings to Iraklion and five to six sailings a week to Khania (port at Soudha). The voyage to both ports takes about twelve hours from Piraeus, either overnight or during the daytime on different days of the week. The cost of first class and tourist class cabins from Piraeus to Crete is about £4 5s. ($10.30) and £2 5s. ($5.20) respectively. Deck class, which means that you will spend the night stretched out alone on a wooden bench or else packed in with a large and varied crowd, costs around £1 5s. ($3). Because of higher harbour expenses the fares for the Crete to Piraeus direction are approximately 10 per cent higher. There are reductions for return tickets, for children, and for some special categories such as clergymen, diplomats, statesmen and professors. Cars cost about £10 ($20–25) for the round trip.

There are also special cruise ships which start both from Piraeus and from Italian and other ports, some of which include Crete in their itineraries. Such ships usually make a very limited stay at Crete and will take on only those who intend to remain with the ship for the complete cruise. In addition to the several tourist agencies which specialize in Hellenic cruises, the following are some lines which in summer provide short cruises from Piraeus and sometimes call in – usually for one day – at Crete:

Chandris Cruises Ltd, 70/71 New Bond Street, London w1; 666 Fifth Avenue, New York.
Kavounides Shipping Co. Ltd (for addresses see opposite).
Holland America Line, 120 Pall Mall, London sw1; Pier 40, North River, New York.
Epirotiki Lines (for addresses see opposite).

Finally, in addition to the above, there are freighters leaving various foreign ports, but these put in at Crete only if they have cargo to discharge or load. The average traveller, therefore, will have little opportunity of reaching Crete by this means. Inquiries could however be made to a travel agent or the appropriate shipping line, taking particular care to verify that the ship will definitely stop at Crete. Such lines include the Swedish S.O.L., the Deutsche-Orient Linie, the Argo Nah-Ost Linie, the Atlas-Levante Linie, Hellenic Lines and the K.N.S.M. Company.

Connections between Crete and other Greek islands

There are a few connections between Crete and other Greek islands, but it must be stressed that schedules may vary from year to year. Even the companies operating the services may change from one year to another. So anyone wanting to take advantage of such connections should wait until he is on the spot – in Athens-Piraeus or on Crete – and learn the exact details from the National Tourist Information offices, the major travel bureaus, or from the harbour-masters. What we give below are the possibilities as they have been in recent years and as they have been planned for the immediate future.

(*a*) There has been one ship that leaves Piraeus (on Monday), sails down along the Peloponnese and puts into such ports as Monemvassia and Neapolis, goes on to the island of Antikithera and then to Khania in Crete. It makes the return trip from Khania, stopping at the same ports, and since the boat takes cars, this offers a fine alternative to combine Crete with a drive through some lesser-known parts of the mainland.

(*b*) There is one ship a week that sails directly from Iraklion to Rhodes: this has been the *Aikaterini*, leaving Iraklion on Sunday at 4 p.m. You must check when on the scene to see if the particular ship can handle your vehicle.

(*c*) There is one ship which makes one sailing each week, in each direction, connecting Crete with Théra (the unique volcanic island, also known as Santorini, due north of Crete) and with Rhodes. En route to and from Rhodes, it also puts in at the three small islands between – Kassos, Karpathos and Khalki. This ship does not call at Iraklion, however; its Cretan ports are Ayios Nikolaos and Sitia, farther to the east along the northern coast. Because of the often uncertain and early departure times from these ports, an overnight stay at one or the other is usually necessary. Again, you cannot count on a particular vessel's being able to handle your car until you are in Greece and Crete and know the exact details.

Since the schedule can vary considerably from season to season – and even from week to week – there is no use giving exact times here. This ship, though, is one that originates at Piraeus, so upon returning to Théra from Crete it goes on back to Piraeus.

Aside from these connections, there are no scheduled links between Crete and other islands, so it is necessary to return to Piraeus, where there are many ships that ply between there and the other islands. However, the adventurous traveller with a little time to spare might eventually find one of the smaller freight or fishing vessels to take him direct to one or other of the islands. These are the boats widely known as *caiques*. It is safe to assume that the *caique* will not set out unless it is going to have a comparatively smooth crossing; no one has more respect for the winds and seas than the native sailor. Fares are somewhat elastic. If it is left entirely to you to decide what the trip is worth, much will depend on how you encountered the crew and your relations with the men on the trip; it may be that you can only pay your debt in wine. On the other hand, you must consider the money and time you are saving by not going via Piraeus.

RAIL

There are, of course, regular international trains to cities such as Athens, Venice or Brindisi, from which you can make air or ship connections with Crete.

ROAD

Many people ferry their cars to Greece from ports such as Brindisi or Venice; and, as described on p. 32, it is possible to ferry a car direct to Crete from other ports besides Piraeus. But more and more tourists are now making the drive overland to Greece and Athens – usually through Yugoslavia. It is a long journey, but the roads are now quite good except for a few stretches. From Piraeus you can then ferry your car over to Crete by the services described on p. 33.

CAR DOCUMENTS

Anyone planning to drive a car to and in Greece is advised to check first with his local automobile association. The following documents are required for taking a car into Greece:

(1) International Driving Licence. If you have come to Greece without this you may obtain one upon presentation of your national driving licence at the Greek Automobile Club,

6 Amerikis Street, Athens. Your passport, two extra passport photos and Drs 100 will be required.

(2) The log book (or registration) of your car.

(3) The green international insurance card issued by your own insurance company.

Upon arrival at the Greek border the Customs officials will allow your vehicle free entry for four months. (This could be extended for another eight months upon application to the Finance Ministry in Athens.) At the same time, an entry will be made in your passport listing various data about your vehicle.

The same regulations governing entry of vehicles into Greece extend to Crete, so that once you are in the country you can bring your car over to Crete without any further documents. However, you will most likely be asked to produce your papers and passport as you disembark on Crete, just to make sure that all is in order. If you have come direct from some foreign port, then you must go through all the formalities at the Cretan port of entry.

PASSPORT AND CUSTOMS

Since Crete is part of the Greek State, there are no special arrangements required for entering Crete other than those required for Greece. A valid passport, in fact, is enough. If you come over to Crete from the mainland, there is not even any question of producing this. For travellers coming to Crete direct from a foreign country there will be the usual passport control and Customs formalities.

While you may take in any sum of money in travellers' cheques and foreign currency, you are only allowed to bring in Drs 200 of Greek money. Only 200 cigarettes (or 50 cigars or 200 grams of tobacco) are admitted free. Cameras, typewriters, field-glasses and similar equipment are supposed to be entered on your passport, and shown on leaving.

As for export restrictions, technically only Drs 200 may be taken out of Greece. There is also a limit on how much olive oil an individual is allowed to take out duty-free. Finally, taking out ancient works of art (these are defined as anything dated before 1830) is prohibited unless you have been given a proper certificate with your purchase.

Anyone planning to stay for an extended period or intending to bring in a lot of special equipment would do well to check first with the nearest Greek Consulate. And when it comes to getting unusual amounts of luggage to Crete, one of the large international freight agencies – such as American Express or Schenker & Co. – can save an individual a great deal of time and temper.

If your stay in Greece and/or Crete is to be of any duration (i.e. for British subjects over three months; for Americans over two months) you must apply for a renewal or extension of your passport privilege at the Department for Foreigners of the Ministry of Internal Affairs (head office at 9 Chalkokondeli Street in Athens; central office on Crete in 25th August Street, down by the harbour of Iraklion).

Foreigners whose stay in Greece has been one year or more must obtain a tax-clearance certificate from the Finance Ministry before they will be allowed to leave. For further information consult the Tourist Organization or Police on Crete. (Indeed, anyone who stays for long in Greece soon learns to save all papers, documents, receipts, forms, seals and scraps of paper picked up along the way. It is astonishing how often these can be required.)

REDUCTIONS AND DISCOUNTS

Certain discounts are available to special classes of visitors to Greece – particularly students, teachers, artists and journalists. Almost all of these, however, apply only to the cost of getting to and from Greece (p. 33) and foreign ports; none apply to transport on Crete itself. Anyone who thinks that he might qualify for a discount should inquire at a travel agent, Greek Consulate or the National Tourist Organization.

There is one pass available to the above-mentioned groups of tourists which is valid on Crete: the one that entitles the holder to free access to the various archaeological sites and museums of Greece. This pass may be obtained upon personal application at the National Archaeological Museum in Athens. Identification of your status is required – either from your passport or some official letter. (You will also need two extra passport photos.)

TRAVEL ON CRETE

SEA

Yachting

Yachting is probably the ideal way to get round Crete. There are small but safe harbours all round the island, and in certain places, such as Iraklion, Khania, Rethymnon, Ayios Nikolaos and Sitia, there are adequate facilities for emergencies and repairs. By putting into various harbours you would have access to every site on the island; no place would be much more than 20 miles from the sea. Sailors should remember, though, that the sea off the north coast can be quite rough, especially during August.

It is possible to rent motor yachts and sailing yachts, with or without crews, in Piraeus, and arrangements can be made through the travel agencies. There is considerable range in accommodation, but when the cost has been divided among a party of six to twelve adults it is less heavy than one might expect. With a cook aboard, doing one's own food-buying and no hotel bills, it might even become a fairly cheap way for a group of friends to get about.

For further information, write to the Yachting Department of the National Tourist Organization, 4 Stadiou Street, Athens.

Caiques

A *caique* is the type of boat used in the local coastal and island traffic. They vary in size from yacht-style boats to plain little fishing boats. All have motors. *Caiques* may vary in comforts and conveniences, but all are perfectly reliable for what they set out to do.

There are two ways of hiring *caiques*. One is to make arrangements through the travel agents on the mainland or on Crete itself. Naturally, the *caiques* they deal with tend to be more elegant than the ones you might pick up for yourself in some little fishing cove.

The second way arises when you find yourself on the coast – whether in a town like Iraklion or in some nameless village-harbour – and you want to get somewhere farther along. You approach the men on the *caique* and ask when they will be moving on; if it is at a convenient time for you, you can perhaps come to terms. In most cases there is no fixed rate, but by consulting the map you may get an idea of what you might have to pay. Much would depend on whether the men were going to make the trip anyway as part of their work. If you have to hire them to make the trip specially for you, you would naturally have to pay more. If you fall into company with a fisherman in some café and he says, 'Come on – let's go!' you can expect to get to your destination for a bottle of wine or two. Assuming that you hire a *caique* for a special excursion to a point some two or three hours' sailing along the coast, you can expect to pay about Drs 300 for the return trip and a short wait while you explore the site. At Ayios Nikolaos there are boats that are available for trips to various sites in that area (pp. 254–6).

BUS

Many people will depend on buses to get round the island. And in spite of the rickety appearance of some of them, they always get to their destinations. There are scheduled connections with practically every village and site on the island, usually departing from the capitals of the four nomes: Iraklion, Khania, Rethymnon and Ayios Nikolaos. Only a very few out-of-the-way places involve any change or wait at a junction, although the independent tourist who is trying to see the most in a limited time might choose to make some connections at various points in order to combine excursions.

The main towns and sites are served by more than one bus a day, but there is usually only one bus a day between the main towns and the smaller villages and sites. Moreover, the time-tables between main towns and smaller villages have been set up for the convenience of the villagers who come into the town early in the morning and go home late in the afternoon – exactly the reverse of most tourists' excursions. By careful planning, combining excursions and possibly a little walking, this difficulty can be overcome.

The island's bus lines operate throughout the year, with the possible withdrawal of an occasional bus to some isolated area. Winter and summer schedules are slightly different. The summer season is from April 15th to October 15th, but very few routes and villages are seriously affected by winter changes.

Buses usually leave from the central squares of the towns and villages. The bus stations in the major towns have been indicated under their respective sections. Tickets are bought at the time and point of departure. Be sure to get there well on time, though. Not only are the buses crowded, but as soon as a bus is filled the driver might decide to depart.

Incidentally, when flagging a bus down on the road, get right out there and wave. Don't assume that the bus will stop because you are at a bus stop.

TOURIST COACHES AND GUIDES

The private tourist agencies operate various kinds of tours, using buses or other vehicles; the fees and schedules vary, depending on how many people are involved. English-speaking guides are included, and such tours have certain advantages for some people. Ask the National Tourist Office to recommend you one. Of particular interest is the weekly tour arranged by the Creta Travel Bureau to a typical village for local music, dancing, wine and snacks.

Large parties, incidentally, could make their own arrangements and hire buses from the transport companies; Greeks call a heavy, modern touring bus a 'pullman'. Private guides – speaking the foreign language desired – are available at the convenience of individuals or small parties. The National Tourist Organization and the private agencies can contact such guides. Prices depend on a number of factors, but typical might be Drs 125 for up to four people for a 2-hour tour of the Iraklion Archaeological Museum or of Knossos; or Drs 250–300 for a full-day excursion to Phaestos (and related sites) or to Mallia and Gournia.

TAXIS

In certain situations hiring a taxi is the best way to get to some place. It is not as extravagant as it may sound; nor will it mark you as a 'rich tourist'. Greeks use taxis at the drop of a hat, and think nothing of it when three or four people decide to share one and avoid the crowded buses. In the large towns it is easy to hire a cab, and even comparatively small villages support at least one cab. Foreigners sometimes cannot understand how an isolated village can support some mammoth American vehicle, but in places where no private individual owns a car it is a necessity to have some means of transport.

As some excursions take longer than one would wish, owing to the fact that bus schedules are arranged for the villagers and not for tourists, an excursion which might take three days to make by depending on buses could be done in one day if you had a taxi at your disposal. When three or four people share expenses the cost can be quite reasonable. In addition there are valuable 'fringe benefits' – such as the taxi-driver knowing many people and cafés and sites en route.

Official rates are given below, but, to avoid misunderstanding, any major trip should be discussed with the particular driver before setting out. This is where the Tourist Information Office or the Tourist Police make their usefulness felt.

The normal charge is Drs 3.20 per km. for the first 5 km. After that the charge is Drs 5.80 per km. Naturally there is also a charge for the driver's waiting-time at sites. These rates are for taxis taking five to six passengers; there should be no extra charge for reasonable amounts of baggage, nor does the rate fluctuate with the number of people.

CAR HIRE

In Iraklion and Khania and at their airports it is possible to hire a car to drive yourself. This can be arranged through the National Tourist Organization or the private travel agencies in these towns; during the busy tourist season it might be best to make arrangements before arriving on Crete. Most of the cars available are recent European models.

Car-hire rates fluctuate, but are usually worked out on a basis of about Drs 250–400 per day plus an additional charge per km. Petrol is not included, full insurance protection is extra and a refundable deposit is usually required – as much as Drs 1,500 or more. Special rates are available for long periods. British readers will want to ensure that the V form is accepted.

MOTORING

Each year more and more visitors from abroad are discovering the pleasure that can be had from touring Crete by car. It is expensive, of course, to bring a car over to Crete, or to hire one, but in the end it may repay you. If you have only three to five days, it probably will not be worth bringing a car over. But anyone planning to spend a week or more, with a family or party of friends, may discover that it is a most reasonable proposition. Certainly your own car will allow you to see places and things that could not be managed in a limited time with other forms of transport.

Petrol and oil are available all over the island – including several of the better-grade American and European brands. There are plenty of filling stations, but it is well to keep as full a tank as possible, especially in the remoter districts. Petrol is sold by the imperial gallon and costs from Drs 25 to Drs 28, depending on the grade.

In the smaller villages filling stations offer little except petrol and oil, but there are plenty of repair shops in the larger villages and towns. You will not get the *most* expert service and repair work in the world, but the men are certainly experienced with European and American cars.

Crete has its share of bad roads – but also its share of good ones. From Khania in the west to Sitia in the east the main coast road is entirely asphalt; there is a new asphalt road from Iraklion to Phaestos; and there are several other stretches of asphalt around the island – some of them in the most unexpected places. In fact, over the last few years there has been a great deal of road-building; this means both that many roads may be vastly improved and also that you may be held up by extensive road works. After these 'first-class' roads come the good 'secondary' hard-packed dirt roads; they can get a bit dusty during the dry season and a bit slippery in the rainy season, but by and large they are good solid roads. Here and there is a washboard stretch, now and again a patch under repair – but you get along. And finally there are one or two stretches to sites described in this book which, frankly, are very bad roads. Yet with a little patience you can get there. The heavy low-slung American car is apt to be at a disadvantage on these stretches, but most of the taxis on Crete are just such vehicles and their drivers are able to penetrate into the most isolated spots. The author of this book, moreover, can speak from experience. In the course of four months' excursions to some very isolated sites, he never ran across a road that couldn't be taken. It is largely a matter of being willing to crawl. Considering Crete's situation – geographically, historically, economically – the island has better roads than one has a right to expect.

Driving is on the right. Roads are not as well marked as one might like them to be. Curves, bad gradients, soft shoulders, hazardous conditions – you cannot count on signs for any of these.

Nor will crucial turnings always be marked; you will have been directed to go straight ahead to the site you want, and two seconds later there will be a fork – one road as good as the other, and with no sign to indicate which leads to your destination.

As for asking directions, care is needed. The average villager can only estimate distances or times, and usually his estimate is based on the way he knows best: a donkey trail, overland. Your destination is always 'straight ahead'; it is assumed that you know about those forks and turnings. Roads are either 'very good' or 'very bad' – and the native's criteria may not be yours.

Finally, Greek drivers seldom use light or hand signals. They often ignore through traffic, and will turn on to the main road from some little by-road just when you are convinced that you have the right of way. The right of way in Greece, in fact, goes to the fastest and first – except for pedestrians. Pedestrians still have the right of way in Greece, and no matter how frivolous their actions you must make it your business to avoid them if you are behind a wheel. At night oncoming vehicles will blink their lights on and off. During the day the driver of the car in front of you will suddenly halt to chat with a friend at the roadside. Driving through a town's main street is like taking part in an old Keystone comedy – but, somehow, everyone survives.

MAPS

There are various maps of Crete available, with more or less detail, and more or less accuracy. One of the best of the larger-scale maps is that produced by Mathioulakis Publications. It can be found in shops in Athens and Crete, and has the great advantage of being in English and using the Roman alphabet.

MULES AND DONKEYS

For the really determined traveller there is still the mule or donkey. One school of travellers claims that the only legitimate way to arrive in Mediterranean villages is over the trails with a donkey. Quite seriously, if one wants to do much travelling among the mountains, it is a most practical means of getting about. The Tourist Police would help with arrangements for this in almost any village. If it were only the donkey you wanted to hire, you could get one for Drs 100 a day, and if you wanted a man to come along as well it would cost about twice as much. Even these prices could be substantially reduced through clever bargaining. It is even possible to buy a donkey fairly cheaply – Drs 800–1,500, depending on the staying-power of the beast and your own powers of bargaining. With any luck you might sell the animal back for just about what you had paid for it, which would mean you had had free transport – of a sort.

The word for donkey is *zóo* which means 'animal', and to Cretans the donkey is *the* animal.

HOTELS AND RESTAURANTS

Taking the island as a whole, travellers on Crete have a fairly wide choice of accommodation when it comes to sleeping and eating. Outside the principal towns, of course, there is little or no choice in any particular place. However, all accommodation is regulated and inspected by the National Tourist Organization and Tourist Police (as throughout Greece) and standards are maintained in respect of prices and facilities. Incidentally, if one hotel is full, the receptionist or proprietor will usually help you to find a room in another hotel in the neighbourhood.

HOTELS

There are five main classes of hotels. Clean linen and safe water are provided in all, but other conveniences may vary. Categories are assigned on the basis of such things as whether there are a reception hall, telephones, hot running water, etc., not all of which concern all tourists. It might be pointed out that the only first-class accommodation on Crete is to be found at the Minos Beach Hotel at Ayios Nikolaos; the Class A hotels in and near Iraklion; and, to a lesser extent, the Xenia Hotels (officially classed as B). B and C hotels are good, though; Class D and E can be spartan. The official hotel list, which is obtainable from National Tourist Offices, gives only the A, B, C, and a few D, hotels. The word for hotel, by the way, is *xenodokhio*.

The following average prices have been given per room as this is the way Cretan hotels operate, whether it is a luxury single room with a bath or a four-bedded room in a Class E hotel.

AVERAGE PRICES (DRS)

	Single room		Double room		Full board	
Category	With bath	Without bath	With bath	Without bath	Single	Double
Class A	200	120	300	210	300–525	500–700
Class B	120	80	170	120	200–300	320–470
Class C	90	65	120	95	190	300
Class D	—	45	—	65	—	—
Class E	—	40	—	60	—	—

These prices are subject to change, obviously, and vary from town to town, but they indicate relative costs. Since there are often little misunderstandings arising from this very matter of hotel bills, we single out several points:

(a) Certain hotels – because they are newly built or have made extensive alterations – may make a surcharge beyond the usual rate for the class.

(b) Service charges (up to 15 per cent in the better hotels) and Municipal Taxes are included in these prices. Tipping is at the discretion of the individual (see note on p. 56).

(c) Tourists taking rooms without private baths or showers can usually make arrangements for these: the usual rates are about Drs 12 for a bath and Drs 7 for a shower.

(d) Heating is not included in the prices quoted: the charge is about Drs 10 for a single room, Drs 15 for a double room, per day.

(e) If your hotel does not have a restaurant, and most of the cheaper ones do not, you can usually send out for breakfast. It will consist of Turkish coffee (unless you specify Nescafé or 'American') and some sort of bread with jam or honey; and will cost about Drs 10–15.

(f) Several hotels on Crete offer lower 'off-season' rates during the months from November to February.

Two of the most attractive hotels on Crete offer *pension* terms. One is the Minos Beach Hotel, at Ayios Nikolaos, which in the few years since it has been established has become a popular spot for a very international set. In addition to the beach and recreation facilities such as boating and water-skiing, it provides individual cottages – built and furnished in the Greek island style – each with its own terrace, shower or bath, and a sense of privacy. Bed and full board for one is about Drs 525 per day; for two it is about Drs 700. (This works out at about £4–5 per person, which is very reasonable for what you get.)

And at the beach of Mallia there is the Pension Grammatikakis – not as elegant as the Minos Beach Hotel, but no less a favourite with those who have frequented it. It offers bed and full board at about Drs 210 for one, and Drs 325 for two.

In recent years there has been a great deal of hotel development, and several bungalow-type hotels have been established to exploit the fine beaches along the north coast to the east and west of Iraklion (see list of hotels under Iraklion). There is also the Aptera Beach outside Khania; and a bungalow development is being built outside Ierapetra (on the south coast). The advantages of these hotels are obvious: although convenient for the towns and sites, they have fine swimming, facilities for excursions and boating, and are located in quiet situations. Generally terms are either half or full board.

BOARDING HOUSES

In Iraklion, and to a lesser extent Khania, there are several pensions and private homes where you can stay for about Drs 30–40 for a single room and Drs 50–60 for a double room; arrangements can also be made to take meals for about Drs 30–35 per day. The office of the National Tourist Organization will assist in locating such people.

TOURIST PAVILIONS

Strategically located at various tourist attractions throughout Crete are the Tourist Pavilions, erected by the National Tourist Organization and the local authorities. Most travellers use them only for welcome refreshment during a day's excursion, but some of them provide overnight accommodation during the summer season for about Drs 30–50. The one at Phaestos is especially well known, and is the only one to take overnight guests throughout the year. Those now in at least limited operation include the ones at Phaestos,

Matala, Psykhro (near the Dhiktaian Cave), Khora Sfakion, Xyloskalon (at the top of the Gorge of Samaria) and Arkadhi Monastery.

VILLAGE ACCOMMODATION

In some villages there are modest little inns. Beds cost from about Drs 20 to Drs 25 per night and, although little else is provided, these places are perfectly reliable.

And even in the more isolated villages, where there are no commercial inns, you can always be sure of finding a bed for the night in someone's home. The local Tourist Policeman will usually see to this for you. If he isn't around ask for the *próedros* – the president of the local community. And if *he* isn't available, almost anyone in the local café will be willing to help you. Once you have begun to seek lodging, you had best resign yourself to accepting hospitality. If people seem to be giving up their own beds, if they obviously bring out the best family linen, if they insist on putting themselves out in many little ways – accept it all graciously; they do it because they want to.

What you pay – and whether you pay – for such accommodation depends largely on the circumstances under which you approached the particular village. If you have simply walked out of nowhere, sought a bed for one night, and intend to pass on the next morning, then Drs 15–20 will probably be expected. If you have been spending some time in the neighbourhood, have come to know some of the villagers and are all but invited to spend a night or so, then you will probably 'feel' whether your host is going to be insulted when you try to force money on him. One way round such situations is to indicate that it is 'for the children' – not just payment for goods received. The more time you happen to pass with a village and its people, the more you are likely to be indebted to their hospitality in ways that you cannot repay with money.

MONASTERIES

There remains one other possibility for overnight shelter: the monasteries. In certain isolated places they may be the only convenient shelter – and certainly the most interesting. They are often quite comfortable, and sometimes meals are provided. There is no rule against women being received as guests.

Overnight lodging and a meal for the wayfarer are traditionally provided free by monasteries. But as the Cretan monasteries are poor and struggling, it is equally traditional to leave some payment. As with Greek hospitality in general, much depends on the circumstances. If you arrive and simply use a bed, then you should offer to pay or at least leave some offering in the chapel. If you have received some special services from the abbot in charge or one of the monks, then offer some gratuity directly to him; if he refuses, there is nothing you can do.

YOUTH HOSTELS

At present there are youth hostels in Iraklion, Khania and Ayios Nikolaos. Prices are around Drs 15 for a bed; showers, use of kitchen and meals are extra. Normally you have to be able to produce a Youth Hostels Association membership card if you want to stay in one of these hostels; you can obtain membership of the Greek Youth Hostels Association for Drs 65 (Drs 210 for Americans) from their headquarters at 4 Dragatsaniou Street, Klafthmonos Square, Athens.

CAMPING

There are at present only two official camping sites in Crete: one about $2\frac{1}{2}$ km. east of Rethymnon and the other 3 km. east of Khania (for details see under those towns). However, more and more people each year are camping at various places around Crete.

The first thing to do upon arriving is to go to the nearest office of the Tourist Police or the Tourist Organization, describe what you have in mind and get information about possible locations and restrictions. This is best done in person, on Crete itself; if you write in advance you may get a letter full of misleading information owing to their having a totally different conception of your needs. You will find, in general, that you will be given complete co-operation by the local authorities and inhabitants. The former may forbid you to set up your tent in the middle of some historic site, and the latter may not want you camping in their olive groves, but you will certainly find a location. There is an almost limitless choice of scenic spots – whether on the coasts, in the mountains or along the roadside. The basic problem is to avoid intruding on someone's private property.

Water could become a problem, but springs are never very far away. Check with the local people; failing anything else, you can make arrangements with one of the village boys to haul you a couple of buckets per day – in fact they will probably insist on this. Fruit and vegetables in season will be easily come by from local farmers, and other provisions can be obtained in near-by villages. The larger towns and villages will have equipment such as lanterns and cooking-stoves and rope.

RESTAURANTS AND CAFÉS

If there is one thing that Greece and Crete have an abundance of it is eating and refreshment places and most of them are open seven days a week. The quality and atmosphere may vary, but no one need ever go hungry or thirsty; even the meanest village will have a café or two where some sort of meal can be scraped together. Incidentally, 'café' is literally *kapheneíon*, but in the villages it may be called *magazí* – 'the shop'.

In the larger towns restaurants are classed 'A', 'B', 'C', etc., depending on the extent of the menu, the facilities, the atmosphere, and so on. However, although there is a wide gap between the best and the worst, the majority conform to a general pattern. Some may have white tablecloths, some will have bare wooden boards; some offer a large choice of foods, some can offer only what they have on the stove at the moment. The foreigner will be well received in all and should try as wide a range as possible.

A more detailed discussion of the Greek menu and Cretan specialities follows on p. 112. It is customary in Greek restaurants to go into the kitchen – or over to the cooking area – to see what is on the stove. Besides ensuring that you get what you want, it saves a struggle with the menu. Simply point to what interests you, try to find out what it is and indicate whether or not you want it. And if you don't like what is brought to your place, don't hesitate to express your disapproval; Greeks send food back for all sorts of reasons.

In addition to the restaurants, there is a class of eating-place known as a *taverna*. Although these cannot offer a choice of menu comparable with real restaurants, they can produce all kinds of interesting meals – cooked to your personal taste. Almost every little café, too, can offer something to eat: hard-boiled eggs, bits of meat, cheese, olives, bread, vegetables and fruits in season. Even when drinking, it is customary to munch something: a bit of cheese, fresh artichoke leaves, tomato slices; these are known as *mezés*, or *mezedákis*. Similar hors d'œuvres served before meals are called *orektiká*.

Prices vary, but not greatly. It is quite usual to spend less than Drs 35 in moderate to better places; beer or wine would add a few drachmas more. Service is usually included in the bill: 10 per cent, or 15 per cent in some of the more stylish places. (For tipping see p. 56.)

NIGHTLIFE

Particular facilities for nightlife will be indicated under each centre, but a few general remarks might be made about the possibilities. Essentially, outside the few bigger towns – where, to be sure, most visitors will be at night – tourists will have to make their own nightlife and it will be of the informal, impromptu variety: late meals, lingering drinks, moonlight strolls. Only Iraklion, Khania and Rethymnon have organized night-clubs, and even these are largely limited to music and dancing. There are cinemas in the larger towns, where mostly foreign films are shown; these are in the original language, with Greek subtitles. If you are lucky, you may just run into the odd folk-dance performance or folk-music concert. What it comes down to, then, is dancing, from a stylish nightspot in Iraklion to a roadside *taverna*, from a foxtrot to a folk-dance, from watching to joining in. As for girls, anyone who needs a guidebook to find them is wasting his time.

PRACTICAL INFORMATION

CLIMATE

Crete has one of the most favourable climates of the Mediterranean, with mild to hot weather prevailing for most of the year. Tomatoes, and swallows, flourish all the year round in a few places. In general, you can count on almost three hundred days of sunny, clear skies each year, with moderate temperatures. For those who have the whole year to choose from, May or September is recommended as the ideal time to travel on Crete.

Spring moves in during April, and the rains usually stop by the end of the month; quite literally, barely a drop of rain falls during May, June, July, August and September. During the peak summer season, the visitor is advised to avoid ambitious expeditions during the middle of the day, when the temperature on the plains ranges from 80° to 100° F., but that still leaves many hours for sightseeing. Evenings, too, are generally mild, cooling to 60° to 75° even during the hottest spell. Fortunately too, cool breezes play along the coasts and through the mountains, thus breaking the dead heat. Autumn is mild. Winter can occasionally be severe – especially the end of January and early February. Freezing temperatures are rare, though, in any locale where the traveller is likely to be. Mountain winters can be rough, and snow covers certain slopes and trails, making travel impossible. Snow is all but unknown in the coastal regions.

There are two minor divergences from this climate-pattern; neither should deter the prospective visitor. One is the hot, dry sirocco that occasionally sweeps up from Africa and can be a minor nuisance. The other consists of earthquakes, but these occur so infrequently and are so slight as to count for nothing in the traveller's plans.

HEALTH AND DRINKING WATER

All the large towns have hospitals. Iraklion has full medical facilities, including X-ray and surgery, in its public hospital and several private clinics.

Doctors are either on hand or on call in all villages; a phone call, a taxi-ride – and a doctor will be there. Many of the doctors have studied in England, America, France or Germany, so language will probably not be a problem.

The larger towns also have chemists selling more or less all the familiar medicines; these shops, by the way, are marked by a red cross. People intending to go off on their own and into the hills might well take along a small first-aid kit. Anyone with special needs or worries should naturally consult his own doctor before leaving for Crete.

There is good, safe drinking water in plentiful supply over the entire island and throughout the year. All the towns and larger villages have chemically treated supplies, while fresh springs are abundant elsewhere. In the towns bottled mineral water (*metallikó neró*) is available; and even in the most obscure and isolated villages there always seems to be some sort of bottled lemonade.

TOURIST INFORMATION

Information of every kind may be obtained from the National Tourist Organization of Greece. Its main Offices in Athens are at 2 Amerikis Street and at 4 Stadiou Street. Other offices in the world's principal cities include:

London: 195–7 Regent Street, London w1.
New York: 601 Fifth Avenue, New York 10017.
Ottawa: 215 Metcalfe Street.
Paris: 3 Avenue de l'Opéra.
Rome: Via Bissolati 78–80.
Frankfurt-am-Main: Bethmannstrasse 50–54.
Brussels: 62 Boulevard de l'Impératrice.
Stockholm: 2 Grev Turegatan.

Greek Consulates and Embassies in all cities will assist the prospective visitor. There are also, of course, private travel and tourist agencies.

Once in Crete it is possible to get help and advice from several sources. The following towns have Tourist Offices:

Iraklion: 25th August Street.
Khania: Post Office Building, Tzanakaki Street.
Ayios Nikolaos: Temporarily c/o Tourist Police (see below).

If you want to know where there is to be some village festival, or clear up a point about an obscure Byzantine chapel, or make contact with the local authority on cheeses, antiquities or caves, go to one of these offices.

Another official institution which you may find yourself relying on during your stay on the island is the Tourist Police. This is simply one of the main branches of the Greek National Police and is to be found all over Greece. Its members wear a greenish uniform, and are identified by the words 'Tourist Police' on their sleeve. In addition, those who speak a foreign language wear the flag of that nation on their jacket. (English-speaking ones wear the American flag.) Tourist Police are to be met all over the island and will do anything possible to help the traveller. They can help you find a room in a villager's house, arrange a ride over the mountain with some local lorry-driver or find a boy to guide you to an isolated chapel. Main offices of the Tourist Police are:

Iraklion: King Constantine Avenue.
Khania: Karaiskaki Street.
Rethymnon: Kefaloyianni Square.
Ayios Nikolaos: Near the 'bottomless' pool.

Incidentally, any complaints you may have, about prices or anything else, should be directed to the Tourist Police.

MUSEUMS AND MONUMENTS

Specific information about museums and sites will be given where they occur in the routes section. Here we only wish to point out that they are open throughout the year – with, at most, slightly reduced hours during the winter season from October 1st to March 31st. Some museums – including the Iraklion Archaeological Museum – are open on Sundays and public holidays until 1 p.m. only. And note, too, that this museum is closed on Monday afternoons and the Khania Archaeological Museum all day on Mondays. Many museums are also closed at Christmas, New Year, Greek Easter March 25th and October 28th. Admission charges vary from Drs 5 to Drs 10. For details of a free pass available to certain classes of visitors, such as students, teachers, artists and journalists, see p. 37.

MONEY CHANGING AND BANKS

The Greek drachma has been fairly stable for some years now. As with all currencies there may be minor variations in the exchange rate according to where you make the transaction – in banks, travel agencies, hotels, etc.

The maximum amount of drachmas that a foreigner is allowed to bring in or take out is 200. If you should overstock, it is possible to buy back your own currency, but only at the Bank of Greece. You must produce the receipts of your original purchase of drachmas, and you will lose about 1 per cent on the transaction.

If for any reason you have to send money out of Greece to some other country, this may also be done through the Bank of Greece, and here again you will need to take all your documents and receipts.

Above all, the traveller should work out his own personal system for making conversions and relating values. For example: with the English £ at around Drs 72, one drachma is about 3d., Drs 10 about 2s. 9d., Drs 50 about 13s. 9d. and Drs 100 about £1 7s. 6d.; with the U.S. $ pegged at around Drs 30, one drachma is about 3 cents, Drs 10 about 33 cents and Drs 100 about $3.33.

The Greek drachma – often known colloquially as a 'franc' – is made up of 100 lepta, which makes 50 lepta worth about a penny-halfpenny or one and a half cents. The coins now in circulation include 10-, 20- and 50-lepta pieces, and 1-, 2-, 5-, 10- and 20-drachma pieces. And beware! Several of these are almost the same size and are easily confused. There are also notes to the value of Drs 50, 100, 500 and 1,000.

Banks are open from Monday to Saturday from 9 to 1, except for the public holidays listed on p. 59. Travellers' cheques can also be cashed in hotels, restaurants, souvenir shops, etc.

SHOPPING AND SOUVENIRS

Villages and the smaller towns can provide little beyond the basic amenities, but several of the larger towns offer a full range of shops and services – including laundry and dry-cleaning, films and photographic supplies, chemists and jewellers, clothing and hardware, local and foreign – especially American – cigarettes. Many of the manufactured items will bear familiar names, since Greece is forced to import a great deal. Dry-cleaners are surprisingly cheap, laundries surprisingly expensive. In general, prices are usually marked – and fixed (see Bargaining, opposite). Many of the better shops now have some English-speaking personnel, and people around will always help you with any difficult purchase.

With regard to souvenirs and handicrafts, Crete's specialities include knives, hand-woven materials, bags, carpets, lace, embroideries, shawls, hand-made gold and silver jewellery and ceramics. The larger towns have a wide selection in the shops; if you are lucky you may be able to pick up some things in the villages. The Cretan knives are of particular interest. Some of the imitations of Minoan artwork are fairly attractive. Among the best buys are textiles – wool, linen, silk, cotton, embroideries, knitwear, lace – made into handbags, rugs and various articles of clothing. Much of it has been produced in the villages on the old looms and with the old patterns.

With the exception of certain holidays (p. 59), shops are open every day except Sunday, although certain ones manage to open even then – little meat shops, for instance, or village shops that are practically homes and that seem to be open round the clock. But in the towns some shops (including foodshops, barbers, etc.) close on Wednesdays at noon, while others close on Saturdays at noon. In general, shops open at 8 a.m., close for the long siesta at 1 or 2 p.m., open again around 4 or 5 p.m., and close for the night at 8 p.m. Pavement kiosks in the larger towns are open at almost any time of the day or night; here you can get cigarettes, toilet articles and cosmetics, pencils and postcards, sweets, etc., and sometimes postage stamps.

BARGAINING

Many tourists believe that haggling is a required constituent of all transactions in Mediterranean regions and are more or less nervous of it according to their individual aptitude for this pastime. It may not be entirely avoided, but it need not be so unnerving; we give here a list of goods and services and show how the custom applies.

Hotel Rooms: These charges are fixed by law and are exhibited as a matter of course. Extra fees are for extra services, such as heating.
Restaurants: Prices are clearly marked on menus. Where there are no menus you may find yourself paying a few drachmas more than a native – but only a few.
Bus and Taxi Fares: These are officially fixed, although for a long trip by taxi it is a good idea to come to some arrangement with the driver before you start.
Groceries, Fruit, etc.: Prices in shops and markets are usually clearly

marked. It is as well to memorize standard prices of a few basic commodities and allow for small differences according to locality.
Souvenirs: Prices will usually be marked. This is a competitive business and shop-owners must keep a constant watch on prices. If a shop-owner knocks 10 – or even 30 – drachmas off an article he has been asking Drs 120 for, it may be that he has seen you waver – and he may need the sale more than you realize. Haggle if you feel like it, and see what happens.

Other Goods: You need a lantern or a stove for camping, so you go to a hardware shop. You are quoted a price that is Drs 30 more than your Greek friend told you it would be. It may be that your Greek friend doesn't know the real price. But if he did, and if the dealer is in fact trying to get Drs 30 more from you than he would from a native Cretan, you must just decide how much it is worth to you and play the game on that basis. Nor should you feel that you might have been cheated when the price is reduced. That is why you are haggling. And for all you know the shopman may need your money so badly that he is prepared to cut down on his fair profit.

If you should really feel that you have been cheated, you should quietly ask for a receipt – completely itemized – before handing over your money. Then take the receipt to the Tourist Police at the first opportunity, and you will have their assistance.

TIPPING

Tipping often presents a problem to tourists. On Crete many people will be helpful to you and there will be occasions when you just do not know whether to tip or not. Cigarettes, particularly American or English ones, are always welcome. Take with you a stock of cigarettes in packets of 5 and 10, and you will easily be able to get over the difficulty of tipping. It is also possible to give a tip and indicate that it is for the children.

Hotels: There is a 10 per cent, and in some cases, a 15 per cent service charge on the bill, but it is customary to give a few drachmas to anyone who has been particularly helpful – the man who carries your bags, and the chambermaid, for instance.

Restaurants: After a meal it is customary to tip over and above the service charge included in the bill. Give your waiter, personally, a few drachmas extra when he returns your change, or leave the tip on the plate with the bill. It is important to know that drachmas left on the table are considered to be the property of the water-boy. It is usual to leave two drachmas for him as well if the party consists of two or three people. In little *tavernas* or cafés where it is obviously the proprietor himself who is serving you, tipping is not customary.

Taxi-drivers: You are not expected in Crete to give taxi-drivers any sort of percentage of the fare, but it is usual to give them a few drachmas.

Ladies' Hairdressers: For a shampoo and set the correct tip is 5–8 drachmas to the hairdresser in charge, and 3 to the assistant.

Shoeshine Boys: They usually get a 50-lepta tip. The shine itself costs about Drs 2.

Cinema Usherettes: It is usual to give the girl who shows you to your seat a drachma or so.

SPORT

SWIMMING

Crete is ringed by beaches – some like Pacific lagoons, others of a harsher grandeur, but all attractive in their various ways – and they will be mentioned in their proper places. Here we simply point out that the main towns have a few public beaches with full facilities; at the less frequented beaches, the usual precautions are advised.

WATER-SKIING

Water-skiing facilities are available at the Minos Beach Hotel at Ayios Nikolaos, the Blue Sea Motel at Stalis, 31 km. east of Iraklion and at the Creta Beach and Knossos Beach hotels near Iraklion.

SKIN-DIVING

This latest international sport can be practised on Crete. In addition to the chance delights of underwater flora and fauna, there are several places where submerged remains may be examined: Arvi, Olous at Elounda, Limin Khersonisou, Matala, Nirou Khani and Rethymnon. Masks and harpoons and such gear can be purchased in Iraklion and Khania; anything in the way of air tanks or SCUBA gear would have to be brought over from the mainland. (Nikos Kartelias has a shop at 3 Karageorgi Servias St, Kastella-Piraeus, which will rent all necessary gear.)

TENNIS

Both Iraklion and Khania have private tennis courts. If you happen to be travelling with your gear, inquire at the Tourist Office.

WALKING AND CLIMBING

For those who would like to see something of Crete on foot, there are touring and climbing clubs in Iraklion and Khania (p. 121 and p. 211), which arrange frequent excursions – some involving only a few hours of walking, others quite ambitious climbs. Foreigners would always be most welcome and contacts can be made through the Tourist Office. For those who prefer to go alone and would like some hints from men who have actually walked over much of Crete, the following books are best: Pendlebury's *The Archaeology of Crete*, Grantham's *Minotaur and Crete*, Brewster's *The Island of Zeus*, Trevor-Battye's *Camping in Crete* and Fielding's *The Stronghold*. There are several quite rewarding climbs to be made on Cretan peaks, but most people go to the mountains to enjoy their beauties rather than for spectacular ascents. Snow stays on some peaks through much of the year and these can be cold and windy. Proper preparations should be made before setting out. The single most attractive climb – the ascent of Mt Idha – is described in some detail on pp. 168–72.

HUNTING

There is a fair amount of small game on Crete, including rabbits and hares as well as partridges, woodcock, ducks, thrushes, etc. It is forbidden to shoot the wild goat of Crete – the *agrími*. Seasons are observed, and a licence – costing Drs 170 – is required. The Tourist Police in Iraklion or Khania will give you information; there is officially a requirement that a foreigner must have been resident for 6 months before being entitled to a licence.

FISHING

Although the coastal waters in this part of the Mediterranean are no longer as productive as might be expected, there is still some fairly good fishing for the amateur. No licence is required, but anyone intending to use fishing guns or spears should consult the Tourist Police or Harbourmaster about restrictions.

PUBLIC HOLIDAYS

We list here the official Greek holidays on which banks, museums and many shops are likely to be closed:

Jan. 1st – New Year's Day.
Jan. 6th – Epiphany.
Last Monday before Lent.
Good Friday.
Easter Monday.
Mar. 25th – Greek Independence Day.
May 21st – St Constantine.
Aug. 15th – Assumption of the Virgin Mary.
Oct. 28th – *Okhi* Day (Second World War episode).
Dec. 25th – Christmas Day.

HOLIDAYS AND FESTIVALS

Hardly a day passes on Crete without a celebration in honour of somebody or something – a saint, a village festival, a harvest, a patriotic event. Each nome (p. 105) has one place – either a chapel, a monastery or a village – where on major saints' days the people bearing the name of the saint gather. These 'name-days' are far more important to Greeks than their birthdays. Often dancing and general celebration take place on the night preceding the actual church observances, and extra services are run on the regular bus routes. Sometimes festivities are extended over two or three days, and the lavish Cretan hospitality sets itself no limits.

Those dates which are official holidays are also listed above. As celebration of certain festivals may vary from year to year, inquire at the Tourist Office for details.

Date	Occasion	Where and How Observed (Nome given in parentheses)
Dec. 30th– Jan. 1st	New Year	In homes, cafés, hotels and public assemblies: observed by feasting, card-playing and gambling, and rituals such as opening the windows at midnight to let the evil spirits out.
Jan. 6th	Epiphany	At harbours and sea-shores: a cross is thrown into the sea to bring luck and blessings.
2 weeks before Lent	Carnival *	Cities like Iraklion and Rethymnon make the biggest display, but eating, drinking and good spirits are general throughout the island.
Last Monday before Lent	Clean Monday *	This marks the end of Carnival and the beginning of Lent: no meat is eaten, but a feast is contrived all the same. Kites are flown – by all ages.

Date	*Occasion*	*Where and How Observed* (*Nome given in parentheses*)
(See note on Greek Easter)	Lent *	Observed by everyone to a certain extent, but a Holy Week of almost total fasting is the culminating feature of Lent.
See note below)	Good Friday to Easter Monday *	On Friday evening there is a funeral procession through the streets. On Saturday evening a long church service ends with rejoicing at midnight, the lighting of candles, and fireworks. Easter Sunday is celebrated with eating, drinking, dancing. Many flock to military installations where the soldiers entertain the local population.
Mar. 25th	Greek Independence Day	Observed mainly by parades in large towns.
	Annunciation of Our Lady	Church of Prassa (Iraklion) and Apokorona (Khania).
1st Sunday after Easter	St Thomas *	Monastery of Vrondisi, Ayios Thomas (Iraklion) and Neo Khorio of Apokorona (Khania).
April 23rd (See note below)	St George	Monastery of Epanosifi (Iraklion): religious feast with Archbishop celebrating Mass.
		Selinaris Monastery (Lasithi): religious feast.
(See note on Greek Easter)	Ascension *	Almyros Church near Ayios Nikolaos (Lasithi): service and feast.
		Local dances and fireworks.
May 1st	Spring Festival	Throughout the countryside people picnic, dance and weave flower-wreaths.
May 5th	St Irene	Village of Kroussonas (Iraklion): religious feast.
May 20th–27th	Anniversary of Battle of Crete (Second World War)	City of Khania celebrates with athletic events.
May 21st	St Constantine and St Helena	Name-day of the King.
June 1st–7th	Amateur fishermen's week	Arranged by local Hellenic Club in Ayios Nikolaos.
June 24th	Birthday of St John the Baptist	With bonfires (which are actually observing the summer solstice) on which are burned wreaths of flowers which have been hanging over people's front doors since May 1st. If you are lucky, you may see people jumping the fires.
June 29th	St Peter and St Paul	At various chapels named after these saints.
July 17th	St Marina	Village of Voni (Iraklion): major religious feast.
July 26th and 27th	St Paraskevi and St Panteleimon	Observed at villages of Kounavi (Iraklion) and Fournes (Khania).
End of July	Wine Festival	The city of Rethymnon has instituted a modern festival, with several days of wine-sampling. Dances in Cretan costumes.
Aug. 6th	Feast of the Transfiguration	At a small church on Mt Iouktas (Iraklion). Also observed at Skine (Khania).

Note on Greek Easter: The Greek Orthodox Easter is calculated in a way which baffles all but the initiated. As with the Western Christian Churches, it must fall after the first full moon following the first day of spring, but it must also fall *after* the Jewish Passover. Holidays dependent on Easter (marked with an asterisk), of course, must also fluctuate in relation to this date.

Note on St George's Day: If this festival happens to fall in Holy Week, it is postponed until after Easter. This is because there are so many Cretans with the name Georgios who would not be able to celebrate their name-day with proper enthusiasm during the austerities of Holy Week.

Date	Occasion	Where and How Observed (*Nome given in parentheses*)
Aug. 8th	St Myron	At the village of Ayios Myron (Iraklion): there is a cave where the saint lived, with sacred water.
Aug. 15th	Assumption of Our Lady	At the town of Neapolis (Lasithi): feast starts on 14th with local dances, athletic sports; ends on 16th. At the village of Mokhos (Iraklion): festival organized by Greek Touring Club, with Cretan food, local dances in Cretan costumes, exhibitions of local hand-weavings and embroidery, fireworks. Religious feasts at villages, convents and monasteries throughout Crete.
Aug. 25th	St Titus	Iraklion: religious procession from Church of St Titus.
Aug. 27th	St Fanourios	Monastery of Vrondisi (Iraklion): religious feast.
Aug. 29th	Beheading of St John the Baptist	At Giona, near village of Rodhopou (Khania). Also at various churches named after St John.
Aug. 31st	Holy Sash of the Virgin Mary	Village of Psykhro (Lasithi): religious feast and local dances, hundreds of people descending to the plain on mules.
Sept. 14th	Raising of Holy Cross	Observed in city of Iraklion and villages around Mt Idha. Also at Alikianos (Khania).
Sept. 20th–25th	Sports	Swimming and athletic events organized by local clubs of Ayios Nikolaos (Lasithi).
Oct. 7th	St John the Hermit	At the monastery of Gouverneto and the near-by cave where the saint died (Khania).
Oct. 26th	St Demetrios	Observed at many chapels, as this is a popular name.
Oct. 28th	*Okhi* Day	Observed all over Greece to commemorate the occasion when the Greek Premier replied 'Okhi!' ('No!') to the Italian ultimatum of 1940.
Nov. 7th–9th	Anniversary of Explosion of 1866	Monastery of Arkadhi and at Rethymnon: Crete's own 'national' holiday, with people from all over the island gathering at the monastery (p. 204).
Nov. 11th	St Menas	Town of Iraklion: religious procession for Patron Saint of town.
Dec. 4th	St Barbara	Village of Ayia Varvara (Iraklion).
Dec. 6th	St Nicholas	Town of Ayios Nikolaos (Lasithi).
Dec. 25th	Christmas	This is less important to the Orthodox Church than Easter, but the whole season of Twelve Days is marked here and there, with singing on Christmas Eve. Popular diversions are gambling and fortune-telling. Fear of evil spirits – the *Kalikañtzaros* – prevails.

POSTAL INFORMATION AND TELEPHONES

Every village on Crete has some place where it is possible to buy stamps and send and receive mail. In the main towns you can sometimes buy stamps at kiosks as well as at the post offices (the word for stamp is *grammatóssimo*). Postal rates on Crete are the same as on mainland Greece.

C

Postal Rates

	Letters	*Postcards*
	Drs	Drs
Internal	2½	1½
United Kingdom (Air mail)	4½	3
United States of America (Air mail)	6	3½

Registered Mail

If you intend to send a registered letter, this should not be sealed until the post office official has approved its contents.

Parcel Post

If you are sending a package out of Greece you must be prepared to show the entire contents to the postal authorities: this means un-doing even gift wrappings – often for each individual item. There is also a considerable amount of form-filling, stamping, etc. The Greeks themselves take their various gifts and items to the post office, get them inspected, and do all their wrapping-up there, and this seems to be the easiest way.

Air Freight

Olympic Airways has a surprisingly cheap service for light freight and packages – but only within Greece. It is worth while if you have to get things to and from the mainland while on Crete.

Telephone and Telegrams

There is at least one telephone to be found in every village on Crete and both local and long-distance calls may be made. Local calls cost Dr 1. In the main towns telegrams may be sent from the telegraph offices; in other places this may be done by telephone. From mid-night Saturday/Sunday till midnight Sunday/Monday telephone rates *within* Greece are doubled.

WEIGHTS AND MEASURES

The international metric system is used, officially and generally. The few exceptions that linger among the older folk are noted below.

WEIGHT

Kilo (1,000 grams) = approx. 2.2 lb.
Half-kilo (*missó kiló*) = approx. 1.1 lb.
Quarter kilo (*tetarto*) = approx. ½ lb.

(The *oká* – 1,282 grams or 2.8 lb. – has been officially abolished, but it is still sometimes used by older people.)

VOLUME

1 litre = approx. 1¾ pints
1 quart = approx. 1.136 litres.

Petrol is sold by the imperial gallon. Other liquids are often sold by the kilo. In restaurants wine is sold by large or small bottles or by the glass; but in the wine taverns by the kilo.

LENGTH

1 metre = 39.37 inches
1 kilometre = 0.62 miles (roughly, ⅝ of a mile).

The English yard may occasionally be used by men's tailors or cloth salesmen.

TEMPERATURE

The Centigrade scale is used. To convert Fahrenheit to Centigrade, subtract 32 and multiply by $\frac{5}{9}$. To convert Centigrade to Fahrenheit, multiply by $\frac{9}{5}$ and add 32.

ELECTRICITY

All the larger towns and most big villages have electricity. The voltage is variously 110 or 220, and the current can be either A.C. or D.C., so you should always inquire before plugging in electrical equipment. Anyone planning a long stay on Crete with elaborate electrical equipment would need to bring transformers to convert the voltage. Plugs are usually Continental two-pin size.

TIME

Crete, like the mainland, lies in the Eastern European Zone, two hours ahead of Greenwich Mean Time. Officially, Greece uses the

Continental 24-hour system, where 1 p.m. is '13 o'clock', 2 p.m. is '14 o'clock', etc. But in practice people say 'one this noon', or 'eight this evening'.

All Greece – except Mount Athos – uses the Western Gregorian calendar. With the exception of Easter and its dependent holy days (p. 60), most Greek religious holidays and festivals coincide with those of the rest of Europe.

THE LAND AND ITS RESOURCES

General Situation and Features

Crete lies in the Mediterranean, almost equidistant from Greece, Asia Minor and Africa – a fact which should be kept in mind whenever the point is being made that Crete is the first recognizably *European* civilization. After Sicily, Sardinia and Cyprus, Crete is the fourth largest island in the Mediterranean. It is approximately 160 miles long, and varies in width from about $7\frac{1}{2}$ to 38 miles; its area is about 3,200 square miles. Altogether Crete has some 650 miles of coastline. The north coast is irregular, with five major bays, the chief of which is Soudha Bay, considered to be one of the finest harbours in the Mediterranean. The south coast is less irregular, but possesses no natural harbours of any great extent. Crete is distinguished by several physical peculiarities: its many fissures and ravines (*pharaṅgi*); its upland plains – some quite large, flat and fertile; numerous caves; one freshwater lake and three brackish water-holes (*almyrós*); and many unique species and endemic varieties of flora. The predominant aspect of the island is its rocky, scrubby, mountainous terrain.

Geological Background

Crete's underlying formation is the limestone deposited during the Cretaceous period. In this dim geological past, Crete was part of a great arc of mountains connecting it to the mainland masses of Europe and Asia Minor. For the layman, perhaps the most dramatic evidence for this is the fossil remains of such animals as the dwarf hippopotamus that have been found on Crete – proof, also, that the island was still connected to the mainland up to the beginning of the Pleistocene Epoch. All this only brings us to about $1\frac{1}{2}$ million years before the first men appeared on Crete. In the last several thousand years Crete has been racked by innumerable earthquakes, but the most catastrophic event in historical times seems to have occurred in the sixth century A.D., when some massive submarine movement tilted the entire island on its axis. The western end was raised about 26 ft out of the water, while the eastern end subsided accordingly. Striking evidence for this may be seen at the site of Phalasarna, where the old port facilities are now 150 yards inland, and at

Olous, where the harbour installations are submerged. It has been surmised, too, that Mokhlos Island was joined to the mainland before this event.

The Mountains

If one feature of Crete's geography had to be singled out as the most influential, it would be the mountains. They are not spectacular in height, but they do express the Cretan character. As on the mainland, they have probably influenced the island's history by isolating the various settlements. There are four principal mountain ranges and one is never very far away from them; they are the backbone of Crete.

(1) In the west are the White Mountains (*Lefka Ori:* literally, 'white landmarks'). The highest point is 8,045 ft (2,452 m.) above sea-level.

(2) In the centre is the Idha range, now generally known as the Psiloritis. Its peak, the highest point on Crete, is Stavros – 8,058 ft (2,456 m.).

(3) East of the Idha range are the Dhikti Mountains, the highest point of which is Mount Dhikti – 7,047 ft (2,148 m.).

(4) At the extreme east are the Sitia Mountains, whose highest point, Mount Thrifti, is 4,843 ft (1,476 m.).

In addition to these principal ranges there are the Asterousia Mountains (also known as the Kofinos range), which separate the Messara Plain from the south coast in central Crete. The summit here is 4,039 ft (1,231 m.).

Snow may remain on the highest peaks throughout most of the year.

Flat Land and Plateaux

The largest flat land is the Messara Plain, which is about 25 miles long, and averages 5 miles in width. It runs roughly on an east–west axis in the south-central region of Crete. Rich in history, it is also one of the richest agricultural areas of the island. The other intensively cultivated flat lands are found chiefly on the narrow coastal plains bordering the gulfs along the north coast.

Crete also has three major upland plains – basin-like plateaux formed of irregular mountain masses with flat bottoms that furnish excellent pasture and farmland. The one of most interest to the visitor is the Lasithi Plain below Mt Dhikti, at an elevation of about 3,000 ft. The other two major plateaux are the Omalos Plain west of the White Mountains (about 3,780 ft) and the Nidha Plain on the north-east slopes of Idha (about 4,560 ft). All tend to draw rain and water from the adjacent slopes through pot-holes and the limestone rock strata, the water subsequently running down to the sea.

Water Sources

There are only a few rivers of any consequence on Crete – the Kerides, the Anapodharis, the Mylopotamos, the Yeropotamos – and their watershed basins cover one-fifth of the island and contain the major grain and fruit areas. Although travellers until and even throughout the nineteenth century spoke of an abundance of water on Crete, there has been a drastic decline and most rivers and streams today are small, short and seasonal. The one freshwater lake, Lake Kournas, which is about 25 miles west of Rethymnon, has an area of only some 160 acres. There are several large springs and many smaller ones, and conditions are good for well-sinking. The highly seasonal character of the rains and the scarcity of permanent rivers, together with the cavernous limestone rock-formations throughout the island, make storage dams impractical – at least on any grand scale. Water remains the principal challenge to Crete's development.

Climate

The climate is principally characterized by the dryness that prevails throughout most of the year, the rain occurring largely from October to March. Even then, the rainfall varies considerably over the island as a whole, with the mountain and upland regions getting more than their share, and this wide variation in locale and season plays a dominant role in the type of crops as well as irrigation needs. The prevailing winds blow across the Aegean from the north, often with such force as to keep down tree-growth in many exposed places along the coast. At the same time, these winds furnish power for irrigation in many areas by propelling windmills. Once again, the focus is on Crete's need for water.

Trees and Forest

Now we come to one of the main reasons for the water shortage: there are no really extensive forests left on Crete. Yet the island is reputed to have been covered with dense cypress forests in ancient times, the export of timber being one of the chief sources of Minoan prosperity. Cedars grew, too, and the island was famed for its trees well into classical times. Centuries of subsequent neglect, deforestation, grazing and warfare left Crete denuded. Today small forests of pine, cypress and oak, scattered over the island, cover only about two per cent of the land. The ilex tree is plentiful in the eastern half, the cypress in the western half and upland regions; there are chestnut trees in Selinou Province; particularly noteworthy are the fine old plane trees that flourish near springs and water sources and grow to an astounding size. Olive trees and carob trees are discussed in some detail on pp. 71 and 72.

Flora

Crete provides unusually interesting territory for the botanist, for it has a great variety of flowers, plants, trees, herbs, etc. There are said to be over 1,500 species or varieties, at least 100 of which seem to be endemic or indigenous, or at least varieties and sub-species peculiar to Crete. Quince, for instance, is said to be an indigenous Cretan fruit. Some are more familiar Mediterranean species, modified by the environment; the mountain heights, with their sharp climatic changes, have been the chief influence here. Flowers will be with you wherever you go on Crete. And there are many thorny bushes and spiky plants – hence the high boots worn by the mountain men.

Herbs are among Crete's most distinctive vegetation and if one species of all Crete's flora had to be singled out it should be the endemic herb, dittany (*Origanum dictamnus*, from Mt Dhikti, where it flourished). A plant of the mint family, it is of the same genus as wild marjoram. It is given several names by the natives – *Érondas, Stamatóhorto*, or – as it is most widely known – *Díctamo*. Cretan dittany is mentioned in many classical texts, and it is still prized for its pharmaceutical qualities; it is believed to be of special comfort to women in childbirth. It may be found growing throughout the island, particularly in the mountainous reaches, and even in the gorges and caves. You will find yourself eating it as a flavouring with many of the Cretan foods; it is also popular as a herb-tea.

Fauna

Crete also offers a variety of wild life. The following mammals have been reported by reputable observers in recent decades: shrew, hedgehog, bat, badger, marten, weasel, wild cat, rabbit, hare, mouse and rat. There are no poisonous snakes; tradition credits St Titus with expelling them from Crete (as St Patrick did from Ireland). The fish population is scanty, but there are many butterflies. There are some surprises among the native and migrant birds.

The one really notable and unique animal on Crete is the wild goat – *Capra aegagrus creticus*. Zoologists deny it the rank of a species, but it is not to be confused with the ibex and bouquetin of the European Alps; it is related to the wild goat found in the Caucasus and Mt Taurus and down into Iran and Pakistan. The Cretans refer to it as the *agrími* – a generic word for wild animals – and have admired it since Minoan times, as various works of art in the Iraklion museum prove. It has been known to weigh up to 100 pounds and have horns up to 31 inches in spread, but it is chiefly noted for its nimbleness at racing and jumping across the rocky cliffs of the Gorge of Samaria – its last natural habitat. It is so adept that it would seem almost impossible to catch or kill, but over the years so many *agrími* were taken for their flesh or hides that they almost became extinct. Some years ago, however, the government and local organizations instructed the inhabitants of the region about the need to protect these goats. Hunting was prohibited, strict penalties for poaching were imposed and sanctuaries established on several off-shore islands: Ayios Theodhoros, near Khania; Dia, near Iraklion; and Ayii Pantes, near Ayios Nikolaos. The future of the species on Crete, therefore, now seems secure.

Land Use

Two-thirds of the land area of Crete is taken up by largely barren mountains, leaving only one-third for crop production, although nomadic grazing, wood for fuel, oils, honey and some other produce are also provided by the mountain areas. More crucial is the fact that the best soils for cultivation comprise less than 7 per cent of the total area of the island – and more than two-thirds of these better soils are located in the Messara Plain, where lack of water poses a serious problem. A large percentage of the soil lacks nitrogen and phosphorus, and full advantage is not yet being taken of modern fertilizers and soil conservation techniques. The land problem has been further complicated by the custom of dividing land among children upon the death of the owner or as dowries for the girls. This has reduced the size of the farms and scattered the land in each holding, until the farms have become impossibly small and inefficient.

Animal Husbandry

In the sheep and the goat we see the paradox confronting Crete: they are the mainstays of a way of life, yet they devastate the land. Their meat, of course, provides the staple flesh diet; the wool has a multitude of uses; they provide cheese and milk – you will see very few cows on Crete. For that matter, you will not see many sheep and goats, considering how many there must be, unless you chance across flocks as they are passing to or from spring and winter pastures. Chickens and pigs are fairly plentiful; rabbits less so.

Agriculture

Throughout history – and despite this history – Crete has managed to feed its population. In the sixteenth and seventeenth centuries A.D. under the Venetians, Crete was virtually a garden, famed for its fruit, olives, wines, grain and cheeses, which were exported – together with products such as silk and leather – all over Europe. Today the most remarkable aspect of Cretan agriculture is the extent to which the primitive methods prevail; in many respects, little has changed since Minoan times. Many of the implements used are classic – although tractors and some other farm machinery are appearing on the scene. If you are fortunate enough to observe a grain harvest you will see that the grain is cut by hand, gathered and carried to the threshing floor, where cattle tread it – or perhaps a sleigh is dragged over it. The winnowing is still done by tossing it to the wind until the chaff is blown away. At any time of year you may observe the extremes farmers must resort to for water: a few lucky individuals have small petrol pumps for their wells; some make do with windmills; others use donkeys to turn the crank; but a few are forced to haul water by hand, hour after hour, in the heat of the summer, pouring bucket after bucket into little irrigation ditches. Much of the cultivation, moreover, is on far from desirable terrain – burnt-out soil or mountain-sides.

The wonder of it all, then, is that yields are as high as they are. Crete cannot grow enough grain for self-support, but fresh fruit and vegetables make up a large part of the island's diet. Nuts – almonds, chestnuts, peanuts – provide a supplement. Almost any edible growth is made use of somehow. In the end, Crete is able to export considerable quantities of its vegetables and fruit, largely to Athens.

The Olive

The number of olive trees on Crete is thirteen million. If you keep to the main routes you may find this hard to believe; it is only when you wander in the hinterland and among the foot-hills that you begin to realize how many olive trees there are. They thrive in the most unlikely places – not, as is commonly supposed, because they don't require water, but because their roots strike deep to underground sources. The olives are picked during the winter months and although the oil is widely used on the island there is still plenty left for export. In addition, after the oil has been extracted, the crushed seeds and pulp are dried and pressed and subsequently burned as a cheap, if foul-smelling, fuel. And last but not least, the aged gnarled trees have traditionally provided hiding-places from the oppressors and occupiers of the island.

The Grape

The delicious table grape known as *rosaki* is a favourite for domestic and export consumption, but, in terms of economic value, it is the dried grape – alias the raisin – that has the greatest importance. Thanks to its mild climate and fertile soil, Crete's wines have been noted from earliest times. Dionysus and the grape are motifs of early Cretan coinage, and classical authors often extolled the fine quality of Cretan wines. By the fourteenth century wine was a principal export; vine cuttings from Crete were so highly regarded that Prince Henry of Portugal is said to have sent for plants to stock the island of Madeira. By the sixteenth century the English were foremost among the Europeans who sang the praises of Crete's malmsey. The first English consul on Crete, indeed, was a merchant appointed by Henry VIII in 1522 to supervise the wine exports. But by the eighteenth century Cretan wines had lost their international popularity and were forced out of the market. Today their quality varies considerably; some claim that only the monasteries have first-rate wines – thanks to the care that they lavish. Nevertheless it is still possible to be served with an attractive wine in some isolated *taverna* or home.

The Carob Tree

The carob is a small evergreen tree found throughout the Mediterranean; on Crete it grows most extensively in the eastern part of the island. It has long pods looking like overgrown green beans which are rich in sugar and proteins and have been used since ancient times for animal fodder, human food and fermented beverages. They are still much in demand as fodder. In addition, a gum made from the pods is used in paper-making and tobacco-curing, as a stabilizer in food products, and as a celluloid in photographic supplies. Sometimes the actual pods are exported for these purposes, but usually it is only the gum that has been extracted. The bean has many names, including 'Saint John's bread', for it was the carob that St John the Baptist ate when he wandered in the wilderness. This is an interesting example of a crop, all but unknown to most of us, providing an income for a whole people. But, in fact, we have all come in contact with the carob; the carat, standard unit for precious stones and gold alloys, is derived from the Greek *kératon* – 'little horn' – the carob bean that once served as a standard measure.

Mineral Resources

Both copper and iron have been mined on Crete, even in modern times, but it seems probable that the Minoans imported the bulk of their raw ores. Stone quarries and gypsum mines, in any case, are all that operate today; in 1967 it was announced that new deposits of gypsum, of considerable economic value, had been discovered in eastern Crete. Surveys have also turned up some lead, talc, manganese, lignite, sulphur, zinc, gold, silver, tungsten, platinum, emery, graphite, tin and magnetite. But these latter deposits are unlikely to be worth mining.

Occupations

By far the majority of Cretans are engaged in agricultural occupations; most are self-employed, eking a living out of scattered plots of land. Outside the few large towns the visitor will hardly be aware of any other occupations. There are some, though. In addition to the hundreds of olive-crushers and grape-pressers and distilleries that require operators at harvest time, there are a number of small factories and plants. Most employ only a few people and utilize little power or equipment, but they process foods, produce soap and make building materials. Then there are harbour installations to be manned, as well as numerous garages and repair shops in the towns. And a stroll through the side-streets of towns like Iraklion will reveal many other crafts and trades being practised. Crete has always been famous for its metalwork – especially its knives. Once, too, the black mulberry tree and the silkworm were cultivated on Crete, and the island could boast of a domestic silk industry. What the foreigner seldom gets a chance to see are the many people working at small home 'industries': spinning, weaving, knitting, embroidering, basket-making and turning out various other handicrafts and tourist articles. But as Crete advances into the twentieth century, more and more Cretans find employment in transport, trade, government and office work.

Human Resources

As with any organic society, the real potential finally lies in the people. Crete's population today numbers about half a million, in comparison to the up to a million inhabitants that some scholars say were there during the peak of the Minoan civilization. Because of the climate, soil and harbour facilities, the majority live in clusters along the north coast. Less than a quarter – including over 50,000 inhabitants of the rich Messara Plain – live in the southern half of the island, where Ierapetra is the only large town. Many mountain dwellers, however, traditionally descend to the lower villages and coastal towns for the winter. The capital resources of Crete are largely in Iraklion, Khania and Rethymnon, which results in a concentration of the educated and skilled in these towns. Athens, too, has come to represent an irresistible magnet for the young and ambitious.

CAVES AND MYTHS

The caves of Crete are among its most remarkable attractions. They are of every conceivable size and location. Some are simple grottoes – mere holes in the ground or on the sides of mountains. Others are many-chambered, with complicated passages, stalactites and stalagmites, or pools of water. Some have been thoroughly explored and have yielded rich archaeological treasures; others have barely been looked into. As recently as 1961, for instance, a large cave was discovered on the Omalos Plain and the first investigators, spending a whole day there, estimated its length at 20 km. and its depth at 1,000 m.; they also reported an internal river or lake.

The first settlers on Crete probably used the caves as dwellings. Gradually they came to use them increasingly as religious shrines and burial sites. Finds from some of the caves have been most valuable in piecing together Crete's history – from fossil remains of prehistoric animal life to human skulls and bones, and later to votive offerings of pottery and bronze. The caves attracted pilgrims and petitioners long after the Minoan era, and even now some of them are still approached with veneration. In addition they have provided a refuge for the islanders in times of trouble – as for instance the Cave of Melidhoni (p. 199).

But, exploring aside, it is the mythical associations of the caves that generate the most controversy. Take the matter of Zeus' birthplace. There are many caves throughout the ancient world that claim to be the site. Obviously, in such a matter, everything depends on the classical source that you accept. Hesiod in his *Theogony* seems to link Zeus with the Dhiktaion Cave at Psykhro. But many students in this field (Robert Graves, for one) dispute this cave's right to the honour. And technically – i.e. on the basis of geographical allusions – the Cave of Zeus should be farther east. Another strong candidate is a cave near Arkalokhorion, which was frequented and famous during the first millennium of Crete's history; some scholars have begun to advance this cave as the site of a Zeus cult.

And even after reaching agreement as to where Zeus was born, a second question arises as to whether he was brought up in the same cave. In the end neither 'true believers' nor classical scholars can decide, and the Tourist Organization has the last word. For them Zeus was born in the Dhiktaion Cave (p. 164) and was brought up, under the protection of the *Curétes*, in the Cave of Idha (p. 171).

There are many other myths involving the caves of Crete. Minos was said to have returned every nine years to the birth-cave of Zeus, where he was re-consecrated by Zeus and given a 'refresher course' in law. Elsewhere it is mentioned that the sixth-century Cretan mystic, Epimenides, slept fifty-seven years in the Cave of Idha. Several myths and legends are also attached to the Cave of Eileithyia (p. 242), a cave which is easily accessible from Iraklion. And finally, a cave on Mount Iouktas is claimed as the burial site of Zeus – although not by the mainland Greeks of classical times, for whom Olympian Zeus could never have died.

Those who have had no experience of cave-exploring are advised not to go unattended. Some of the caves are soon explored, but others are true labyrinths. Candles and strong flashlights are minimum requirements; rolled newspapers, ignited, provide a clear view for a short time. A good length of string is a necessity for ambitious expeditions; rubber-soled shoes and a light stock of food and water are also advised.

HISTORY

With every year that passes, our knowledge of the Minoan era is having to be reassessed, for modern archaeology and scholarship do more than reveal the history of a place such as Crete; they force a continual reappraisal of this history. The earlier concept of a unique and indigenous Minoan civilization has been revised. Crete has now been placed in the Mediterranean and Near East complex, and this whole world, in turn, is viewed as a dynamic process, not as a set of building-blocks.

It is not surprising, therefore, that some of the theories and conclusions of Sir Arthur Evans have had to be modified. The problem of chronology, however, always seems to remain. 'Minoan' was the name given by Evans to the specifically Cretan culture that would otherwise be classified as Copper and Bronze Age. Evans decided – and not altogether arbitrarily – that there had been three definite periods: Early, Middle and Late Minoan, each of these being subdivided into three phases. The findings of archaeologists since Evans's pioneering days have necessitated many adjustments in his dating, but one of the most recent and authoritative chronologies assigns the following dates:

	Began		*Began*		*Began*
	B.C.		B.C.		B.C.
EM I	2500	MM I	1950	LM I	1550
EM II	2400	MM II	1850	LM II	1450
EM III	2100	MM III	1750	LM III	1400

Not all scholars or published accounts agree on this, and in any case there will probably have to be further adjustments. Therefore, since the average layman cannot always be sure which chronology has been used in assigning dates to artifacts and sites, a different scheme has been adopted for this book. It is one accepted by some scholars in the field and, based upon internal evidence from the principal sites, it uses the terms Pre-, Proto-, Neo- and Post-palatial, covering the following periods:

	B.C.
Pre-palatial	2600–2000
Proto-palatial	2000–1700
Neo-palatial	1700–1400
Post-palatial	1400–1100

Not all of Crete, of course, participated in this recorded culture from the outset. In the early centuries it seems to have been confined mainly to eastern and central settlements; only gradually was there a spread to the west. Moreover, even where several sites are contemporary, they are not necessarily at the same stage of development.

STONE AGE (?–2600 B.C.)

I. PRE-NEOLITHIC

On some of the other Greek islands there have been finds indicating Palaeolithic inhabitants. But although fossil remains of animals indicate that Crete was once attached to the mainland of Europe and Asia, there is no evidence that man arrived on Crete before Neolithic times.

II. NEOLITHIC (5500–2600 B.C.)

In general, archaeologists postulate that the first people to settle in Crete were seafarers or semi-nomadic groups from Asia Minor and/ or North Africa. An early date for their arrival would be between

6000 and 5000 B.C. Their way of life must have been quite primitive at first: hunting and fishing, using stone and bone tools, making simple clay pottery, dwelling in or near caves. Later migrants introduced elementary agriculture, domesticated animals, decorated pottery and simple dwellings of clay bricks on stone foundations. They soon turned to making a variety of vases and clay figurines of familiar animals. From the finds of small steatopygous idols, known from many primitive cultures, it is suggested that they worshipped some aspect of the maternal fertility goddess. Most important for what was to come, some of the earliest settlements were at Knossos, Mallia, Phaestos and Ayia Triadha, as well as at such sites as Katsamba, the caves of Eileithyia and Trapeza, and on the Akrotiri peninsula near Khania.

COPPER AND BRONZE AGE: THE MINOAN ERA (2600–1100 B.C.)

I. Pre-palatial (2600–2000 B.C.)

Cretan culture was developing naturally through late Neolithic stages when, about 2600 B.C., new waves of settlers begin to appear. This was not an invasion and the Neolithic population was only gradually absorbed by the newcomers who were, in any case, most probably close relatives. Where these new people – or peoples – came from cannot be said for certain. But certainly in the next few centuries Crete was to show many influences from Anatolia, Syria, the Cyclades, Egypt and Libya. Whatever cultures they brought with them, however, the peoples intermingled, and the new environment stimulated an individual culture that we know as 'Minoan'. (The Minoans, by the way, were short, the men averaging just a few inches over five feet.)

Copper was worked (there was a mine on Crete) and later bronze. How much trade there was is not certain, but obsidian knives from the earliest times have been found – and obsidian had to be imported, probably from the islands of Melos and Yali (south of Kos) or Anatolia. A new artistry appeared in the treatment of pottery – the incised Pyrgos style, the painted Ayios Onoufrios style, the spiny-shelled Barbotine style and the Vasiliki 'flameware'. The handling of metals and stone revealed an advance in craftsmanship, and the carving of ivory, rock-crystal, precious and semi-precious stones in the sealstones indicates a remarkable sensitivity. The circular and vaulted tombs that first appear at Krassi and Leben and then on the Messara Plain have not only yielded many of the treasured possessions buried with the dead – jewels, tools, seal-stones, vases – but their construction suggests relationships with the later 'beehive' tombs of Mycenae.

The major sites such as Knossos and Phaestos remained settled, but the principal centres of life and culture through most of this period were on the Messara Plain and at the eastern end of the island (sites such as the islands of Mokhlos and Psira, Vasiliki, Kato Zakros and Palaikastro).

II. PROTO-PALATIAL (2000–1700 B.C.)

The construction of the first palaces at Knossos, Phaestos and Mallia shortly after 2000 B.C. accompanied what would appear to have been a rather sudden concentration of power in the ruling families at these settlements along with a general shift of vitality to central Crete. And it is no coincidence that these palaces were in the most productive regions of Crete. A more systematic and hierarchic society came into being. Increased trade with Egypt, Asia Minor, Africa, the Aegean islands and the Mediterranean world in general laid the foundations for the Minoan maritime state ('thalassocracy') as well as providing immediate cultural and commercial gains. Situated in the centre of major sea routes, Crete was something of a 'middleman', importing tin and copper, processing them to make bronze and then exporting the products as far as Troy and Italy in ships made of native cypress and cedarwood. Incidentally, the Keftiu who appear in Egyptian tomb-paintings are generally accepted to be Minoans; most likely, too, they are the same people as those from the island of Kaftor mentioned in the Bible.

A native hieroglyphic script – perhaps derived originally from Egypt – was in use by at least the year 2000 B.C. There were many achievements in arts and crafts – stone-carving, goldwork, jewel-lery, sculpture, pottery (most notably the Kamares polychrome style and 'eggshell' ware).

In about 1700 B.C. the main palaces seem to have been struck by an earthquake, but there is no break in the continuity of Minoan culture. What appeared about this time, though, is Linear A, a script probably used to record commercial and administrative affairs. Scholars have not agreed on what language is recorded by Linear A; Indo-European and Semitic languages have been put forward as candidates.

III. Neo-palatial (1700–1400 b.c.)

The palaces at Knossos, Phaestos and Mallia were reconstructed and additions brought about the grand structure we know as a Minoan palace: several storeys, majestic stairways, great courts, murals, corridors, columns, workshops, ritual chambers, together with all the technical achievements that would mark them as advanced in many parts of the world even today. There seems to have been a concentration of power at Knossos, but numerous towns and villas, as well as paved roads, irrigation works and other structures throughout the island indicate the extent of wealth and energies during this period.

It should be remembered, however, that most of the refinements were confined to the palaces and upper classes; there are no grounds for thinking that the mass of Cretans enjoyed any of this style or comfort. Their life was probably at least as good as that of most people of their day, but most Minoans were farmers and workers who supported the society that culminated in the Priest-King of Knossos, the legendary Minos. ('Minos', by the way, was probably a generic title, like Pharaoh, and applied to several rulers.)

The epitome of aristocratic refinement is to be seen in the role that women seem to have enjoyed in the life at court. This is the sophisticated Minoan social life that can be deduced from frescoes and other remains. Crete was not a matriarchal society, however, even if some women at the palaces may have had a fair amount of independence and influence.

The Mother Goddess was worshipped, with symbols such as the double axe, the pillar, horns, the dove, snakes and flowers. The familiar Snake Goddess was only one of various manifestations of this Mother Goddess, the object of devotion throughout much of the ancient world at this time. The Minoans adopted most of their symbols, but probably developed some rituals on their own; their bull-leaping, for instance, may have been involved with some religious ceremony.

By now Crete was one of the chief maritime powers in the Mediterranean. Its influence can be detected in the finds of artifacts in many distant corners of the ancient world. There is one theory, too, based on resemblances of burial structures and some few artifacts, that Cretan merchant ships went through the Straits of Gibraltar and up the coast of Europe as far as Scandinavia. The discovery of stone markings very similar to the Minoans' double axe at Stonehenge has even suggested to some a Cretan architect. But even if the Minoans were not physically present in these lands, they took part in the widespread trading operations of the time. For example, Crete imported amber that came down across Europe on the amber routes from the Baltic.

Crete's far-ranging ships not only enriched the island's economy but they protected the island to the extent that the great palaces needed virtually no special fortifications, though undoubtedly they had a defensive warning system along the coasts. Minoan society, indeed, is characterized more as a vast commercial complex than as a militaristic power. All the arts and crafts were practised. Vase-making particularly flourished, with decoration becoming more naturalistic in its use of marine and floral motifs.

Around 1500 B.C. the Linear A script was adapted to record a new language, at least at Knossos. Until 1953 the revised script was known only as Linear B, but, primarily owing to the efforts of Michael Ventris, it is now accepted to be recording an early form of Greek. The extant records are largely inventories and other such mundane accounts, but the implications cannot be dismissed. If Greek was being spoken, there must have been mainland Greeks on Crete – and in positions of some influence. If so, they were most likely the Achaeans of Mycenae. It has long been accepted that the Minoans were involved with the Mycenaeans. What is now coming to be recognized is that the Mycenaeans played a more active role in Minoan life (at least at Knossos) and from an earlier time than had been supposed.

In about 1400 B.C. Knossos and many of the other centres of Minoan society seem to have been simultaneously overwhelmed. The most generally accepted theory now is that there was a catastrophic explosion of Théra (Santorini), the volcanic island due north of Crete, accompanied by a rain of volcanic matter, a tidal wave and an earthquake on Crete itself. Some scholars think that invaders or rebel forces attacked and burnt the palaces; still others have suggested that a natural disaster merely exposed the island to new influences. Sir Arthur Evans and his supporters believe that, whatever the calamity, it marked the effective end of Minoan society and culture. According to this view, 'squatters' took over the abandoned palaces, merely biding their time until the coming of the Dorians some centuries later.

IV. Post-palatial (1400–1100 b.c.)

Whatever or whoever was responsible for the collapse of the distinctive Minoan culture, the Achaeans were certainly on the scene during the years that followed. Although some of the peculiarly Minoan social, religious and artistic patterns seem to have been broken up, the arts and crafts did not completely disappear. At least parts of some of the sites – including Knossos, Tylissos, Ayia Triadha, Palaikastro – were restored and reoccupied. Some of the Minoans seem to have founded new villages elsewhere on the island, especially in eastern Crete.

With the balance of power shifted to the mainland, the commercial importance of Crete disappeared, although the island still exported and imported. And when the Mycenaean Greeks undertook the expedition against Troy, Crete joined in the struggle, led by King Idomeneus.

The real significance of the struggle at Troy, however, was that it signalled the disintegration of the Bronze Age world, already weakened by wars, economic strains and general social stresses. New peoples were on the move and power was shifting throughout much of the ancient world during the thirteenth and twelfth centuries b.c. Among the people on the rise were the Dorians, one of several Greek tribes from the north-western Balkans who had been encroaching on the Aegean world for some time. By the end of the twelfth century, the Achaean strongholds had been totally overrun by the Dorians, and the Mycenaean domain, including Crete, lay exposed. The Bronze Age had ended.

IRON AGE: THE GREEK WORLD (1100–67 b.c.)

I. Sub-minoan – Geometric – Orientalizing – Archaic
Periods (1100–500 b.c.)

Although it has been claimed that Knossos was destroyed in the twelfth century b.c. along with other Achaean strongholds, this is not generally accepted. In any case, the coming of the Dorians to Crete was not marked by widespread destruction, nor was it sudden. Crete, rather, went into a state of gradual decline, during which some of the major sites were deserted. As the Dorians moved on to the island, there was probably little organized resistance and so little need for violence. The native population, however, was reduced to a serf class, so some of the Minoans took refuge in hill sites. Others withdrew to sites in the far east of the island, where for hundreds of years they kept alive some of their Minoan heritage, thus becoming known as Eteocretans, or the indigenous Cretans. (See the remarks on Eteocretans under Sitia, p. 263, and Praisos, p. 270. Or see Homer, *Odyssey*, Book XIX.)

For a while Crete was lost in the Dark Ages that settled over much of the Greek world. The island was isolated and inactive, although such arts and crafts as vase-making were kept up and, if anything, stimulated by the new Dorian forms. Iron, meanwhile, was gradually replacing bronze. Then some of the old sites were reoccupied and there were new signs of life in western Crete. As Crete renewed contact with the outside world, influences from the Near East – in particular, Syria, Phoenicia, Assyria and Egypt – appear. And out of the mixture of the various elements – from Minoan to Dorian to Near Eastern – a new culture emerged; it can be thought of as starting about 900 B.C. It was no longer a specifically Cretan culture, for Crete was now part of the broader currents known as the Geometric, Orientalizing and Archaic periods. In the case of its pottery and sculpture, however, Crete made distinctive contributions. Sites such as Lato, Dreros and Prinias witnessed notable architectural achievements.

Perhaps most surprising is to find on Crete the full-fledged Dorian social system similar to Sparta's, with the Dorian aristocrats ruling over the native serfs and the young male citizens raised in communal houses to be warriors. The Dorians on Crete were especially advanced in their constitution and laws, too, judging from their reputation and such evidence as the Code of Gortyna (p. 176).

II. CLASSIC – HELLENISTIC PERIODS (500–67 B.C.)

In the end, though, the Dorians were unable to consolidate their governments or resources, and each city-state went its own way. During the great days of the Attic-Athenian civilization, Crete remained a provincial outpost, sharing in neither the struggles nor the glory. It is tempting to speculate as to why Crete failed to develop into another Athens – but then who else did? Crete had had its day. Yet the Greeks of the classic age paid their respects to Crete, for they saw it as the source of much of their culture, especially in the matter of myths and the law (pp. 95–6). During this period Crete produced nothing notable of its own, but trade brought a certain prosperity and there was also some building. Cities issued their own coinage. Knossos, Gortyna and Kydonia exercised some rule over lesser settlements. Around the year 300 B.C. certain cities in the west – Elyros, Lissos, Hyrtakina, Tarrha, Syia, Poikilassos – formed the Confederation of Oreioi, with Gortyna, and Cyrenaica under King Magus, joining later.

During the next 250 years Cretan cities and settlements made and broke alliances with various Mediterranean powers – Sparta, Macedonia, Egypt, Rhodes. There were continual feuds, skirmishes and wars, and the island came to be known as the haunt of lawless pirates, mercenaries – and liars! In actual fact, there was a fair amount of building during the twilight years of the Hellenistic period, but Crete as a whole declined. By the first century B.C. the Romans were interfering more and more in the island's quarrels. Rome was perturbed, moreover, by its alliances with such foreign powers as Mithridates the Great from Pontus.

ROMAN AND BYZANTINE ERA (67 B.C.–A.D. 1204)

I. ROMAN OCCUPATION (67 B.C.–A.D. 395)

The Romans came to settle the island's feuds; they stayed to conquer. After sporadic campaigning for three years – with Quintus Caecilius Metellus gaining the final triumphs – they acquired another province. Gortyna became the capital of Crete and Cyrenaica (part of North Africa). The Romans had ambitious plans for Crete, and after initial repressions prosperity of a sort was established. There was extensive building at Gortyna and elsewhere on the island, including an impressive settlement near Knossos. The Romans left their familiar landmarks all over the island – villas, mosaics, temples, sculptures, aqueducts, roads and brickwork. The Apostle Paul is supposed to have made his first landing on European soil in about A.D. 47 at Kaloi Limenes ('Fair Havens') while on his way to Rome as a prisoner. Tradition has it that he appointed Titus as Bishop of Gortyna, and it was Titus who spread the Christian faith on Crete.

II. FIRST BYZANTINE PERIOD (A.D. 395–824)

With the division of the Roman Empire into the western and eastern sections, Crete fell under the sway of Byzantium. Christianity prospered, with considerable building of basilicas; the most notable was Ayios Titos at Gortyna, around the sixth century. In the political-economic sphere Crete was virtually an abandoned outpost. Trade routes shifted, and the Arabs slowly absorbed the Mediterranean territories.

III. ARABIC OCCUPATION (A.D. 824–961)

Abou Hafs Omar, having been driven out of both Spain and Alexandria, came to Crete with his band of brigands, attacked and destroyed Gortyna and overran the island, establishing a fort at Rabd-el-Kandek – the nucleus of what was to become Iraklion. During the next century or so Crete was used by the Arabs as a pirates' base; all attempts to regain the island for Byzantium failed. There was no colonizing on any scale, but there were some intermarriages and conversions.

IV. SECOND BYZANTINE PERIOD (A.D. 961–1204)

Eventually the Byzantine general, Nikiphoros Phokas, liberated Crete. It is said that he catapulted the chopped-off heads of his Muslim prisoners against the garrison. Aristocratic families from the Greek mainland, Christians from eastern territories and European merchants were 'imported' to effect a revival of Crete. A variety of feudalism developed, the former Muslims being retained as slaves. Phokas, meanwhile, had moved on to become (in 963) one of the great Byzantine emperors – and patron of one of the monasteries on Mount Athos. Crete once more had a place on the perimeter of affairs.

VENETIAN OCCUPATION (A.D. 1204–1669)

Byzantium fell during the Fourth Crusade, and Crete was 'given' to Boniface of Monferrato, who in turn sold it to the Venetians for a thousand silver marks. In the meantime the Genoese had set themselves up there, and together with the native Cretans they resisted the Venetians. But in 1210 Jacopo Tiepolo was appointed first Governor and the Venetians began their long occupation. They named the island and its capital city 'Candia' and set to work to organize, fortify and adorn their new territory. Many of the fortifications and castles remain to this day. The island was divided up on feudal principles: six sections, corresponding to the six quarters of Venice, were thrown open to Venetian colonizers and entrepreneurs. But the native Cretans were never quiet for very long and there were several bloody revolts. The Venetians had hoped to impose their own way of life, but actually many of the Italian colonists joined the Cretans in revolting against the unjust taxes and privileges of the Mother City, Venice. In fact, it became clear that the Venetians were there to convert only one thing: produce into gold.

With the decline of the Byzantine Empire and the fall of Constantinople in 1453, Crete had become a refuge for artists and scholars from the mainland. Orthodox monasteries, schools, literature and painting flourished, borrowing details from the Venetians but essentially preserving Greek traditions (see p. 97). Now and again the Cretans pressed their attacks on the Venetian overlords. In certain parts they practically had self-rule; but also many Cretans had accepted positions and privileges from the Venetians – the barriers were falling down.

In the meantime, during the sixteenth century pirates under the Turkish 'Barbarossa', Khair Eddin, were ravaging the Cretan coastal towns. The Venetians set about restoring and enlarging the various walls and forts. The Turks had come to see Crete as one of the last barriers to the west and in 1645 they mounted a fleet and took Khania; Rethymnon fell the next year, and in 1648 there began the epic siege of Candia (Iraklion).

For the next twenty-two years all Europe waited and watched what was probably the longest siege of its kind in history. Candia was the last outpost of Christianity against the Ottoman Empire in that part of the world, and when its downfall seemed imminent Pope Clement IX appealed for aid. Louis XIV sent a French force under the Duc de Beaufort, but it was wiped out. In the final two years Candia's defence was undertaken by Francesco Morosini, but he was finally forced to surrender. The Turks let the defenders leave with honour, and most of the Cretans deserted the city. Some Cretans went to settle in Mani, the southern tip of the Peloponnese, and also in the Ionian Islands; from Mani, some moved on to Corsica, where a variation of the Cretan dialect has been reported as surviving until quite recently.

TURKISH OCCUPATION (A.D. 1669–1898)

I. YEARS OF SUPPRESSION (A.D. 1669–1821)

The island was once again divided among foreign conquerors and administrators – this time the Pashas. There were, however, no great numbers of Turkish colonists.

At first the Cretans willingly traded Turks for Venetians. But relations soon deteriorated. The Turks took over the cities, the Cretans clung to their mountains and the Janissaries roamed at will. Under the non-administration of the Turks, agriculture and commerce declined, roads fell into disrepair, walls and forts crumbled and building largely ceased – even the mosques were converted churches. Taxes and tariffs took so much that the Cretans lost all incentive; the population declined, and earthquakes and insurrections defeated construction.

In spite of this sad history, however, it is estimated that by the mid-eighteenth century there were 60,000 Christians and 200,000 Muslims on Crete – and almost all of the latter were converted Cretans! This may not be one of the proudest statistics of Crete's history, but for most people it was a simple question of survival. Moreover, many of them were Muslim in name only; the Orthodox faith was practised and sustained. Nor were the Cretans entirely passive during these years. There were several uprisings, the best known being the one led by Daskaloyiannis in 1770. Unfortunately, though, mountaineers like the Sfakians, who raided and then retired, brought persecution and bloodshed to the exposed villages.

II. YEARS OF REVOLUTION (A.D. 1821–98)

With the uprising against the Turks on the mainland in 1821, Greece set off on the road to independence. Crete joined in, but was unable to keep up the pace. When the new Greek state was proclaimed in 1832, the Allied Powers ceded Crete to the Egyptians – who had actually been called in by the Turks to put down the revolution in 1824. But by 1840 the Turks were back in possession.

The nineteenth century on Crete is one of the most shameful episodes in Great Power politics. Decisive action by England, France, Italy and Russia – acting in consort or in any combination – could have resulted in the final handing over of Crete to Greece. Instead there were compromises, intrigues, rivalry – and inaction. But on Crete there was insurrection and bloodshed. Every decade had its uprising, but these fail to tell the full story of suffering and slaughter. The rallying cry during these years was 'Freedom or Death'; for most Cretans there was only the latter.

Finally, in 1898, after a relatively minor incident – which happened to involve loss of life among some of the British soldiers stationed on Crete – the Allied Powers stepped in, forced the Turks to leave, and granted the island autonomous status under a High Commissioner, Prince George, younger son of the Greek King.

TWENTIETH-CENTURY CRETE (A.D. 1898–Present)

I. Towards Union (A.D. 1898–1913)

Prince George was warmly welcomed in December 1898; in the next year a Cretan assembly met to draw up a constitution and a new spirit of order and co-operation prevailed. Many Cretans refused to settle for half, however; they wanted union with Greece or no outside interference. Turmoil set in once more and in 1905 Eleftherios Venizelos led an abortive revolution. Venizelos, a Cretan, was destined to become the only modern Greek statesman who can be classed in the grand European tradition. His ancestors, it is true, had come from the mainland, but Venizelos, born in 1864 at Mournies (p. 222), was forged in the Cretan struggles. A staunch republican and politician, he first raised his banner by forming a party pledged to seek union with Greece. In 1905 he convened a revolutionary assembly at Theriso (p. 222), in violation of the government of Prince George and the Allied Powers. When he resorted to arms he was beaten down, but he forced the retirement of Prince George and gave notice that Venizelos and Crete would be heard of some day soon in the parliament of Greece. Eventually he had his way; he was Premier of Greece during several tempestuous administrations; he was listened to at the Treaty of Versailles; he lost a great deal, for himself and for Greece, but the net gain was the modern Greek nation.

After the 1905 revolt, the next few years were merely a biding of time until Crete could openly be taken into the Greek nation. Finally in 1913 – and not until the whole Balkan region had been embroiled in a war – the union of Crete with Greece was officially recognized.

II. Settlement – and Occupation (A.D. 1913–44)

Crete quietened down and went unscathed during the First World War. But in 1923 it was exposed to another severe strain by the exchanges of population between Greece and Turkey. The Turkish population – about 11,000 – left, and about 13,000 Greek refugees from Asia Minor came in their place. So once more Crete settled down, to build and prosper. Agriculture and commerce were increasing; archaeology and tourism gave promise of a new future. Then in 1941 the Second World War descended on Crete, first in the person of British troops driven from the Greek mainland by the invading Germans. The British decided to make a stand, and on May 20th the German paratroops and gliders began to land. The British forces were assisted by the Cretan citizenry, using any weapon they could get their hands on, and for several days the Germans got the worst of it. After the war, in fact, it was revealed that the German High Command regarded the Cretan airborne operation as something of a disaster, owing to the high mortality rate. But once the Germans held the airport at Maleme, west of Khania, reinforcements poured in. By May 30th the battle of Crete was over. Thousands of British troops managed to get across the mountains to the south coast and were taken off to Egypt. Many failed to get away.

For the next three and a half years Crete was an occupied land. At times it was a bitter one, with forced labour, insufficient food, deprivations of all kinds and punitive retaliations against many villages. The Cretans continued the struggle as guerrillas and partisans, helped by special British agents, against the German and Italian troops. The latter occupied the eastern end of Crete. The most famous incident of this period was the kidnapping of the German Commandant Kreipe, who was then taken off to Egypt by an English submarine. With the end of the occupation in October 1944 – after the Germans had made a last-ditch stand at Khania – Crete surveyed the damage. Iraklion had been particularly hard hit, and so had several other coastal towns; many villages lay in ruins; transport, roads and commerce were idle; food was a pressing problem.

III. POST-WAR YEARS (A.D. 1944–PRESENT)

The United Nations moved in to save Crete during the first months of peace, but the islanders soon recovered their equilibrium. In the next few years, although there were still some lingering conflicts between the several resistance groups, Crete even had an advantage over mainland Greece in avoiding civil war. With its commerce and agriculture restored, Crete in fact began to attain new levels of prosperity and construction increased. Further excavations, with publicity for the archaeological sites, has brought increasing numbers of tourists to the island; the future of Crete may well lie in its past.

HISTORY OF EXCAVATIONS

One of the most frustrating sensations while exploring some ancient site is to know nothing about the circumstances of the excavations themselves. When were the remains discovered? Who excavated them? For how many years have visitors been able to view them as we know them today? Such questions often rush to mind, and usually must remain unanswered. Here we offer a brief survey of the exploration and excavation of Crete in order to put the whole field into some perspective. For it is one of the most common fallacies in the entire realm of archaeology to say that until Sir Arthur Evans excavated the great palace at Knossos no one had ever suspected that Crete had a past. According to this version, Evans was the first to stumble on to Crete, the first to dig, the first to reveal the existence of a Cretan culture; before Evans there was nothing but vague mythology and a few classical allusions.

It is true that Evans was the first to advance the evidence and concept of a peculiar Minoan civilization. But the plain fact is that Crete had never been completely lost to men's eyes or minds. Indeed, the list of those who had come to Crete before Evans is a long and honourable one, which includes the Homeric heroes as well as Schliemann. In the *Iliad* and the *Odyssey*, Crete appears only indirectly, but it is cited as the home of populous cities – respectively 100 or 90, only a few of which are named – and as a land of great wealth. (In Hesiod, on the other hand, Crete is a land of the gods; it is he who sets the tone of mythology that is later associated with Crete.) The disguised Odysseus pretends to have come from there – he even mentions the Cave of Eileithyia; and part of Menelaus' fleet is blown ashore south of Phaestos – but in general Crete is a distant prospect.

By the time of the classical mainland civilization the Cretan cities and their glories were all but legendary, although one,

Gortyna, was still to enjoy a revival. Numerous classical sources refer to Crete: historians, commentators, geographers, travellers. To men such as Thucydides, Aristotle, Apollodorus, Diodorus Siculus, Pliny, Strabo, Appian, Ptolemy, as well as many others, Crete was a very real place, even if all their facts were not quite correct. But Strabo, in the first century B.C. gives quite accurate distances between Cretan sites.

After the Roman occupation of the island, Crete passed into obscurity. The *Stadiasmus*, an anonymous 'Admiralty Chart' of the sixth to eleventh centuries A.D., mentions many places and routes on Crete, but like much of the Mediterranean world Crete fell into disrepair. For hundreds of years its cities and sites, temples and tombs were abandoned to the ravages of time and climate, earthquakes, marauders and – perhaps most destructive of all – Cretans themselves, seeking materials for new structures.

The arrival of the Venetians in the thirteenth century provided both losses and gains, but at least Crete re-entered the awareness of the western world. The Venetians' name for the island, 'Candia', began to appear in dispatches, and men passing through the eastern Mediterranean on the way to the Levant or Asia often made a point of calling at Crete. The Italian Buondelmonti, in the fifteenth century, was among the first to record his visit; he was able to say of Gortyna that he 'counted two thousand columns and statues upturned by time. For grandeur it is the equal of our Florence.' Belon and Belli in the sixteenth century; Boschini and Lithgow in the seventeenth; Tournefort, Savary and Pococke in the eighteenth; Tancoigne, Olivier, Sieber and Hartley in the early decades of the nineteenth – these are only a few of the men who set down their impressions of Crete. In addition, scholarly works such as those of Meursius (1675), Dapper (1688), Cornelius (1755) and Hoeck (1823–9) kept the academic light burning for later archaeologists.

With the publication of Robert Pashley's *Travels in Crete* in 1837 a new era began. Pashley was one of England's indefatigable scholar-travellers; after finishing his book the reader is left feeling that there was nothing for anyone else to discover. He had in fact a remarkably high score in his identification of sites. However, when he reaches what he feels is 'undoubtedly the site of Knossos', he says, 'All the now existing vestiges of the ancient "metropolis" of Crete are some rude masses of Roman brickwork ... ' The fact is that Pashley, like his predecessors, had no idea of how much he was missing; despite all they did see and despite all they knew of Crete's past, they lacked one simple tool – the spade.

Pashley was followed by men such as Raulin and Spratt, just as knowledgable in their own ways, so that by 1870 most of Crete had been brought into the area of the *known*. But what all these men had settled for were fragments protruding above ground, or random surface finds of artifacts. Some were scholars, of course, and cited a classical allusion for every remain they saw; at most they might dig up a column or a sarcophagus. Yet if none excavated, as we understand the term today, some of them certainly looked very hard, and turned up things that provided material links to Crete's past. From the time of Pashley on, there could be no doubting the existence of historical Crete; it was only a question of digging it up.

Two events in the year 1878 gave the impetus to Cretan archaeology. One was when a Cretan merchant and amateur archaeologist (most fittingly named Minos Kalokairinos) was digging in an olive grove a few miles south of Iraklion, not far from the known Roman ruins. His spade struck a buried structure, and before long he was uncovering extensive walls, stones with masons' marks on them, and huge storage urns. W. J. Stillman, an American archaeologist-journalist, who had once served as consul on Crete, went off to explore with Minos. Before they could proceed much farther the Turkish authorities put a stop to the excavations, but not before Stillman had sent out various dispatches. Heinrich Schliemann read the accounts and in 1886 he arrived in Crete, determined to buy the land concerned. He was unable to come to terms with its owner, however, and abandoned his 'hope of discovering the original home of Mycenaean civilization'. What Minos Kalokairinos had excavated, by the way, were store-rooms of the palace of Knossos.

In that same year a group of prominent Cretans formed an association to advance the education and culture of the islanders. Within a few years they were concentrating on preserving the historical and archaeological remains, collecting antiquities and generally encouraging excavation. (From this enterprise, incidentally, developed the Archaeological Museum in Iraklion.) The guiding spirit behind all this was Joseph Hadzidakis of Iraklion. Scholar, active archaeologist, first curator of Cretan antiquities, not the least of his achievements is the aid he lent to the various foreign archaeologists during the early years of 'digging up' Crete.

In the meantime – starting in 1884 – an Italian mission was

travelling about the island making significant discoveries of both epigraphical materials and ancient sites. To the Italians, in fact – headed by Professor Federigo Halbherr – should go the credit for the first really sustained and professional excavations on Crete. By 1900 parts of Gortyna, the Caves of Idha, Eileithyia and Kamares, many tombs and other sites had been revealed by the combined efforts of Greek, Italian and other foreign archaeologists.

Then came the spectacular excavations at Knossos. Sir Arthur Evans had originally come to Crete in 1894 in search of linguistic materials. He was looking for sealstones with pictographs, and in the course of his searches he uncovered several sites, explored caves and tombs and made finds that were later to occupy many other archaeologists. After several attempts he was finally able to buy the entire plot of land at Knossos. There, armed with his personal fortune, his knowledge and his insight, and aided by a staff of technicians, archaeologists and artists, he supervised the literal unearthing of Minoan civilization. It was to take many decades, and the whole world looked over his shoulder. It is little wonder that Evans has come to stand as the Columbus of Crete, but it does not belittle his achievement to recognize all those who had gone before.

From 1900 onwards, the excavation of Crete proceeded by leaps and bounds, stimulated by the finds at Knossos. Some were the results of individual quests; others came about through patient searching by teams of archaeologists. The Greeks were active throughout the island, finding the tombs of the Messara and the *megarons* of Tylissos, Nirou Khani and Amnisos. The Italians were uncovering many sites; concentrating on the Messara, they excavated Phaestos, Ayia Triadha and Gortyna. English archaeologists spread over the island and were particularly active in eastern Crete, as well as exploring caves generally. The French undertook such sites as Mallia, Lato and Dreros. Americans excavated Gournia, Mokhlos and Psira. By 1940 the major patterns of Cretan archaeology had been established.

Excavating has by no means ceased. Even during the German occupation it went on to some extent. The Greek government and various archaeological missions from foreign lands bear the burden of the expenses now, and some of the glamour may seem to have passed. But to dedicated archaeologists the day-to-day finds at even some of the more modest sites can be exciting. And since the war there have been some quite dramatic finds, at both old sites and new discoveries – such as those at Katsamba, Leben, Phaestos, Knossos Vathypetro, Phourni near Arkhanes and, above all, the unearthing of a great Minoan palace at Kato Zakros.

With the refinement of techniques, e.g. stratigraphic excavation (the precise recording of levels), and new dating methods, some of the previous conclusions about the history of Crete have had to be modified. Crete now stands like some great jigsaw puzzle: most of the pieces are there, but the problem of arrangement still remains. And although it is unlikely that anything as spectacular as Knossos or Kato Zakros lies buried, there is a good chance of major finds yet to come.

ART, LEGENDS AND LITERATURE

Considering its size, its isolation, its unsettled history, Crete has made some truly remarkable contributions to both Greek and Western European culture. The art and artifacts of the Minoan civilization are widely known: vases and ceramics in a dazzling variety of forms, techniques and motifs; sealstones and jewellery with an unusual delicacy of style and observation; statuettes and carvings created with a perception and freedom transcending their times; frescoes almost bewildering in the range and reality of their subjects. These have all been pictured and publicized, although one should still make the pilgrimage to the Iraklion Archaeological Museum to see them in their glory. (The Ashmolean Museum at Oxford has the second finest collection of Cretan art and antiquities, thanks to Sir Arthur Evans's bequests.) Even when adapting or transmitting the art of others, Crete gave its inimitable imprint.

In one medium above all Minoan Crete attained unique dimensions. That was architecture. Its palaces were Crete's distinctive achievement. Nor is there any possibility of confusing Minoan architecture with that of classical Greece; to put it briefly, in place of symmetry there is improvisation. Small rooms and various structures cluster around a central court; additions seem to be accidental; the sites themselves are irregular; the total complex seems to 'erupt' at random levels. Yet the more one examines the different palaces, the more one appreciates the design of the whole.

D

It is dynamic, organic – an architecture that anticipates the modern style of a Frank Lloyd Wright.

As regards literature, the Minoans left none that we are aware of. But when all the evidence is collected who knows how influential – even crucial – Crete was in transmitting the alphabet to the western world? One thing seems certain: the Minoans must have had a rich stock of folklore if they were anything like their descendants. Songs, tales, ballads, proverbs, popular lore of every kind, were surely passed on orally from generation to generation. And, of far more importance than a barren legacy of fragments and minor texts, Crete left a vital corpus to the classical world – and to our own – in mythology.

The traveller to Crete who wishes to recognize its oldest traditions should prepare himself by reviewing these myths. 'Review', because it is surprising how many of the familiar personages and episodes of classical mythology concern Crete. In a book such as *The Greek Myths* by Robert Graves, almost every page contains at least a passing allusion to Crete. It must, however, be admitted that many of these myths were transplanted to Crete long after the decline of the indigenous culture. On the other hand Crete must have offered a fertile soil for the proliferation of such myths.

There is the birth of Zeus himself, involving Cronus and Rhea, as well as several episodes in his youth; these are associated with specific Cretan caves, although scholars have not agreed as to which is which (p. 74). Later, Zeus returns to Crete, this time in the guise of a bull, carrying Europa on his back; the associations here run through three thousand years of European art. Europa bears Zeus three sons – Sarpedon, Rhadamanthys and Minos. It is the last-named who became the dominating force in Crete's myth-history; the repercussions have never really stopped.

There is a certain ambiguity in the figure of Minos. On the one hand, he is the harsh tyrant whose ships scour the seas while he sacrifices to the Minotaur; on the other hand, he is the just and benevolent lawgiver who attains immortality as a judge in the after-life. But that is only part of Minos' drama. He had a wife, Pasiphaë, who had a god-willed lust for a bull; their union produced the Mino-taur. This was the occasion for the Labyrinth, constructed by the legendary craftsman Daedalus to hide the Minotaur. Then comes Theseus – who would seem to embody some semi-historical figure or event – the slaying of the Minotaur, the flight with Ariadne. Later,

Theseus marries Phaedra, another of Crete's ill-starred daughters, and there follows the classic tale of her passion for Hippolytus. It is an endless thread, indeed. Meanwhile, Heracles had accomplished the seventh of his Twelve Labours on Crete. There is also Daedalus, back in the Labyrinth; his escape with his son Icarus has never ceased to engage man's wonder. In addition there are all the secondary figures – Britomartis, Miletus, Talos the Bronze Monster. Crete may not have given birth to all these gods and heroes, but they have all wanted to claim Cretan ancestry.

At the time of the Homeric Age the balance of power had shifted, but in some versions of the Trojan War the Cretan Idomeneus was accepted as an equal of Agamemnon. Judging from the behaviour of Idomeneus in the *Iliad*, the Cretans had a reputation as rather rugged fighters. This same Idomeneus appears some three thousand years later in a considerably less boisterous setting – Mozart's *Idomeneo*, which deals with his return to Crete after the Trojan War.

With the coming of the Dorians, Crete entered into the mainstream of the cultural world as it was developing in that part of the Mediterranean. There was a minor resurgence of the Cretan genius in ceramics, and, although it cannot be claimed that Crete originated the forms, it certainly contributed its share to the emerging art of the Geometric and Oriental styles. By the seventh century B.C. still another force was at work, this time in the archaic sculpture of the Greek world. Crete has generally been credited with playing a major role in the development of the 'Daedalic' style, which was named after the mythical craftsman. In addition to the Daedalic sculptures on view in Iraklion, there are the 'Lady of Auxerre' in the Louvre, a bronze statuette at Delphi, and figures in New York and other museums.

With the ascendance of the Attic-Athenian culture, Crete was completely overshadowed. It can, however, be fairly claimed that Crete was the cradle of many of the manifestations of the classical civilization. Various students have claimed to see a Cretan influence in much of its art and architecture; certainly it can be said that Crete played a dominant role in its mythology and religion – there was, for instance, a legend that the first priests at Delphi were Cretans from Knossos. Then, too, there is a fragment of a lost tragedy by Euripides, *The Cretans*, that appears to deal with a religious cult. Beneath the classical veneer a Cretan influence often seems to be lurking. Cresilas, the sculptor of the well-known bust of Pericles, was from Kydonia in Crete. There is even a theory that Plato's 'Atlantis' is really Crete. Or take, for instance, one of the most famous Cretans of this period – Epimenides. Said to have flourished around the turn of the sixth century B.C., he came to Sparta and Athens and is credited with shaping the legislation of the times. Numerous works are attributed to him, including the constitution of Crete and mythical-mystical texts. In due time many myths accrued to him, such as that he was a son of Zeus, slept in a Cretan cave for fifty-seven years, had prophetic revelations and was reincarnated. Obviously something of an apocryphal figure, his most famous line, alas, is his claim: 'All Cretans are liars!'

It was in the domain of law, however, that Cretans were particularly honoured. Both Minos and Rhadamanthys were installed as judges in the underworld. Lycurgos, the lawgiver of Sparta, was said to have studied on Crete. Solon also was inspired and influenced by Cretan law; indeed, it was Solon who counselled Athens to bring Epimenides from Crete to help purify the city. Plato and Aristotle paid frequent tribute to Crete. And if more tangible evidence is required, we have only to consider the Code of Gortyna (p. 176), still standing as irrefutable testimony to Crete's pre-eminence.

Gortyna also stands as a symbol of the Romans' ambitions on Crete. They came, conquered and built, but the Empire declined before Crete could contribute to the greater glory of Rome. And Rome did little for Crete. Instead, the winds blew from the East. Paul of Tarsus passed through. Paul's immediate heir on Crete was Titus; his testament is in Acts xxvii and the Epistle to Titus. With the absorption of Crete by the Eastern Empire at the end of the fourth century A.D., the island was left pretty much to its own devices. Church buildings and mosaics seem to have been the sole expressions of any aspirations. The Arabs came and went, from 824 to 961; then mainland Greeks asserted themselves on Crete under the banner of Nikiphoros Phokas. In the thirteenth century all Greece became prey to the plundering Crusaders and warring commercial states of Europe; Crete fell to the Venetians.

For the next four and a half centuries Crete was a Venetian colony. During the first half of this occupation there were frequent and bloody uprisings, but the Venetians imposed their *castelli* and order, and a cosmopolitanism gradually took over in the main city-ports. Yet, somehow, Cretans survived as such, in their language, their religion, their folklore, their dances, their art and their traditions; the people kept their identity. As described in the History section, after the fall of Constantinople in 1453 Crete was one of the last outposts of Orthodox Greek culture; scholars and artists, fleeing from the mainland, often landed there. A fascinating footnote to history, by the way, is the fact that many Cretans, both natives and transients, went on to western Europe, where they played a crucial role in transmitting the actual texts of the classics and promoting Greek studies, thus helping to advance the Renaissance. Venice, in particular, had a large colony of Greeks, among whom Cretans were prominent as printers, copyists and editors. To single out but one, the native Cretan Markos Musuros was influential in bringing out the famous Aldine Press editions of the Greek classics.

Thus, the three traditions met: the indigenous vigour, the links with the West via Venice, and the cultivated forms of Byzantium. The result was Crete's version of the Renaissance during the sixteenth and seventeenth centuries. The literary products of this period are not generally known outside Greece, which is a pity. There is the poetry of Sakhlikis, who recounts his escapades in a Rabelaisian manner. There is a pastoral poem – *The Fair Shepherdess* – perhaps somewhat incongruous on an island of such real shepherds. The most notable work is the long epic poem *Erotokritos* by Vincenzo Cornaros; it strikes those who read it today as a mausoleum of conventions, but it exercised considerable influence on modern Greek literature, and even now can still be heard in the villages of Crete. (Georgios Seferis, the 1963 Nobel prize-winner in Literature, in his poem, 'On a Foreign Verse', speaks of his boyhood in Smyrna and says: ' ... like certain mariners who ... recited to me in my childhood the song of *Erotokritos* with tears in their eyes ... ')

It was the drama, however, that experienced the finest flowering. Eight plays and various interludes (not all intact) have been preserved from the period 1550 to 1670, and if none is a masterpiece – and all are highly derivative – they represent a significant achievement. The finest is *The Sacrifice of Abraham*, attributed to Cornaros. It is in the familiar vein of the medieval mysteries, but individual touches and its insight make it truly Cretan. Two other Cretan plays of distinction are *Gyparis*, a pastoral comedy, and *Erophile*, a tragedy. Some of these plays have been revived by Greek theatre groups in recent years, and it is occasionally possible to see them at some summer festival. *The Sacrifice of Abraham*, incidentally, was presented at Amsterdam in the early 1920s in a Dutch translation by Hesseling.

But it is in another medium that medieval-Renaissance Crete has held the attention of the world: in painting, both of frescoes and icons. Scholars have not yet separated all the strands in the tapestry of Cretan–Byzantine painting; besides indigenous art there is an imported influence. The Byzantine schools of Macedonia and Mistra evidently made some impact; later there was the influence of Italy. Yet it is agreed that there is a recognizable 'Cretan school' of Byzantine art, even though this may be more a style and technique than the work of a circle of friends. In either case, the Cretan spirit speaks with an intense masculine energy. Figures are often exaggerated in length, realistic detail is emphasized, a chiaroscuro effect is achieved by the use of bold colours over dark backgrounds.

When used in a restrictive sense, the term 'Cretan school' refers to the fresco painting that flourished during the fifteenth and sixteenth centuries, although frescoes of other periods – as well as icons of that era – reveal some of the same spirit. Among the six hundred or more chapels and churches on Crete, there are many that still have their wall-paintings intact – albeit restored. The most notable examples are at Kritsa (p. 252), Ayios Fanourios (p. 170), Potamies (p. 161), in the chapels around Kastelli-Pedhiadhos (p. 166) and in the provinces of Amari (p. 196) and Selinou (p. 233). In more accessible places many of these would attract thousands of viewers. In the sixteenth century several Cretan painters worked on the mainland: Theophanes, Anthony and Tzortzis are the best known, and their works – perhaps the master-works of the 'Cretan school' – are to be seen in the monasteries of Mount Athos and Meteora.

By the end of the sixteenth century the Cretan spirit tended to express itself rather in icons than in large-scale frescoes. The tradition, of course, had been long established: recognizably *Cretan* icons can be found from the fourteenth century. Here again mainland influences came into play; by the later sixteenth century Italy – particularly Venice – exercised her spell; and eventually, in the seventeenth century, a Creto–Venetian school flourished in the Ionian Islands. Michael Damaskinos, one of the true Cretan masters, absorbed much from his years in Italy. When he returned to Crete to paint his major works – largely from 1570 to 1591 – he blended the

Italian-Renaissance style with his own Byzantine manner. Finally there came the man who made a bridge between the Byzantine and Western forms, the medieval and modern worlds, the Orthodox and the Catholic – the man from 'Candia' who moved on to other lands but who could never quite forget his homeland – its landscape, its patterns, its eyes: Domenico Theotokopoulos, 'El Greco'. He was born in 1541 and died in 1614. None of his work is to be seen on Crete, but Crete is to be seen in much of his painting. Not all Westerners find the Byzantine iconography congenial, but even for such El Greco vindicates the tradition.

To round out the picture of Crete's peculiar vitality during this period, three other Cretans who left their mark on the world must be mentioned. In 1340 a certain Peter Philargis was born outside Neapolis; he went to study in European universities, advanced in the Roman Catholic hierarchy, and crowned his career by being elected Pope in 1409. As Alexander V he served for only ten months; it is suspected that he was poisoned – a typical end for a Cretan and a pope of that day. Then there was Kyrillos Loukaris (1572–1638), another Cretan who wandered forth to get a European education some two centuries later. A man of true culture and learning, he became Patriarch of Constantinople and took the lead in educating Greeks in their traditions, even to the extent of introducing the printing-press into Constantinople and sponsoring a translation of the Bible into a less archaic, more colloquial Greek. But such activities were too advanced for the times; he only succeeded in offending Orthodox, Muslim and Catholic and he paid with his life. Finally, there was yet another Cretan scholar, whose achievements would seem to have gained him the blessings – or curses – of all faiths. Nathaniel Kanopios was at Balliol College, Oxford, for ten years, until Cromwell expelled him in 1648. In the course of his time there he is credited with having introduced coffee-drinking into England.

By the end of the seventeenth century and with the final conquests of the Turks, Crete once more passed out of the mainstream of European history. Again, though, popular traditions – songs, poetry, music, dancing, folklore of all varieties – kept the Cretan character alive, renewing the life and language of the island. Every event provided its hero, and subsequent songs and epics. The most admired of these poems is *The Song of Daskaloyiannis*, based on the uprising of the Sfakians in 1770. But in the nineteenth century, when the rest of Greece had gained independence and was sharing the artistic harvest of the new spirit, Crete was still occupied territory. Its energies went into the continual struggles and uprisings against the Turks.

Yet when Crete re-entered the Western community in the twentieth century, it produced two great men who achieved international reputations in very different ways. One was Eleftherios Venizelos, whose career is described under the History section. The other was Nikos Kazantzakis. He left Crete as a young man, but he could never get it out of his mind. *Zorba the Greek* and *Freedom and Death* are literally set there; *Christ Recrucified* is animated by a Cretan energy; and even his Odysseus becomes deeply involved with Crete. Philosopher, poet, dramatist, novelist – a genuine man of letters – the translations and the publicity of his last years gave Kazantzakis a somewhat exaggerated status in relation to the total Greek literature of this century. But no one can deny his power, his intensity and the provocative nature of his work.

Nor was he the only Cretan writer of this century. Several others have made significant contributions to Greek literature: Kondylakis, Prevelakis, Dimakis, Hadzidakis, and the poet Odysseus Elytis. In addition, the leading Greek actor of our time, Alexis Minotis, is also from Crete. What is the secret? Why should this small isolated island have produced so many strong art-forms across the centuries – and what do they have in common? It could be that if there is one theme peculiar to the Cretan spirit, one thread that links Minoan pottery, Cretan frescoes and the novels of Kazantzakis, it is an affirmation of life in all its diversity, a spontaneous – yet intense – celebration of man's joys and mysteries.

RELIGION

Commentators on modern Crete all remark on the continuity of Cretan culture. Despite a history of violent disruptive forces, Crete seems to have maintained intact many fundamentals from even the earliest eras. In nothing is this more apparent than in its religious beliefs and practices. The Orthodox Church of Crete is not under the Greek mainland Church but is an autonomous institution which owes its allegiance directly to the Patriarchate of Constantinople. It stresses its own continuity, taking pride in its own faithfulness to the roots and sources of earliest Christianity. For the visitor, Crete provides a fascinating glimpse of age-old sources of the religious impulse and of religious behaviour. To Cretans, who are almost all Orthodox, there is nothing contradictory or curious about worshipping in the ways of their ancestors, but it is one of the most interesting and attractive features of a stay on Crete.

The priest, or *papás*, in his stove-pipe hat and flowing gown, soon becomes a familiar figure as he strides across the fields or sits in the café. In the Orthodox Church, if a priest wants to rise in the hierarchy or to enter a monastery, he remains celibate, but the village priests are allowed to marry and are encouraged to take part in the life of the community. It is therefore no cause for surprise to see a bearded old *papás* showing off his grandchildren. The village priests will often be obliged to do some other work to support their families, despite the fact that they receive part of their salary from the government, since Orthodoxy is recognized as the official State religion. The Church's hierarchy, in fact, has a status analogous to the civil service or the military: the Metropolitan of Iraklion, who is head of the Church on Crete, has the 'rank' of a general – and should even be saluted by members of the military when he passes in his official capacity.

The Greek clergy, by the way, have always been associated with the political and national life of their people. During the centuries of Turkish occupation, for instance, it was the Orthodox clergy who helped to keep the Greeks' identity and aspirations alive, both by word and deed. The Greek Independence Day celebrates the occasion on March 25th, 1821, when Bishop Germanos of Patras raised the flag of revolution at the Monastery of Ayia Lavra on the Peloponnese.

Of the chapels and churches on Crete (there are reputedly over six hundred) many are tiny, and are used only on one day of the year to commemorate a particular saint, or the name-day of the donor. Some are new and have no significance for the visitor. But some are very old indeed, and many of these have frescoes and other works of art that are worth going out of one's way to see. They are to be found everywhere – on the barren coast, perhaps, or high on a peak. They are worth looking into, deserted or not (the key is usually on the ledge over one of the doors), for they have a special atmosphere. Often candles will be burning in the most isolated chapels. The simple icons are often interesting and sometimes, flanking the picture of a saint, many little silver tags are to be seen. These are *támata* or *taxímata* – simulacra moulded in the image of the afflicted part of the body, or an animal, or someone the petitioner wants cured or protected.

LANGUAGE

The history of the Greek language will here be described briefly, in so far as it impinges on modern spoken Greek. One thing should be said at once: there *is* a definite relationship between classical Greek and modern Greek. Having been given the impression that there is little or none, most students of the classical language are amazed at how far it can take them.

After the decline of the classical Attic civilization, a common Greek tongue came into use throughout the Hellenistic-Mediterranean world; this was the *koiné*, the Greek of the New Testament. It is the basis of modern Greek. Over the centuries, through the rise and fall of the Byzantine Empire, a gap developed between the language of the masses and the more refined language of the lettered. The higher clergy especially tried to maintain the archaic Greek, but the vulgar tongue was evolving on its own. Foreign words were absorbed, idioms crept in, and each region developed its own dialect. When the independence of the modern Greek nation was established in the nineteenth century, the movement to impose a unified and purified language gained the support of many educated men; this was the *katharévusa* – the pure, correct, formal language. But for all their sincere intentions, the proponents of this somewhat artificial language were doomed from the start, because the colloquial tongue – despite its inconsistencies – was an organic living language. At the end of the nineteenth century the struggle between the adherents of the two languages was still in full swing, affecting every aspect of national life and capable of causing academic quarrels and popular riots. To a certain degree the struggle is still going on, but the *katharévusa* is now largely confined to the law, science, advanced textbooks, academic circles, government administration and formal use in general. The demotic or 'popular' language is Greek as it is spoken in the streets; among other victories, it has won over most modern creative writers, and it has proved itself an expressive instrument. When a classical Greek drama is performed today, for instance, it is usually in a modified demotic translation. And in recent years the demotic language has begun gradually making more inroads into the school system as well as into the government and administration. Most newspapers used to be written in the *katharévusa*, but today – except for the few that use the straight demotic – newspapers employ a mixed speech, known as *kathomilouméni*.

To understand what it means to have two languages in competition with each other, the English speaker need only imagine all those situations where he employs only the most formal and literary language (legal documents, scholarly papers, formal announcements, conversations with foreign dignitaries) and oppose them to situations where he uses more colloquial and familiar language. In other words, English – as well as every other language – is subject to the same forces. The significant difference, though, is that strict boundaries were never set up between these other pairs of languages, so there has always been some intermingling. Britain could support a Dr Johnson *and* a Robert Burns; America could produce a Henry James *and* a Mark Twain. But the Greek language-psychology found them incompatible. Contemporary educated Greeks, all the same, are finding it easier to bridge the two languages in speech, literature, radio and the theatre. The differences – in sounds, grammar and vocabulary – still exist; everything depends on how much modern Greeks want to make of them.

Few visitors to Greece ever come to grips with the language and fewer still master it. The alphabet defeats most people in the first place. Until one is in control of that there is no gratuitous gain in vocabulary, as is the case when the English-speaking traveller tries other European languages. The result is that most foreigners give up, or at best struggle along with about three words.

This is to be regretted, because the Greeks are among those people who truly enjoy having a foreigner use their language – even when it is not used well. So few do try to use it that the Greeks are pleased when anyone does make the effort. The foreigner need never feel embarrassed while he is learning, and he will never lack encouragement and praise, even though accompanied by good-natured laughter.

Anyone who wants to try to use Greek needs a phrase-book. Several are available; most of them are to be found in the bookshops of Athens. The really ambitious may try to teach themselves Greek before setting out, and there are several courses available. Useful books unclude *Cortina's Modern Greek* and *Modern Greek in a Nutshell*. Record courses include Dover Publications' *Say It In Greek*, the Linguaphone Institute's course, and another by the Institute for Language Study. There is also a small, cheap record, *Pronounce It Correctly in Modern Greek*.

Between phrase-book and complete course lies the dictionary, a necessity for anyone planning to strike out on his own. There are many available – again, mostly to be found in Athens. It is important to make sure you are getting a dictionary of *modern* Greek. Also useful would be *Travellers' Greek*, published by Jonathan Cape, which combines a pocket phrase-book and dictionary in one.

When travelling with a dictionary, it is of little use to hand it to unschooled people and expect them to pick out words for you. They are not accustomed to treating their language as an alphabetical list and are apt to be as baffled as you are by the mass of words. Moreover, just as important as learning the proper sounds of Greek pronunciation is learning the correct syllable to be accented. The accent is a crucial element in the Greek language – a mark is always written over the syllable which must receive the major stress – and when the accent is misplaced it leads either to confusion or to a complete blank. The average Greek finds it hard to dissociate the sounds from the accent. It can be most frustrating when you have taken the trouble to learn some long, difficult word and you know you have the sounds correct – and still no contact is being made. When you finally do shift the accent to the proper syllable, your word will be greeted with immediate recognition and a 'Why didn't you say so?'

There is a distinct dialect spoken on Crete, and as might be expected the farther one goes into the hills the more pronounced it becomes. In the matter of vocabulary, too, there is a rich fund of local words and expressions. The main pronunciation variations are as follows: the Greek *gamma* – γ – thickens into a sound as in 'rou*ge*' before ι, ε, η and υ; the *kappa* – κ – behaves like the Italian 'c', being hard before α, ο, and ω and soft (like English 'ch') before ι, ε η and υ; and the *khi* – χ – ordinarily a guttural 'kh', on

Crete behaves like the Italian 'sc', becoming a soft 'sh' before ι, ϵ, η, and v.

Cretans, like all Greeks, use many nicknames, diminutives and terms of affection. Even the commonest words will frequently have affectionate diminutives, such as '-aki': thus, *nero* is 'water', while *neraki* is more like 'lovely bit of water'. Incidentally, if you meet a Greek whose name ends in '-akis' – 'son of' – the probability is that he comes from Crete.

The English Language

Many of the younger people speak a little English. Some are learning it in school but the majority are studying at one of the many 'institutes', or private evening schools. People of all ages and all walks of life give up a considerable proportion of their time and money to acquire this new way to success. You will be doing a real service by exchanging a few words with such students when opportunity presents itself. However, French still tends to be the second language of the older, educated generation.

Almost every town and village, no matter how isolated, has its 'Greek-American', an ex-immigrant who has returned to live out his retirement in his home town. He will make your acquaintance very quickly, and although his English is not exactly polished it will probably be better than your Greek. He will be of great help, saving you a lot of time and trouble, but you may not gain in the eyes of the other inhabitants of the town or village if you let yourself be monopolized by him. Preserve your independence with goodwill and still seek to make your own contacts.

GOVERNMENT

Crete is one of the eleven major regions under the highly centralized Greek government; and it is from Athens that Crete's ministers of agriculture, education, finance, justice, public works, etc., are appointed, as are the nomarchs, or prefects, at the head of each of the four nomes. The island elects eighteen representatives, or deputies, to the Greek parliament.

Each town elects its own mayor, as do the villages (though 'presidents of the community' might be a better translation of the title, *próedros*). But there is no common legislative body for Crete; the government of the island as a whole is carried on largely by the appointees of Athens. Taxes are collected and disbursed by Athens. The police belong to the national force, too, although the rank and file are usually Cretans who have been more or less permanently assigned to the island. Local teachers must go for their training to Athens after which they may or may not be assigned to Crete.

All this is to a certain extent only a technicality, but the fact remains that the initiative comes from Athens and local responsibility for government and social institutions is relatively small. Crete's true parliament is to be found in its cafés.

PEOPLE AND CUSTOMS

Contemporary Cretans probably represent a mixture of many genes and traits, which makes it all the more remarkable that there is a peculiar people that can be called 'Cretan'. Physical appearances among Cretans, too, vary considerably – from the short wiry 'Mediterranean' to the tall fair 'Dorian'. This second type is only found among certain isolated communities, usually in the mountains, but you can still run into men in the villages who look and bear themselves like gods – whether it be Zeus or Pan. The traditional costume – black knee-length boots, baggy, wrap-around pantaloons, sash, embroidered jacket, black head-wrapping – is generally disappearing, although some of the older men still wear it. Among the younger village men, however, boots and riding-breeches are stylish, as is a black cloth with a little fringe, worn at a rakish angle, for the head.

Women on Crete are not much in evidence. In the villages you will see them lurking in doorways or behind windows, bundled up in rather graceless, timeless dresses. They often go about their work in the fields with their heads wrapped up Arab-fashion. The wearing of black is also common in the villages, though if you happen to arrive at some special festival, you may see women in gay traditional costume. In the larger towns, of course, western clothes have taken over and people dress very stylishly when promenade-time comes on Saturday night.

The old ways, it is true, are gradually dying out, but not without a good deal of delaying action and rearguard tactics. Family ties are still strong and they serve as brakes. Young men's careers are often settled by their parents; marriages are usually arranged, to some degree. (Even the Code of Gortyna (p. 176) dealt, among other things, with the need to marry heiresses within the 'tribe' – to prevent the break-up of families.) The village people, too, are surrounded by rituals and formulas, traditions, superstitions, proverbial ways. And as is to be expected, the younger generation and the urban types comprise the 'modernist' element, often strongly oriented towards America. Yet the dominant tone of the island is set by the conservative, orthodox groups, and the more intelligent and balanced young people do not find it necessary to turn their backs on all the old ways. They are the first to appreciate the traditional social and personal relationships; they still love to dance the old dances, sing the old songs.

Folk Music and Dancing

Dances provide the most authentic evidence of the continuity of Crete's popular traditions and rhythms. Homer in the *Iliad* describes how 'Daedalus in Knossos once contrived/A dancing-floor for fair-haired Ariadne', and the Cretans have always been known for their dances: the *pendozális* – a lively, swinging dance, with the arms interlocked; the *khaniótikos* – a circle dance; the *syrtós* – a sedate circle dance; and many others, such as the *sousta*, *órtzes*, *kastrinós*, *malevysiótikos*, *sitiakós*. A newer favourite is the tango. Today there are groups who revive and perform the traditional dances. But perhaps the really pure Cretan dance is that to be seen in any village café or festival – or, for that matter, in some Iraklion *taverna* – when a man or several men spontaneously move into the centre of the floor and start to dance. And the young people of Iraklion can be just as proud and graceful when they circle in the old dances. It makes no difference that the old melodies are played on electric guitars, or even on a gramophone; the dancing is still performed to the old rhythms. But undoubtedly the most picturesque occasions for the traditional music and dances are at village ceremonies – weddings, baptisms, saints' days.

As for the music of Crete, it strikes the ear as one would expect:

an amalgamation of all the styles and cultures that have entered Crete. Into Near Eastern music the familiar strains of European folk music intrude. If you are lucky, you will see one of the old instruments played – the *lýra*, a small, three-stringed lute-like instrument that is bowed as it is held on the knee. Or you may hear some really old ballads. Most exciting of all are the *mantinádhes*, improvised rhyming couplets that follow the inspiration of some occasion, joyful or mournful. Although traditionally improvised there is actually a repertoire of *mantinádhes* on which to draw. In Iraklion – and possibly Khania – you may also hear *bouzoúki* music. Taking its name from the instrument (something like a mandolin), it has now come to stand more for the mood of the songs and the atmosphere of the places where it is played – a mood akin to jazz 'blues'. Greek music, then, traditional or otherwise, is very much alive, and it will be a long time before American hit songs – which, to be sure, often blare out from some radio – obliterate the old melodies.

The Koumbáros

In Greek life, family loyalties take precedence over all others. This is not so hard to comprehend, but there is one relationship which the foreigner may not have encountered elsewhere but which is essential to an understanding of Greek social-family life. This is the role of the *koumbáros* – technically the best man at the wedding and/or the godfather, but the obligations and significance of his office go beyond anything that most of us know. As best man at the wedding, the *koumbáros* participates by holding the little wreath over the heads of the couple. But that is only the beginning of his bonds with the couple, because, as Greeks tend to stay close to their circle of intimates, the *koumbáros* will probably be the couple's closest friend throughout their lives. Thus, when the first child is born, the *koumbáros* is traditionally asked to serve as godfather. There is also a *koumbára*, the bridesmaid and/or godmother, but like so many female roles in Greek life hers is overshadowed by the man's. She will usually be the wife of the *koumbáros*, if he is married. (On Crete the godparents are also known as the *sýnteknos* and *syntéknissa*.) As a godfather, the *koumbáros* takes on truly serious responsibilities, which he has sworn to uphold in the course of the christening service. As the child grows, the parents will consult the *koumbáros* on all vital matters; and when the child comes of age, he may still turn to his *koumbáros* for counsel. The *koumbáros*, on his side, will have provided aid and favours of all kinds throughout the years. He may be of the same social and economic status as his godchild's family, or he may be of considerably higher standing, but the links are just as strong, whatever the distinctions to be observed. The *koumbáros* will be an honoured guest at family gatherings, but while sharing in the family's lighter moments he does not take his relationship of *koumbáros* lightly.

Hospitality

Greek hospitality is a byword among foreigners; by now everyone except the native has marvelled that the Greek word for 'stranger' – *xénos* – is also the word for 'guest'. But this hospitality is quite complex: on the one hand it reaches out to embrace the stranger–guest, on the other it is restrained by many points of procedure and ritual. For example, when a stranger walks into a village its inhabitants will not speak until spoken to. But once the newcomer speaks he will be overwhelmed with friendly greetings.

Perhaps nowhere is Greek hospitality seen in such intensity as on Crete. There it becomes almost aggressive at times, and the traveller who really wants to understand and take part in local life must be prepared to go all the way. It is no good going into the villages and mixing with the people and then – when the going becomes a bit strenuous – discreetly retiring. If you are welcomed into a home you will be plied with drinks and sweets that must not be refused; you will be given meals that cannot be paid for except with thanks. The less they have the more they will produce for you. Food, drink, flowers, souvenirs – these are their welcome to a guest and should be gracefully accepted. You will find yourself stared at or asked quite personal questions; if you get the impression that everyone for miles around has been called in to 'inspect' you, that is probably exactly what has happened. The greater the number of people who are packed into a small space, whether it is the front parlour or the back seat of a car, the more successful is the hospitality. And everything said here about hospitality becomes still more intense at holidays, especially Easter, when the stranger will find himself truly an honoured guest.

Drinking and Eating Traditions

In view of this great tradition of hospitality it is useful to know about some of the customs and rituals that often accompany a meal. When you enter a private home, for instance, no matter how humble, you will, as a guest, be offered a little glass of *oúzo*; men take it in one gulp, women usually just wet their lips with it. This is followed by a sweet, a little dish of preserves or candied fruit (very sweet!), or a spoonful of vanilla paste. A glass of refreshing water is then brought. Don't feel embarrassed when you alone are treated to this round of good things, while your host and other natives sit by; traditions of hospitality demand this ritual.

If you stay to eat a meal, you may notice several other unfamiliar ways. In the towns, among more sophisticated people, and in restaurants, manners are much the same as everywhere. But if you should become involved with village life or with rural families or festivals, it is as well to be forewarned about several things. There is, for example, considerable eating from common dishes. Plates and bowls are set on the table, you are handed a fork and knife – and it's every man for himself. At a high festive occasion, such eating can become quite intense. Then, a sort of duel with forks may ensue: a man will thrust his fork into a piece of meat and plunge forward, offering it to some table-companion – perhaps you! You are expected to eat it straight off the fork, then swallow a chaser of wine. As a guest, indeed, you will find yourself getting far more than your share of such attentions. You are not expected to return the service at once, but if you are with the spirit of things you will eventually pass your fork round. A banquet like this can become almost aggressive, to put it mildly.

Drinking, as in every land, is surrounded with a great deal of ritual. One is the snack – *mezés* – taken with drinks. Then, too, almost every gulp is accompanied by a toast: glasses are knocked against each other or on the table, a toast is shouted, another is returned, and the drink is swallowed in a gulp. These are a few toasts that might prove useful:

'*Stin iyássou!*': 'Your health!'
'*Iss iyía!*': 'Your health!'
'*Pánta khará!*': 'May you always be happy!'
'*Epíssis!*': 'Same to you!' (used in reply to any toast).
And as do most Europeans, Greeks wish each other 'Bon appétit', which is '*Kalí órexi!*' In the villages it is customary for the host when starting dinner to say '*Kalós orissate*' ('You are welcome') and for the guest to reply '*Kalós sás vríkame*' ('Glad to be with you').

Café Life

On Crete the café is the man's world. If you see any woman in one they will most likely be tourists. Men sit there and nurse a single drink for hours, talking, reading newspapers, watching the world go by. Two active café occupations may puzzle visitors. One is a board game, *távli*, which some will recognize as backgammon; it is played at a furious rate, with much slamming and argument. The other occupation involves the little strings of amber beads which so many men finger while they are sitting or standing about. At first glance they look like rosaries. They are the *kombolóia* – the 'worry beads' – and their function seems to be simply to relieve tension. Men can get quite attached to their 'worry beads' and it is said to be a sign of a well-spent life if a man can show a string of highly polished beads in his later years.

The Vólta

Walking is another feature of Cretan social life. Not tramping overland to get somewhere, but the very special walking known as the *vólta* – the promenade which takes place at given hours along a defined route in towns and villages all over Crete. The basic pattern is for a considerable section of the local population to put on its finery and stroll up and down a certain stretch of the town's main street. The usual time is in the early evening. It is quite a complex social ritual for those involved – who wears what, and who is seen with whom, and who looked at whom, are matters of interest.

Time and Punctuality

If you get to know individual Cretans well enough to make appointments with them it is as well to remember that on Crete 'morning' extends until 12 noon. 'Noon' is from 12 to 3 p.m.; 'afternoon' is from 3 to 7 p.m. If a Cretan says he will meet you 'at noon', he may mean 2 p.m.; 'this afternoon' for him may be 6 p.m.

Roadside Sights

Cretan life takes place largely out of doors. It is particularly fascinating to be present during the summer grain harvest, when the farmers may be seen using tools and techniques that have remained unchanged for thousands of years. Or if you are lucky you may see flocks being moved to or from the summer pastures by shepherds straight out of Kazantzakis. In the fields women often stand guard spinning wool on the distaff – a scene straight off an ancient vase.

If you should want to photograph such scenes you must be careful not to attract attention, for as soon as it is realized that you are going to take their picture your subjects will become stiff and formal. They may even want to go off and put on their Sunday best!

FOOD AND DRINK

Food on Crete

In Greece, as with most national cuisines, many foods that might not appeal to you if taken separately turn out to be most satisfying when blended with a full meal. The notorious resinated wine – *retsína* – is a case in point; by itself, it leaves most foreigners aghast, but when drunk with Greek foods it combines with the other textures and flavours to make a real Greek 'bouquet'.

Some foods are specialities of Crete; a few are even confined to limited areas on Crete. Menus also reflect the season – when something is in season you will see it everywhere; then quite suddenly it will disappear and you switch to another food. (See also the section on restaurants, p. 49.)

Bread

In the villages, people still bake their own bread, so there is variety from house to house. But even in the bakeries of the towns there is a choice. The word for bread is *psomí*, but there are many special words for varieties and local types. On saints' days and special occasions, for instance, there is a slightly sweet bread, *ártos*, which is blessed and then broken to be passed around. And in some villages they make a stone-hard bread – *paximádhia* ('toast'); this must be soaked in water before you can get your teeth into it, and then it goes surprisingly well with the other foods.

Olive Oil

Greeks like a lot of olive oil, but with a little persistence you can persuade them to reduce the quantities for you.

FISH AND FOWL

Fish are more of a rarity than one would expect on an island. But they will be very fresh when you do have an opportunity to try some. The *barboúnia*, a red mullet, is especially good. Try shrimp or shellfish, if you are lucky; try octopus or squid, if you are brave. Chickens are available and eggs are plentiful.

MEAT

The staple meat is some form of lamb-sheep-mutton – usually very good. Diced, and placed on a little spit, it is called *souvlákia*. Charcoal-grilled chops are known as *brizóles*. And what we should call offal is wrapped round a large spit to make up what is known as *kokorétsi* – and, despite the sound of it, it is delicious. Veal and beef are obtainable in the towns – even some pork. But lamb is the thing to eat if you are living off the land.

PREPARED DISHES

A great favourite is *mousaká*, made in a casserole of layers of aubergine, chopped meat, macaroni or potato, and egg. Or there are *dolmádes*: vine leaves stuffed with ground meat or rice – especially delicious when served with a lemon-egg sauce.

VEGETABLES

There are plenty of tomatoes, cucumbers and courgettes. Aubergines, too, are widely eaten, and a variety of green beans. In the spring, Cretans enjoy eating raw artichoke leaves.

FRUIT

The prices fall rapidly from day to day as the various fruits come into full season. Oranges, peaches, water-melons, grapes and bananas are the most common; there are also quinces, pears, apples, mulberries, apricots, cherries. Try the less familiar ones – fresh figs, or pomegranates.

DESSERT

Most of the typical Greek sweets are some variety of *baklavá* – a flaky layered pastry with finely chopped nuts, soaked in honey; most foreigners find it excessively sweet. There is also *halvá* – a mildly sweet, crisp paste made of honey and sesame seeds; *loukoumádhes* – doughnut-like lumps, covered with honey; and *bougátsa* a pancake with a cream or cheese filling. In the villages one can sometimes get *tigharítes*, a typical Cretan delicacy, which is a plain flour pancake covered with honey and sesame.

CHEESE

There are a variety of goats' cheeses, but the best-known and best-liked are *anthótiro, mizíthra, manoúri, graviéra* and *kefalotíri*.

Regional Specialities

IRAKLION NOME

Stiffádo (meat with onions and spices).
Dolmádes or *dolmadákia* (vine leaves stuffed with rice).
Giouvarlákia (meat balls with rice and sauce).
Tirópita (fresh cheesecake).
Fresh grapes: *rosakí* and *sultaniá*.
Oranges from Fodhele.
Mageirítsa (soup of lamb's liver, vegetables, rice, and eggs – traditional on Easter Eve).

KHANIA NOME

Honey from Akrotiri and from Sfakia.
Wines and chestnuts from Kissamos.
Olive oil of Apokorona.
Chochlioí (snails with potatoes).
Boiled *radíkia* (herbs) as salad.
Oranges and tangerines.
Kallitsoúnia (mint-flavoured cream-cheese pastries – traditional Easter food).

RETHYMNON NOME

Pork with *máratha* (herbs).
Chochlioí.
Mizíthra (white soft cheese) with honey.
Graviéra (cheese) from Mount Idha.

LASITHI NOME

Grilled fish.
Local cheeses.
Wine from Mouliana.
Soumádha (a drink from almonds).

Drinks

Oddly enough, water is the 'national drink' of Crete. Cretans like it cold and they like to savour its taste. They like compliments about it, too. (See remarks on drinking water, p. 52.)

WINE

Cretan wines have not the quality of good Continental wines, but they go with the local food. *Retsína* is not nearly so popular on Crete as it is in Athens. Ask for *aretsínoto*, unresinated wine. Two of the better Cretan red wines are *Broúsko* and *Kíssamos*. Often a good white wine called *Minos* is obtainable; others are *Gortinos* and *Phaestos*. The sweet dessert wine *Malevízi* is a specialty; and local vermouths and Greek brandy should be tried.

BEER

Beer is popular; it seems to be quite fashionable in the restaurants. Brands of beer available are Alpha, Fix and Amstel. They stand up surprisingly well to better-known brands.

OÚZO

Oúzo is *the* Greek spirit; it is made by distilling the crushed mash after the wine-juice has been pressed from the grapes, with anisette added to give a slight flavour. On Crete the men are distinguished from the boys by drinking *rakí* (known as *tzikoudiá* on Crete). An even stronger spirit is *mournóraki*.

COFFEE

In spite of the claim just made for water, coffee-drinking will strike the visitor as the national pastime, and most foreigners come to enjoy the ritual, the locales – and sometimes the coffee. For Greek coffee is served Turkish style: in a small cup with the muddy lees in the bottom, and usually very sweet. You soon learn how to make the little cup last an hour. As for the dregs, plan to stop about two-thirds of the way down! As a rule, the sugar is boiled together with the coffee. If you don't want any sugar, ask for *skétos*; if you require just a little, say *me olíghi*; medium, *métrios*; sweet and well boiled, *glykí vrastós*; and very sweet, *polí glykós*. These are only some of the gradations. The waiter will bring you sweet coffee unless you indicate otherwise. In the better restaurants or cafés you may be able to order a cup of 'American' or 'French' coffee, but in many cases this will turn out to be Nescafé, although espresso coffee is now being served at some of the smartest restaurants and cafés. If you send out for breakfast, be prepared to get Turkish coffee unless you have made yourself very clear on the point.

INTRODUCTION TO ROUTES

The centres and routes described in this section are shown in the Diagram of Routes on p. 118. The plan has been to start with Iraklion and the various excursions that use this city as a base. Route 1 described after this is to Phaestos, followed by excursions from Phaestos to sites on the Messara Plain. Route 2 describes the trip from Phaestos up through the mountainous centre of Crete to Rethymnon. Starting again from Iraklion, Route 3 moves westwards along the coast to Rethymnon; Route 4 continues on to Khania, which then becomes the base for excursions to Khora Sfakion, the Gorge of Samaria and north-west Crete. From Iraklion again, Route 5 goes eastwards to Mallia and Ayios Nikolaos; and Route 6 continues east to Sitia, which is the base for various excursions into eastern Crete, including Kato Zakros. In the text, links between the main routes and cross-references between the excursions are indicated. In general, the excursions cover places that are either not conveniently placed along the main routes or would take too much time to visit when travelling from one centre to the next.

Distances given along the routes refer to the distance along the direct route up to that point and do not include detours. In some instances, particularly in remote or mountainous regions, distances are only approximate.

On the Chart of Excursions, facing p. 29, distances are one-way from the centre indicated. The times allocated for excursions assume that private transport is available (i.e. your own car, hired car, or taxi) and are minimum times for visitors rather than the time recommended for maximum enjoyment. The number of days allotted to each centre refers to the minimum time for seeing the most important sights within the city and does not include excursions.

Diagram of Routes

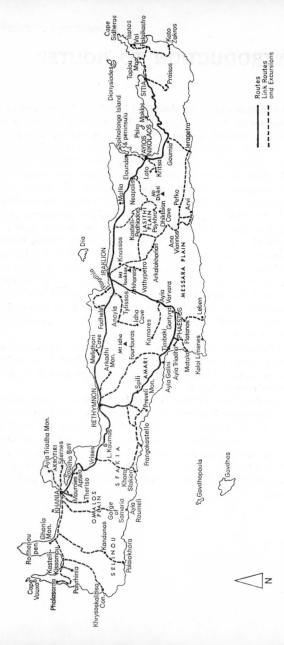

Routes
Link Routes and Excursions

N

IRAKLION

Iraklion is the largest and best-known town of Crete, its commercial capital and the focal point for most visitors to the island. Although the town itself lacks ancient remains, it has more historical attractions than many people realize. Above all, it houses the world's supreme collection of Minoan art and is the gateway to Knossos, the foremost Minoan site.

Population 64,492.
Air and sea connections
See pp. 32–5. Iraklion Airport is on the road to Mallia and Ayios Nikolaos, and the Olympic Airways terminal is in 25th August Street (*Map* **7**). The Efthymiadis Lines, which run the car ferries to Piraeus, also have their offices in 25th August Street.
Information
National Tourist Organization of Greece: 25th August Street (*Map* **6**).
Tourist Police: King Constantine Avenue (*Map* **16**).
Hotels
Class A: *Astir*, 25th August Street (Ayios Titos Square) (restaurant).
        Astoria, Liberty Square (restaurant, swimming-pool).
        Atlantis (opening soon, near the Archaeological Museum).
Class B: *Ariane*, Theotokopoulou Street.
        Castro, Theotokopoulou Street.
        Cosmopolite, Evans Street.
        Esperia, Idomeneos Street.
        Xenia, Archbishop Makariou Avenue (*Map* **3**) (restaurant).
Class C: *Domenico*, El Greco Park.
        El Greco, 1821 Street.
        Galini, in the suburb of Poros.
        Iraklion, Kalokairinou Avenue.
        Knossos, 25th August Street.
        Minos, Archbishop Makariou Avenue.
        Nicas, Liberty Square.
        Palladion, Handakos Street.
        Park, Koronaiou Street.
        Poseidon, in the suburb of Poros.
        Selena, Androgeo Street.
Class D: *Florida*, 25th August Street.
        Hellas, Kantanoleon Street (near Telegraph Office).
        Phaestos, Tsakiti Street.
        Rex, King Constantine Avenue.
        Venetia, Kalokairinou Avenue.
Class E: *Aegypt*, Matiou Street.
        Arkadhi, Kalokairinou Avenue.
        Diethnes, Handakos Street.
        Emporikon, Vikela Street.
        Ethnikon, Evans Street.
        Helvetia, Xopatera Street.
        Idaeon Andron, Perdikari Street.
        Khania, Kydonias Street (near Telegraph Office)
        Moderno, Kalokairinou Avenue.

Along the north coast on either side of Iraklion there are several new hotel-establishments of the type which have bungalows and a central building with restaurant and other facilities. They are normally open only during the summer season from April to October.

Class A: *Creta Beach*, 6 km. west of Iraklion.

Class B: *Amnisos Beach*, 8 km. east of Iraklion.

      Blue Sea Motel, at Stalis 31 km. east of Iraklion.

      E.O.T. Motel, 8 km. east of Iraklion

      Knossos Beach, 12 km. east of Iraklion.

      Mallia Beach, 35 km. east of Iraklion (under construction).

Boarding houses

As noted on page 46 there are several of these in Iraklion; inquire at the Tourist Office for a list. Prices are approximately the same as for Class E hotels.

Youth hostels

There are two youth hostels in Iraklion; the main one, which is open all the year round, is situated in Handakos Street. See note on p. 48 for regulations.

Restaurants

There are countless restaurants and eating-places in Iraklion, not all first-class, but offering a wide choice in menu and atmosphere. At the places listed below regular meals can be obtained at more or less regular hours. There are also numerous cafés and sweetshops where cold drinks, coffee, ice-cream, cakes, yoghurt and light snacks can be bought, especially round Liberty Square and Venizelou (Fountain) Square, where people sit in the cafés till very late on summer evenings.

Apart from the hotels that have restaurants, the best known restaurants and those offering the largest choice of dishes are:

Caprice, Venizelou (Fountain) Square.

Knossos, Venizelou (Fountain) Square.

Glass House, Archbishop Makariou Avenue, overlooking the harbour (*Map* **2**).

Ionia, Evans Street.

Besides these there are many other smaller restaurants and *tavernas*, including the *Kallithea*, near Liberty Square, *Kostas* and *Klimataria*, Daidalou Street, *Ligeros*, Patros Antoniou Street, *Kastella*, Archbishop Makariou Avenue, *Lakis*, Evans Street, *Voyatzis*, Knossos Avenue.

In addition to trying some of the above, no one should leave Iraklion without visiting one of the little eating-places lining the street known as 'Dirty Alley'. This connects Market Street with Evans Street, one block up from the main crossroads of the city. It provides a fascinating glimpse of a fast-disappearing world. Each little restaurant jostles the next, spilling out on to a narrow street filled with smells, noise and people. The food is appetizing – especially the charcoal-grilled meats. To sit over a meal here is to realize that you are indeed on a unique island.

There are also several outdoor *tavernas* on the outskirts of Iraklion on the road to Knossos, such as the *Kolobotsis*, *Tzobanakis* and *Verikokes*.

Dining and Dancing

There are a few places in and around Iraklion that offer music and dancing as well as food. When spirits get high enough there is likely to be dancing at almost any *taverna*, but the places listed below make a special feature of dancing.

Glass House restaurant (see above). Ideally situated overlooking the harbour, it is well patronized, particularly in the summer.

Taverna Ariadne, on the road to Knossos about 5 km. from Iraklion. This also has a restaurant and is open only during the summer season. It has a delightful garden and often provides musical entertainment as well as an orchestra for dancing.

Zorbas, Ikarou Avenue. Usually has a floor show.

Dionyssos, El Greco Park.

Stamna, Epimenidou Street.

Vrakhas, Archbishop Makariou Avenue, *Kallithea*, near Liberty Square, and *Erotokritos*, Handakos Street, are popular with Cretans and likely to provide some authentic music and dancing.

There are also several dancing-places for young people on the way to Knossos.

Entertainment

There is a special organization of young girls, the Lyceon Ellinidon, who study and perform the authentic Cretan dances. Shows with costumes, music and dancing can be arranged through the Tourist Organization, but they are too expensive for any but largish parties.

One of the most interesting opportunities at the moment is the chance to hear a talented young man who sings the old Cretan poem, the *Erotokritos*, while accompanying himself on the lyra ; consult the Tourist Office to discover where he may be performing.

Cinemas

During the winter, film shows are indoors (beginning about 4 p.m. on weekdays and 2 p.m. on Sundays). In summer, films are shown out of doors (beginning at 8 p.m.). Many of the cinemas are in Liberty Square. Tickets run from about 5 to 10 drachmas ; it is also usual to give the usherette a small tip (about Dr. 1).

Consulates

The following countries have consulates in Iraklion : Belgium, Denmark, Finland, Netherlands, West Germany. Inquire at the Tourist Office for their addresses.

Churches

In addition to the many Greek Orthodox Churches, there is a Roman Catholic Church on Patros Antoniou Street (*Map* **5**), and a Protestant congregation holds private gatherings (inquire at the Tourist Office).

Clubs and Institutes

There is a Chamber of Commerce which would welcome contacts with visiting businessmen, socially or otherwise. There are various language institutes, whose members are always glad to have opportunities to speak English and to hear it spoken. If you are interested contact the Tourist Office. There are also branches of the Greek Touring Club and the Greek Alpine Club (see under Sport and Swimming below).

Shops and Souvenirs

Everything said about shops, services and souvenirs on p. 54 applies especially to Iraklion as the biggest town on the island. Of special interest to tourists will be Alexiou's Bookstore and Ekthesis Vivliou, two bookshops in Venizelou (Fountain) Square, which have a good selection of books, periodicals and daily papers in English and other languages ; newspapers from abroad are also available on Liberty Square. Iraklion also has the largest selection of souvenirs on Crete – ranging from cheap tourist items to authentic native handicrafts to genuine antiquities.

Sport and Swimming

There is a private tennis club on Beaufort Avenue, behind the Archaeological Museum ; if you just want to play the odd game, you are welcome, but for a longer stay you would have to become a member.

The Greek Touring Club arranges excursions around the island ; so, too, does the Greek Alpine Club, with its emphasis on walks and climbs. The Tourist Office can provide further information about both clubs.

The local boys swim in the harbour but visitors will prefer one of the near-by beaches. Closest is the one at Poros on the outskirts of the town on the way to Mallia and Ayios Nikolaos, although it is not a particularly attractive beach. Farther along in the same direction is Karteros – better known as Florida Beach – and beyond that a beach run by the National Tourist Organization (E.O.T.). These beaches have cabins and refreshments, and frequent buses run to them from the centre of Iraklion. There is also a beach at Stomion about 5 km. to the west of Iraklion which has facilities. But all along the north coast there are good places for swimming, more or less frequented, especially to the east of Iraklion – as far as the beautiful beaches of Stalis and Mallia.

For further information about sports facilities on Crete see p. 57.

Buses

Buses for the various towns, villages and sites leave from several points in Iraklion. These bus stations are listed below:

Kornarou Square: Knossos.

Khania Gate: Phaestos, Timbaki, Matala, Platanos, Apesokarion, Antiskarion, Tylissos, Anoyia, Rogdhia, Fodhele, Zaros, Kamares.

Near Xenia Hotel: Rethymnon, Khania.

Beaufort Avenue: Psykhro and Lasithi Plain, Mallia, Ayios Nikolaos, Ierapetra, Sitia.

Kainouryia Gate: Ano Viannos, Kastelli-Pedhiadhos.

Kallergon Square (near El Greco Park): Arkhanes.

Taxis and Car Hire

The main taxi ranks are at Liberty Square, Kornarou Square, Khania Gate and near El Greco Park (for charges, etc., see p. 40). There are many agencies where cars can be hired (see p. 41); it might also be worth inquiring at the Caprice Restaurant.

HISTORY

Iraklion's history is best revealed through the changes in its name. In Minoan times it was at most a minor port for Knossos, and if it had a name it is unknown today. Later the Greeks knew it as Heraklium or Heraklia – where Heracles landed to perform his Seventh Labour – but it was still not much of a city. When the Arabs conquered the island in A.D. 824, they chose to make a fort in its harbour, and called it Rabd-el-Kandak; Phokas liberated it in 961, and by this time the Arab name began to be corrupted by the local dialect into something like Khandax. And when the Venetians took over early in the thirteenth century they named it – and the entire island – Candia. (Shakespeare knew it as 'Candy'.) Candia-Iraklion became one of the great Venetian strongholds; but in spite of its fortifications, it fell to the Turks in 1669 after a twenty-two-year siege that occupied Europe's attention (p. 85). During the next two centuries the city must have been known by many names, but by the nineteenth century the islanders seem to have been calling it Megalo Kastro ('Great Castle'); it is either by this name, or as Candia, that it is referred to in travellers' accounts. Finally, when Crete gained its union with Greece, the city was officially named Iraklion – although there are still elderly islanders who prefer to call it Candia or Kastro.

In the last few decades it has become the island's centre of transport and communications as well as the market for central and eastern Crete. Each year sees it grow more modern, but it still retains something of a Near Eastern bazaar atmosphere. And, although most travellers tend to treat Iraklion strictly as a gateway to Minoan culture, we hope to show that it has historical landmarks of its own to interest the thoughtful visitor, as well as modern diversions.

MUSEUMS

Archaeological Museum
Map **15**

Hours
NOTE: The museum is closed on Monday afternoons and all day at Christmas, New Year, Greek Easter, March 25th and October 28th.
April 1st–Sept. 30th Weekdays 8–1, 3–6.
                       Sundays and public holidays 10–1.
Oct. 1st–March 31st Weekdays 9–1, 3–5.
                       Sundays and public holidays 10–1.
Entrance charge: Drs 10. Free on Thursdays and Sundays.
Fee for taking photographs: Drs 10.
Director: Dr Stylianos Alexiou.

By far the most important 'sight' in Iraklion itself is the world-famous collection of Minoan art in the Archaeological Museum, a relatively modern building just off Liberty Square. As the world's unrivalled collection of Minoan art and culture, this museum would require several days to be explored properly. But the major finds are well displayed in rooms arranged chronologically and geographically, and there are labels in clear English so that the visitor with a limited schedule can move through in a fairly short time and still obtain a good impression of the highlights. Ideally, you should visit the museum both early in your stay on Crete and then again after you have seen the sites themselves.

For a thorough study of the collection and its background, the visitor should buy the official guide by the museum's director, Dr Stylianos Alexiou. (There is an English-language edition available in the museum's entrance hall.) In the description that follows, we single out only the principal displays and the most striking individual pieces.

ROOM I: NEOLITHIC AND PRE-PALATIAL PERIODS (5500–2000 B.C.)
Case 1: Neolithic vessels, ritual objects and tools from Knossos and the Cave of Eileithyia.
Case 2: Neolithic and sub-Neolithic pottery from Knossos, Phaestos and Phourni, and a stone figurine.
Case 3: Pre-palatial pottery from burial caves, including some in the Pyrgos style and in the Ayios Onoufrios style (these being among the oldest painted vases in Europe).
Case 4: Pottery from the Leben tombs.

Case 6: Pottery in the Vasiliki style – a mottled flameware produced by uneven firing.

Case 7: Stone vases from the cemetery on the island of Mokhlos: note especially the handle carved in shape of a recumbent dog (an identical one was found during the recent Zakros excavations); included in this case are some of the earliest examples of carved stone vases.

Cases 9, 11–17: Finds from the *tholos* tombs of the Messara, including sealstones, vases, pottery, idols, jewellery, weapons and tools.

Case 10: Pottery from Palaikastro: note the model of a four-wheeled cart; also the clay bowl with a shepherd and his sheep.

Case 18: Sealstones from central and eastern Crete.

ROOM II: PROTO-PALATIAL PERIOD (2000–1700 B.C.): KNOSSOS, MALLIA, PEAK SANCTUARIES

Case 19: Vases, pottery and moulds from Mallia: note vase in form of Mother Goddess.

Case 20: Small jugs and bell-shaped figurines from Gournes and Tylissos.

Case 21: Votive figurines of men, women and bulls; vessels from the peak sanctuary of Mt Kofinos in the Asterousia Mountains.

Cases 22–23: Polychrome vases in Kamares style and 'eggshell ware' from Knossos.

Case 24: Clay model of sanctuary from Knossos and votive offerings from eastern Crete.

Case 25: The *Town Mosaic*, made up of several small earthenware plaques depicting Minoan structures; the modern reconstructions at Knossos have drawn heavily on these plaques. Also here are examples of early writing on Crete.

Case 27: Vases in the Kamares style from Knossos.

Case 28: Sealstones of the Proto-palatial period from Knossos, Mallia and elsewhere.

Case 29: Pottery from Knossos.

ROOM III: PROTO-PALATIAL PERIOD (2000–1700 B.C.): PHAESTOS

Case 30: Vases of the Kamares style; a utensil, probably a charcoal pan.

Cases 31–36: Kamares pottery: note the clay idols and rhytons.

Case 39: Vases in barbotine style – decorative relief produced by pinching wet clay or adding thin strips.

Case 40: Clay sealings from Phaestos.

Case 41: The *Phaestos Disc*: found in 1908, it is a terracotta disc about 6 ins in diameter, with hieroglyphic or pictographic characters imprinted on both sides and spiralling into the centre. It was made by punching a set of 45 characters into the clay, which might seem to qualify it as one of the earliest examples of 'printing' with movable type. It is dated at about 1700–1650 B.C. It is believed that the text has some religious significance – perhaps a hymn – and there seems to be a rhythm to the order of the signs. Many scholars have suggested decipherments and translations, but none has been generally accepted.

Case 42: Altars and offering tables from Phaestos.

Case 43: Vessels of remarkable shapes and decoration: note a vase from Phaestos with added clay flowers, perhaps imitating metal or stonework.

ROOM IV: NEO-PALATIAL PERIOD (1700–1450 B.C.): KNOSSOS, PHAESTOS, MALLIA

Case 44: Pottery including inscribed vessels from Knossos.

Case 45: Vases, wool-holder and lantern case from Knossos.

Case 46: Pottery from Knossos; vases used for libations in the worship of snakes.

Case 47: Sceptre and other objects from Mallia.

Case 49: Pottery and inscribed objects from Phaestos.

Cases 50, 55: Sacral relics from temple repositories at Knossos: note especially the snake goddesses and the faience plaques representing the deity as a cow suckling a calf and a wild goat caressing kids. See, too, the stone cross and the balance weights.

Case 51: A remarkable bull's head rhyton from the Little Palace, Knossos.

Case 52: Swords from Mallia: note the acrobatic figure in gold foil on one pommel; also the highly decorated miniature objects.

Case 53: Tools and domestic implements from Knossos.

Case 54: Vases from temple repositories of Knossos.

Case 56: The *Bull jumper*: unique ivory acrobat from Knossos.

Case 57: The *royal gameboard*, about the size of a chessboard, made of inlaid ivory, found at Knossos.

Case 58: Ritual stone vessels from Knossos.

Case 59: Alabaster rhyton in the form of a lioness's head.

E

Room V: Late Neo-palatial Period (1450–1400 B.C.):
Knossos

Cases 61, 66: Stone friezes and vases, including some excellent examples from Knossos.

Case 62: Stone lamps from Knossos; Egyptian objects crucial to dating Minoan civilization.

Case 65: Neo-palatial seals from several sites.

Case 69: Clay tablets inscribed with Linear A and B.

Room VI: Neo-palatial and Post-palatial Periods
(1450–1350 B.C.): Cemeteries

Case 71: Idols representing a ritual dance, a cult scene and pottery from the vaulted tomb of Kamilari near Phaestos.

Case 72: Clay and stone vases from the royal tombs at Isopata, near Iraklion, and Knossos.

Case 73: Vases from cemeteries at Knossos: note idol of goddess carrying infant.

Case 74: Note cosmetic box depicting capture of a wild bull.

Case 75: Bronze vases and utensils from cemeteries at Phourni, near Arkhanes, and Knossos.

Cases 77, 85: Bronze weapons, bronze helmet, golden cup and vases from Knossos cemeteries.

Case 78: Note the helmet made out of boar's tusks from near Knossos: unique on Crete, most likely imported from the mainland.

Case 79: Libation vases from Phaestos: note glass vessel.

Cases 80, 82: Jugs and vases from tombs of Katsamba.

Case 81: Lids of jewel boxes, ivory handle of a mirror, mirrors and necklaces from the tombs near Knossos.

Case 84: Spear-heads, swords and daggers from tombs near Knossos.

Cases 86, 87: Jewellery from tombs at Knossos, Phaestos and elsewhere: note the fine granulated work and the gold rings.

Case 88: Jewellery, ivories and mirror from the *tholos* tombs of Arkhanes.

Room VII: Neo-palatial Period (1700–1450 B.C.): Central
Crete

Case 89: Vases, stone lamps, ritual vessel of obsidian from Tylissos and Nirou Khani.

Case 92: Votive offerings from various caves.

Case 93: Note carbonized wheat and figs on bottom shelf.

Cases 94–96: Three of the masterpieces of this museum, black steatite vases with relief carvings from the Royal Villa at Ayia Triadha: the *Harvesters' Vase* (Case 94); the *Chieftain's Cup* (Case 95); the *Rhyton of the Athletes* (Case 96).

Cases 97, 98: Swords and double axes from Arkalokhorion cave.

Case 99: Bronze talents (i.e. currency ingots) from Ayia Triadha.

Case 100: Bronze tools and weapons from Ayia Triadha; potter's wheels and tools from Vathypetro.

Case 101: Gold jewellery from central and eastern Crete: among so many prizes, we can only single out the incomparable 'honeybee pendant' from Khrysolakkos, near Mallia.

Case 102: Votive idols from Ayia Triadha: note especially the triton shell carved from liparite.

And, round the room, note the large bronze double axes from Nirou Khani.

Room VIII: Neo-palatial Period (1700–1450 b.c.): Kato Zakros

These are the most spectacular of the finds at the recently excavated palace site of Kato Zakros (pp. 263–6). All the various ceramic and stone vessels on display are worthy of attention and appreciation, but we single out the following displays:

Case 105: Stone vases and a bronze utensil.

Case 108: Pottery, a little stone column, stone vases.

Case 109: Libation vase of rock crystal.

Case 111: Libation vase with relief representation of a Minoan peak sanctuary: note the incredible liveliness of the goats.

Case 112: Bronze swords and double axes.

Case 113: Copper ingots and elephant tusks; of the pottery note the replica of the famous Marseille jug.

Case 115: Bronze saws.

Case 116: Libation vase in form of a bull's head.

Case 117: A head of a cat, a little silver vase, ivory fragments, a shell vase in faience, a butterfly, double axes and shells.

Case 118: Libation vessels of stone and faience from the palace treasury.

Note, too, on the wall a spiral-decorated frieze in relief from the palace 'banquet hall'.

Room IX: Neo-palatial Period (1700–1450 b.c.): Eastern Crete

Cases 119–22, 125–6: Stone lamps, bronze figures, libation vases and offering tables from Palaikastro, Gournia and island of Psira.
Case 123: Figurines and sacred insects, models of shrines.
Case 124: Ivory idols of children, miniature works, seal impressions.
Case 127: Tools and weapons.
Case 128: A fine collection of sealstones.

Room X: Post-palatial Period (1400–1100 b.c.)

Cases 130, 131: Clay rhytons, goblets and pottery showing Mycenaean characteristics.
Case 132: Women in sacred dance, incense burners.
Case 133: Clay figures of goddesses carrying sacred symbols on their heads.
Case 135: Votive figurines of goddesses with unusual head-dresses.
Case 137: Offering tables, sacred horns with socket for double axe, jewel box with contents.
Case 138: Double vases from Knossos, clay *larnakes* and figurines.
Case 139: Necklaces and moulds.
Case 140: Offering table from Phaestos; goddesses and models of shrines, libation vase in form of human head, and stone altar decorated with double axes and horns in relief from Knossos.
Case 142: Figurines of goddesses and ritual vessels.
Case 143: Votive figurines, sacred swing, sacred ship.
Case 144: Bronze weapons.

Room XI: Sub-Minoan and Early Geometric Period (1100–800 b.c.)

Case 146: Vases, figures of horses, bronze tripod.
Case 147: Votive figures in bronze.
Case 148: Model representing a chariot drawn by oxen; clay statuettes of goddesses in benediction: note three with movable feet.
Case 149: Interesting clay figurines from Inatos cave.
Case 153: Iron weapons and tools; brooches.
Case 154: Cult objects, including clay model of house or sanctuary.
Case 158: Jewellery, statuettes and offerings from Inatos cave.

Room XII: Late Geometric and Orientalizing Periods (800–600 B.C.)

Case 159: Unusual Geometric pottery with blue and red on white.
Cases 163, 168: Orientalizing and Geometric tomb vases.
Case 164: Bronze belt with relief carving from near Knossos.
Case 166: Funerary urns from Knossos cemeteries.
Case 169: Bronze decorations from Idhaean cave; 'master of animals' in relief carving.
Case 170: Jewellery of the Geometric period.

Room XIII: Minoan Sarcophagi (1400–1100 B.C.)

The sarcophagi here belong to the Post-palatial Period; they are either of the 'chest' or of the 'bath-tub' shape. The legs were drawn up tightly – hence the small size. The later ones are decorated in the so-called decadent style.

At the end of Room XIII a staircase leads to the upper floor.

Room XIV: Minoan Frescoes (1600–1400 B.C.)

Most of these come from Knossos, Ayia Triadha and Amnisos. The original fragments are clearly distinguished from the restored parts. Some of the most interesting are noted below:

From Knossos

Relief of a bull's head.
Prince with feather crown.
Fresco of the bull games.
Processional fresco with rhyton-bearer.

From Ayia Triadha

Wild cat and pheasant.
Religious procession.

From Amnisos

White and red lilies.

Also here (Case 171) is what is considered perhaps the most valuable item in the museum – the *sarcophagus* from Ayia Triadha. Discovered in a tomb about 100 yards to the north-east of the Villa, the sarcophagus is carved from limestone with a surface coated with white plaster. It is painted to show the religious rites for the dead and thus represents one of the major sources for speculations on Minoan religion and rituals. It dates from about 1400 B.C.

Room XV: Minoan Frescoes (1600–1400 b.c.)

From Knossos

'The Parisian' – probably a priestess.

Room XVI: Minoan Frescoes (1600–1400 b.c.)

From Knossos

Bluebird (from the garden fresco).

Room XVII: The Giamalakis Collection

Dr Giamalakis, an Iraklion physician, was one of the few individuals allowed to purchase Minoan art, and over the years he amassed an important collection. It has been acquired by the museum and is being displayed in its entirety.

Case 178: A bronze statuette of a man carrying a lamb on his shoulder: exact date and provenance are uncertain.

Case 191: A finely chiselled diadem of the goddess as queen of the animals, and other jewellery.

Room XVIII: Minor Arts of Archaic, Hellenistic and Roman Periods

As the title of this room indicates, it contains a diverse collection of pottery, glass vases, bronze and clay figurines, armour, jewellery and coins, covering the periods from the seventh century b.c. to the fourth century a.d.

Down on the ground floor, there are two rooms of sculpture.

Rooms XIX and XX: Sculpture from Archaic, Classical, Hellenistic and Graeco-Roman Periods

These friezes and sculpture are mainly from such sites as Prinias, Gortyna, Eleftherna, Dreros, Palaikastro and Praisos. Although their aesthetic values may not impress greatly they are of particular importance in tracing the development of Greek sculpture.

Historical and Ethnographic Museum

Map 4

Hours

April 1st–Sept. 30th Weekdays 8–1, 3.30–6.30.
Public holidays 9–1.
Oct. 1st–March 31st Weekdays 9–1, 3–5.
Public holidays 10–1.

The museum is closed all day on Sundays and at Christmas, New Year, Greek Easter, March 25th and October 28th.

Entrance charge: Drs 10.

Taking up where the Archaeological Museum leaves off, this is a collection of art, historical mementoes and handicrafts dating from the first years of the Christian Era. It thus reveals the continuity of Cretan culture from that period on into Medieval, Renaissance and Modern times throughout the island's lulls and storms. It is housed in the former home of Andreas Kalokairinos, a student and benefactor of Crete's heritage.

BASEMENT

Here are remains of the early Christian and Byzantine periods as well as sculpture from the Venetian period and some Turkish remains from Iraklion.

GROUND FLOOR

This houses a collection of early Christian objects found at the Basilica of Ayios Titos at Gortyna (p. 176); also icons and frescoes from various churches and monasteries of Crete. These latter are of particular interest to students of Byzantine painting from the fourteenth to the sixteenth centuries.

UPPER FLOOR

Here are some interesting manuscripts, books and maps associated with Crete's past; examples of popular wood carvings and textiles; and a reconstruction of a Cretan rural home, furnished as it would have been about 1900. Of particular interest to many will be the reconstruction of the study of Nikos Kazantzakis, Crete's gift to modern letters (p. 100), with his furniture, belongings and books.

Basilica of St Mark
Map 12
Hours
Daily 10–12, 3–7, except Sundays and public holidays.
Entrance charge: Drs 5.

Since this old Venetian church was restored in 1961 (p. 137), it has housed a collection of reproductions of early Byzantine frescoes from the churches and chapels of Crete, an exhibition sponsored by the Society of Cretan Historical Studies.

The thirty-odd copies of frescoes from Cretan churches – some of which are quite remotely situated – show the artistic flourishing of Cretan painting in the thirteenth, fourteenth and fifteenth centuries. Among its more distinctive characteristics is the dark background. It is hoped that this exhibition will encourage some people to seek out the churches themselves around the island. In addition to the pamphlet about these reproductions (in English, French and Greek), various comprehensive works on Cretan–Byzantine painting are available at the entrance, including a new edition of the catalogue by Gerola (in modern Greek, a translation of the Italian original) of the frescoes of Cretan churches; and the standard work on the subject, *La peinture murale byzantine de l'île de Crète* by C. Kalokiris.

PRINCIPAL SIGHTS

The major sights of Iraklion are described below, following a route from the harbour up to the centre of the town and radiating from the crossroads at Nikiphorou Phoka Square (familiarly known as 'where the traffic policeman stands') (*Map* 14). Directions from this crossroads are given, assuming each time that you are standing with your back to 25th August Street, which leads up from the harbour.

Harbour

Since Iraklion is traditionally approached by sea, we begin with the view as you enter the bay. Just off to the east is the barren island of Dia, named after the nymph – one of Zeus's extra-marital amours – cast there by Hera. The English-speaking community call it Dragon Island because of its shape. It is now a refuge for the *agrími* or wild goat (p. 69). To the west of the city the land rises steeply, with the remains of a Venetian fort, the Palaikastro, to be seen; above this is the village of Rogdhia (p. 159). Inland and to the west is the prominent cone of Mt Stroumboulas; more central are the peaks of the Idha range and the Zeus-profile of Mt Iouktas (p. 156). The city itself is most dense around the harbour, but over-flows on to the inclined plain that is backed by the mountain spine of Crete.

Ships tie up in the New Harbour, which has been dredged and enlarged over the years and is still developing its facilities. The entrance to the inner and older Venetian harbour – now used for yachts and smaller ships – is guarded by the impressive Venetian Castle.

Venetian Castle
Map 1

The Arabs may have been the first to build on an islet here – now joined by a mole to the mainland; then came the Genoese with a simple fort; and finally the Venetians worked on the ambitious fort we see today, constructing the major part between 1523 and 1540. It has twenty-six chambers and its battlements are worth a visit: the Lion of St Mark recalls the old glory. It is in a good state of preservation and visitors may inspect the whole castle. The Venetians expended a great deal to improve this harbour; little remains except one of their sixteenth-century *arsenali* – great vaulted chambers with arcades, now a warehouse.

Venetian Wall

The dominating structure of Iraklion is the Venetian Wall. First erected in the fifteenth century, these ramparts were greatly enlarged and improved in the sixteenth and seventeenth centuries; Michele Sammicheli of Verona, one of the leading sixteenth-century military engineers, came in 1538 to supervise. These walls were considered the strongest of their day in the Mediterranean world; in spite of the long siege by the Turks (p. 85), they are well preserved and enclose the main part of the city. They have a perimeter of about 5 km., several fine bastions, and the deep moat is visible; dwellings and plant growth have spread on to the ramparts and down into sections of the moat.

There are three main gates:

(1) The Gate of the Pantocrator, or Panigra Gate – now best known as the *Khania Gate* – serving as gateway to the west. Carvings date it at about 1570.
(2) The Gate of Gesu (Jesus), or *Kainouryia Gate*, with ornate stonework and decorations. Dated from 1567 to 1587.
(3) The *St George Gate*, or Porta del Lazzaretto (lepers once crowded outside this gate). Dated at 1565, it has two old fountains that were originally elsewhere in Iraklion and offers a view of the Fortress of St Demetri and the east walls.

One of the bastions, the *Martinengo* (*Map* 22), holds the grave of Nikos Kazantzakis (1883–1957), the celebrated Cretan–Greek author. Because of his somewhat unorthodox beliefs and writings the Greek Church refused to bury him with its full rites. Now he

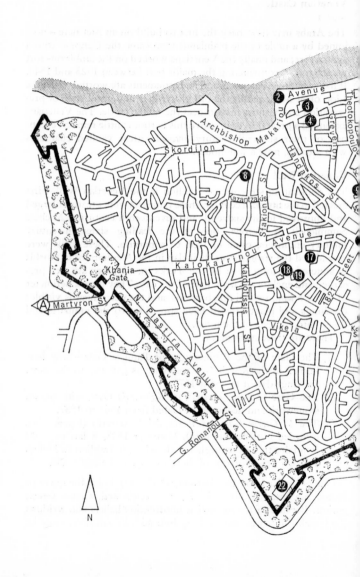

Iraklion

1 Venetian Castle (p. 133)
2 Glass House Restaurant
3 Xenia Hotel
4 Historical and Ethnographic Museum (p. 130)
5 Roman Catholic Church
6 National Tourist Office
7 Air Terminal (Olympic Airways)
8 Priuli Fountain (p.139)
9 Telegraph Office
10 Ayios Titos Church (p. 136)
11 City Hall (Armoury) and Loggia (p. 136)
12 Basilica of St Mark (pp. 131 & 137)
13 Morosini Fountain (p. 136)
14 Nikiphorou Phoka Square (Traffic Policeman)
15 Archaeological Museum (p. 123)
16 Tourist Police
17 St Katherine Church (p. 139)
18 Ayios Menas Church (p. 139)
19 Ayios Menas Cathedral (p. 138)
20 Post Office
21 Santa Maria dei Crociferi (p. 139)
22 Martinengo Bastion (p. 133)

A route to
Tylissos (p. 198)
Fodhele (p. 159)
Rethymnon
Khania
Mt Idha and Kamares Cave (p. 168)
Gortyna, Phaestos and Ayia Triadha (p. 172)

B route to
Knossos (p. 140)
Arkhanes, Mt Iouktas and Vathypetro (p. 156)
Ano Viannos and Arvi (p. 165)

C route to
Airport
Lasithi Plain and Dhiktaian Cave (p. 161)
Mallia (p. 241)
Ayios Nikolaos
Sitia

100 200 300 400 500

metres

lies under a massive but simple, rough native stone. On it an inscription from his own works reads: 'I hope for nothing. I fear nothing. I am free.' It is also possible to visit the 'birthplace' of Kazantzakis in the street now named after him, but it seems unlikely that any of the original structure is contained in the house now standing there. The reconstruction of his last study in the Historical and Ethnographic Museum (p. 131) is more stimulating.

Church of Ayios Titos
Map 10

Proceeding from the harbour, you climb 25th August Street up to the centre of the town. (This is the street on which are the shipping lines' offices, tourist agencies and banks.) About halfway up, you reach the large Hotel Astir on the left. It faces the Square of Ayios Titos (St Titus), named after the patron saint of the island, whose church dominates the square. An early Greek Byzantine church on the spot was used by the Venetians; earthquakes, fires and restorations followed, until the Turks made a major reconstruction as a mosque in 1862, thus accounting for its unusual shape. Its two most famous treasures – the icon of Messopanditissa and the head of St Titus – were taken to Venice when Iraklion fell to the Turks. In 1966, however, a reliquary containing the skull of St Titus was returned by Venice, so it once again reposes in its rightful home.

Venetian Armoury and Loggia
Map 11

Off Ayios Titos Square is the Venetian Armoury, now the City Hall. The armoury backed on to the once renowned Loggia. Constructed early in the seventeenth century in a 'mixed Renaissance' style, it disintegrated, owing largely to earthquakes; the last war finished it off for the most part but it has recently been reconstructed and will be put to some civic use. In the north wall of the armoury is the small fountain of Sagredo.

Fountain Square
Map 13

Higher up along 25th August Street is Venizelou Square – commonly known as 'Fountain Square' after the delightful fountain erected in 1628 under the Venetians. Francesco Morosini, the Venetian governor-general at the time, is credited with supervising its

construction, as well as that of the Loggia, the armoury, an aqueduct from Mt Iouktas to Iraklion and several other fountains. (This
Morosini should not be confused with his nephew, the famous
Proveditore Generale who surrendered Iraklion to the Turks in 1669
and later led the attack on Athens during which the Parthenon was
so badly damaged.)

The four lions on the fountain date from the fourteenth century
and were probably brought from another Venetian fountain. There
was once a statue of Neptune on the top. The eight lobes or basins
have bas-reliefs, not especially fine workmanship but worth a
close look: nymphs, tritons, dolphins, bulls and mythical marine
animals, some playing musical instruments.

Across from the fountain is the *Basilica of St Mark* (*Map* 12),
which contains the exhibition of copies of frescoes in the churches
of Crete (p. 131). Built in 1239 under the Venetians, it was reconstructed after an earthquake in 1303 as the Church of the Duke,
with a campanile (since destroyed); under the Turks it was trans-
formed into a mosque. It has now been restored to the original
Venetian style, and is used as an auditorium for lectures and con-
certs.

Just to the north-west of Fountain Square (that is, a few yards
back down 25th August Street) is *El Greco Park*, a modern public
garden with a bust of El Greco. There are public lavatories beneath
the park.

King Constantine Avenue and Liberty Square

Continuing up along 25th August Street, you arrive at the 'crossroads with the traffic policeman' at Nikiphorou Phoka Square
(*Map* 14). Turn left and go along King Constantine Avenue, where
the better shops are found on the left and administrative buildings
on the right. At the entrance to one of these latter – the *Court House*,
the middle of the three – is a Venetian portal from the destroyed
monastery Church of St Francis. The old Turkish barracks once
stood along the right-hand side of the avenue; these were replaced
by the present buildings, which house the government offices.
On the left-hand side, incidentally, were found some of the few
Byzantine remains in Iraklion.

Continuing down King Constantine Avenue, you come out on to
Liberty Square, with its cinemas and cafés. On Sunday and holiday
evenings their patrons spill out over the streets, and here is where

you sit to watch the *volta*, or promenade. At the far left of the square, where the road swings down through the St George Gate to the east, is the *Archaeological Museum* (p. 123). In its garden is a monument, in French, to the Duc de Beaufort and the French troops who lost their lives in 1668 while trying to lift the siege of Candia.

Across from the centre of Liberty Square, with its trees and flower garden, is a terrace with a life-size statue of Eleftherios Venizelos and, at the edge, a portrait bust of Nikos Kazantzakis.

Market and Kornarou Square

Back at the 'traffic policeman crossroads', the street that bears to the left is officially 1866 Street, but no one can fail to recognize it as the market. A stroll down its length must be made. At the far end is Kornarou Square, where the *Bembo Fountain* (1588) stands; the headless statuette built into it is Roman, brought from Ierapetra. The Bembo Fountain stands hidden by a café, through which you must pass to see it; beside it is another café, this one formerly a Turkish fountain. At the far side of the square is the former *Church of San Salvatore*; once part of the Augustinian monastery, it became the Mosque Validé, and is now a school.

Church of the Madonnina

Returning to the 'traffic policeman crossroads', straight ahead opposite 25th August Street you enter 1821 Street. On the corner, right, is what is left of the Church of the Madonnina, or Virgin of the Forum; it has been claimed that this was built by Nikiphoros Phokas after his liberation of Crete in 961. Little remains, in any case, except parts of the roof that now cover shoe repair shops and cafés.

Cathedral of Ayios Menas
Map 19

Back once more at the 'traffic policeman crossroads', keeping your back to the harbour, you turn right down Kalokairinou Avenue, a street lined with shops of all kinds. After four blocks turn left into Ayii Dheka Street, which emerges into the Square of Ayia Ekaterini, where stands the Cathedral of Iraklion, Ayios Menas. Erected between 1862 and 1895, it is remarkable largely for its six icons by Michael Damaskinos. A contemporary of El Greco, he too was known in Italy where he went to study and paint. These six icons, dating from about 1580, are his masterpieces and were brought here from the church at Vrondisi (p. 170). The icons are named: *The Burning Bush, The Last Supper, The First Oecumenical Synod, Noli me tangere, The Adoration of the Magi* and *The Sacred Mass.*

To one side of the cathedral is the little eighteenth-century *Church of Ayios Menas (Map* **18**); it contains some notable wood carvings, as well as icons by the Gastrophylakes brothers. If it is not open, you may get the key from the staff at the cathedral.

Church of St Katherine
Map **17**

Off this same square, in a lower court, is the Church of St Katherine. It dates from 1555, and is of a plain, relatively pure style except for the elegant seventeenth-century doorway. During the sixteenth and seventeenth centuries, this was the site of the Mount Sinai Monastery School, a centre of the Cretan 'Renaissance', where paintings, theology and humanistic studies were taught. It has been claimed that El Greco studied here as Domenico Theotokopoulos before he left for Italy and Spain, but this is largely speculative. Much more certain as pupils here were the other major figures of Crete's Renaissance: Cornaros and Khortatzis, the dramatists; Damaskinos, the painter; and Meletios Pigas and Kyrillos Loukaris, theologians and patriarchs.

Other Sights

These are the principal landmarks of Iraklion, but there are still other, if minor, sights. There are several charming little fountains – for instance, the *Fountain of Priuli (Map* **8**), dating from 1666. There are remains of other churches – one is *Santa Maria dei Crociferi (Map* **21**) in the south-east area of the town, dating from the early fourteenth century. And everywhere, in addition, are the pleasures and surprises of contemporary Iraklion.

EXCURSIONS FROM IRAKLION

See Chart of Excursions, facing p. 29, for other places of interest on the routes from Iraklion in addition to the excursions described on the following pages.

Knossos

Knossos is, of course, the goal of all visitors to Crete, and it lives up to its reputation. There will always be some who feel that Sir Arthur Evans carried his reconstruction rather too far, but no one ever leaves without being impressed by the majesty of the site. While its breadth and complexity are apparent even to those who merely stroll through, a guided tour is the only way to grasp the details of the site. Private guides may be hired through the National Tourist Organization; the fee for taking up to four people through a normal tour of two to three hours is about Drs 125. A possible alternative would be to go through with Pendlebury's *Handbook to the Palace of Minos: Knossos with its Dependencies*, which guides you through the site in a clear manner, satisfying both to the scholar and the curious tourist.

Route
Leaving Iraklion by King George Avenue off Liberty Square (Route B on town plan), you continue through the suburbs of the city until you reach the site of Knossos. As Knossos is only 5 kilometres from Iraklion, some people may consider making the pilgrimage by foot. (Apropos of pilgrimage, Kazantzakis describes his own journey to Knossos in his autobiography, *Report to Greco*.)
Bus
Buses leave for Knossos from Kornarou Square in Iraklion about every twenty minutes, joining King George Avenue at the edge of the town. Several tourist agencies arrange guided tours to Knossos with their own buses.
Hours
April 1st–Sept. 30th   Weekdays 7.30–1, 2–6.
                                      Sundays and public holidays 10–1.
Oct. 1st–March 31st   Weekdays 8.30–1, 3–5.
                                      Sundays and public holidays 10–1.
Closed at Christmas, New Year, Greek Easter, March 25th, and October 28th.
Entrance charge: Drs 10. Free on Thursdays and Saturdays (except for organized groups).

[1 km.] To the left, a paved road descends into a ravine and leads eastwards to the plateau of St Nicholas, from which there is a fine view of the town and bay. Not far from here were the remains of the *Tomb of Isopata*, a remarkable domed tomb from the middle Minoan period. What little survived when Evans excavated it was destroyed, accidentally or otherwise, under the German occupation; now you must see it through the restoration drawn by Piet de Jong, one of Evans's assistants, in the Iraklion museum.

From this point you could walk across the fields to Knossos, inspecting the remains of other tombs in the region. But it would

take a knowledgable guide to locate them – and all their valuable
yields are in the museum.

Continuing along the main road, you wind up and down through
the suburbs of Iraklion.

[4 km.] On a curve to the left you pass a *Sanatorium* (built by the
donations of Greek–Americans), which commands a fine view
across the valley of Kairatos, where Knossos lies. Many tombs
were discovered when the sanatorium was being built after the
Second World War.

[4¾ km.] Continuing on several hundred metres, you should begin
to look up to the field on the right for the red-roofed structure that
covers the well-preserved mosaic floor of the Roman *Temple of
Dionysus*. To visit this, you may park just along the road before the
5-km. stone and scramble up the slope – taking care to avoid the
barbed-wire fence – and walk the several yards across a field. These
mosaics and a few other odds-and-ends are all that survive of the
Colonia Julia Nobilis, a colony of Roman veterans who settled here
after the conquest of the island (p. 83); although they could
hardly rival the glory of Knossos, it must have been a fairly
ambitious settlement. Proceeding on along the main road just a few
more yards, you pass a side road that leads off to the right past the
gatehouse and up to the *Villa Ariadne*, built by Sir Arthur Evans
for his private residence. During the war it became the headquarters
of the German commandant, but it now belongs to the Greek
Archaeological Service. And just a little farther down the main
road, again on the right, is the entrance to the *Little Palace* (p. 154).

[5 km.] A stretch of little coffee-houses along the main road pro-
claims your arrival at *Knossos*. Just across from the first of these
cafés, to the left of the main road and below it, you can see the
remains of the old Minoan road, but there is no access to the site at
this point. For that, you proceed on to the white pavilion at the car
park. There is a souvenir shop here with a handsome choice of
handicrafts.

HISTORY OF KNOSSOS EXCAVATIONS

It had long been known that there must once have been a place
called Knossos; by the last half of the nineteenth century there were
frequent reports of finds in the area, but they were usually remains

of the later, Roman structures. After the revelations of an amateur Cretan archaeologist, Minos Kalokairinos, Schliemann tried to acquire the site, but it remained for Evans to begin the real excavations in 1900. Week after week produced some amazing find; year after year continued to reveal the immensity of the site. Evans soon realized that if the various levels and the general complexity of the structures were to be presented – not to mention protected from the elements – there would have to be a certain amount of reconstruction. Working carefully with all the fragments and evidence available – cf. the Town Mosaic in the Archaeological Museum – Evans supervised the restoration of considerable parts of the palace: columns, window casements, stairways, walls. All these were rendered in reinforced concrete, and whenever possible actual remains were incorporated in the restoration. Over the decades, Evans was assisted by a staff of archaeologists, architects and artists. In 1960 there began a scholars' dispute that might have appeared to cast doubt on the whole site of Knossos. In point of fact it concerned such matters as chronology, the script and the relationship between Minoan Cretans, Mycenaean Greeks and other Mediterranean and Asiatic peoples. Whatever the final adjustments, the achievement of Evans can in no way be diminished. Excavations continue, under the British School of Archaeology, and still turn up valuable finds both at the palace and in the surrounding fields.

PALACE OF KNOSSOS

Before plunging into the labyrinth, it seems best to have some general concept of what you will be seeing. First, it must be emphasized that what the visitor tours at Knossos today are largely the remains of the great palace that arose during the Neo-palatial Period – approximately 1700 to 1400 B.C. At the same time, remains from both earlier and later periods are everywhere, the Cretans themselves having continually built upon and absorbed previous structures. (Scholars' estimates of the population of Knossos, as both palace and dependent city, range from 30,000 to 100,000; the complete city must have spread over many surrounding acres.) What we see, then, is a great sprawling palace complex, amazingly modern in its treatment of space and terrain. This is not the Greece of classical proportions, but Knossos never was that; the amalgam of periods and structures we view is a legitimate effect.

As the archetype of the Minoan palaces, Knossos has at its heart the great central court, used for everything from religious rituals to moonlight strolling. (The great courts at Mallia and Phaestos, incidentally, are each as impressive in their own ways.) And like the other Minoan palaces, Knossos has no particular walls or defences. Its location, on a relatively modest mound in a valley, hardly made it impregnable; but as signs and remains of fortifications are slight, it evidently relied for defence on sea power, coastal installations – and reputation.

In addition to being the residence of the royal family and their circle of attendant nobles and functionaries, the palace served as the Sacred Precincts, and many rooms and remains are associated with the Minoan religion. There were little chapels and shrines everywhere, as well as lustral baths used for purification during sacred rites. Other indications of the religious atmosphere that must have pervaded the palace are the sacred pillars, the carved signs and symbols, the double axes, as well as all the artifacts, such as Snake Goddesses, now in museums. This great complex also housed the commercial and industrial quarters, with their administrative adjuncts. There were sizeable store-rooms for basic foods, and workshops for many of the common crafts. There are also indications that a close check was kept on such affairs: included here are the inscribed clay tablets that are just beginning to yield information about the Cretans of those days.

Most of the works of art and craftsmanship have had to be removed to the Iraklion museum. But the original drainage pipes function, and bathtubs are in place, as well as the gigantic urns and jars (*pithoi*) – some 7 ft high and 15 ft in girth. The original frescoes are in the museum; what you see at Knossos are copies of reconstructions, although the parts that had been found are distinguished from what is conjecture. (Two Swiss painters, the Gilliérons, father and son, are responsible for most of the imaginative restorations, based on surviving fragments and archaeologists' hints.) Perhaps the most dramatic original still in situ is the throne – generally conceded to be the oldest throne in Europe. It is made of gypsum, is well preserved – and you may sit on it!

The drainage and sanitation systems were probably superior to any known in Europe until the nineteenth century. Particularly notable is the system around the Queen's quarters. Remains in her toilet room suggest that there might have been running water from cisterns on a higher level, and the lavatory itself has the means for flushing as well as drains and a sewer. And the hydraulic science displayed on the East Bastion is quite amazing: the channel bordering the stairs is constructed so that it breaks and governs the flow of water.

Still another distinguishing feature of these palaces is the method of lighting. Building on several storeys as they did, the Minoans solved their lighting problems by leaving open courts and shafts so that the light could illuminate the lower quarters. The stairways, too, are remarkable. Some were narrow, but others were on a grand scale, no doubt with an eye to their function in ritual processions.

The amazing thing about all these technical accomplishments is that the Minoans combined them with artistic refinements. There are drainpipes – and the frescoes; a network of roads – and the Snake Goddesses. Is it any wonder, then, that such a complex structure and habitation gained the reputation of being a labyrinth? Think of the effect such a place must have had on passing travellers or captured enemies. And, perhaps more to the point, there is a pre-Hellenic word *labrys*, meaning 'double axe', and a pre-Hellenic ending *-nthos* (a survival in such sites as Tyrinthos or Korinthos): Knossos was literally a labyrinth, 'the house of the double axe'.

DESCRIPTION OF SITE

In the 'guided tour' that follows, the main rooms and features of the palace are keyed to the site plans on pp. 146–7 and p. 149. These show the basic ground-floor layout and the Piano Nobile. However, owing to the several overlapping levels of the palace, the visitor will find himself constantly moving from one level to another, in what sometimes seems to be a rather confusing fashion. This reminds us, by the way, of another distinctive feature of Knossos: a Minoan viewing the palace from the valley of Kairatos, just below to the east, would have looked up at a four- or five-storey structure, including those storeys built into the hill's slope.

Entrance and South Wing
(See plan on pp. 146–7)
You approach the palace from the official entry pavilion by a path that leads past a bronze bust of Sir Arthur Evans (1) and then across

Knossos: Ground Floor

1 Bust of Sir Arthur Evans
2 West Court
3 Walled Pits
4 West Porch
5 Corridor of the Procession
6 South Propyleum
7 South Entrance
8 Corridor of the Lily Prince
9 Central Court
10 Staircase

11–17 See Knossos, Piano Nobile (p. 149)

18 Stairs
19 Corridor of the Magazines
20 Foundations of a Keep
21 North-west Portico
22 Lustral Area
23 Theatral Area
24 Ancient Road
25 Propyleum
26 Pillar Hall
27 Northern Entrance
28 Ramp
29 Throne Room
30 Ante Chamber
31 Staircase
32 Foundations of Shrine
33 Lobby of the Stone Seat
34 Room of the Tall Pithos
35 Temple Repositories
36 Pillar Crypts
37 Site of Greek Temple
38 Grand Staircase
39 Hall of the Colonnades
40 King's Room (Hall of the Double Axes)
41 Queen's Megaron
42 Bathroom
43 Queen's Toilet Room
44 Closed room
45 Eastern Portico
46 Potters' Workshop
47 Court of the Stone Spout
48 Giant Pithoi
49 East Bastion
50 Corridor of the Draughtsboard
51 North-east Hall
52 Kennels
53 Royal Pottery Stores
54 Corridor of the Bays

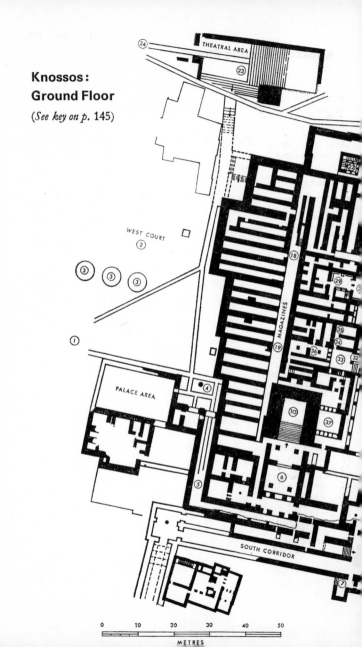

**Knossos:
Ground Floor**

(*See key on p.* 145)

THEATRAL AREA

24

23

WEST COURT

2

3   3   3

1

PALACE AREA

4

MAGAZINES

18

29

19   35

34

36   33   32

10   37

5   6

SOUTH CORRIDOR

7

0   10   20   30   40   50

METRES

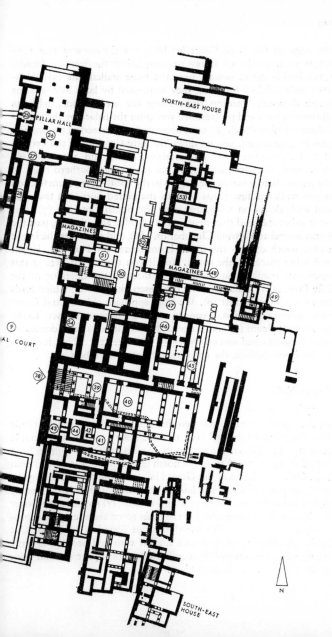

the edge of the West Court (2) by a paved causeway that runs across to meet the causeway running below the western façade. Over beside the causeway, note the large walled pits (3); whatever their original function, they were used by later Minoans for waste disposal. Turning right along the west façade, with its distinctive bays and projections, you enter the palace by the single-columned West Porch (4), once decorated with frescoes; proceeding past its guardroom, you go down the long Corridor of the Procession (5), also once lined with frescoes. At the end, you turn left, then right, then left, and come out on to the southern edge of the palace. Before turning left again to the South Propyleum (6), you might walk the few yards over to the sacred horns on the edge and look down on what was once the South Entrance (7): this once led to the road that went across a bridge and viaduct, past the Caravanserai and Spring Chamber (p. 154), and on across the island to the south coast – the main thoroughfare for Phaestos, Egypt and other places to the south. And if you turned left here at this south-east corner, you would come through the Corridor of the Lily Prince (8) (so named after the fresco found here), which leads into the Central Court (9). We shall approach this Central Court from another direction, however, so we go back some paces to the South Propyleum (6) and proceed through it (also once decorated with frescoes) and ascend the open staircase (10) which leads up to the Piano Nobile, the level with the state chambers.

Piano Nobile

(See plan opposite)

At the top of the stairs, you pass through a porch (11) and vestibule into the tricolumnar hall (12), to the right of which lay a temple treasury (13). Down the centre of the Piano Nobile runs a long corridor (14), entered from the north left corner of the tricolumnar hall. Off to the left was the Great Hall (15); proceeding along the corridor you come, on the left, to the sanctuary hall (16). Directly across from this are the terrace and rooms (17) reconstructed over the Throne Room complex; in the main room are a series of reproductions of some of the noted frescoes found at Knossos. Out again on the terrace, you take a right turn and proceed down a narrow flight of stairs (18), coming down on to the ground floor at the Corridor of the Magazines.

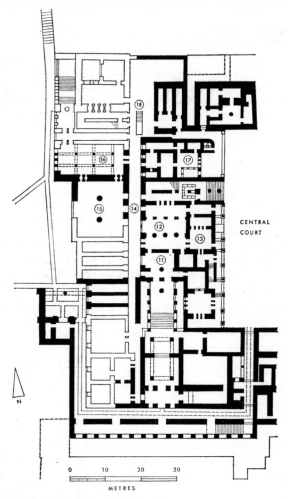

CENTRAL COURT

N

```
0        10        20        30
METRES
```

Knossos: Piano Nobile

11 Porch
12 Tricolumnar Hall
13 Temple Treasury
14 Corridor
15 Great Hall
16 Sanctuary Hall
17 Reconstructed Terrace and Rooms
18 Stairs

North-west Wing
(See plan on pp. 146–7)

The Corridor of the Magazines (**19**) never had access to daylight, so it must have required lamps or torches. Below the paving of the corridor and in some magazines were found sunken chests, which must have held valuables. Many of the great jars which held wine and oil have been mended and put back in their original positions; you may note some black, greasy gypsum slabs, where the burning oil ran when the palace was destroyed. It was in rooms along this corridor, too, that were found some clay tablets inscribed in Linear B. At the north end, turn right past a magazine (where tablets inscribed in hieroglyphics were found), then right, and then left. When you come to a wooden door on your right, turn left and go along an inclined path, to the right of which are foundations of an old keep (**20**), which once contained six deep pits. At the end of the path turn right, then left to pass through the North-west Portico (**21**). Outside to the left, roofed in, is a lustral area (**22**), used originally for ceremonial purificatory bathing. You leave the palace proper here and walk slightly west to the so-called Theatral Area (**23**).

Theatral Area
Originally this was only a flat paved area, but eventually stairs were added on the south side and then on the east side. It has been surmised that this area was used for dances and ceremonies. Leading westwards from this area is the ancient road (**24**), often called 'the oldest road in Europe'; it is still well paved and drained, and traces of houses are to be seen on either side. This road once joined the major Minoan road to the north and to the Little Palace (p. 154).

North Quarter
You return to the palace and walk along its north side and enter through the remains of the propyleum (**25**) into the Pillar Hall (also known as the 'Customs House') (**26**), with its large square piers. The Northern Entrance (**27**) leads from here direct by a ramp (**28**) to the Central Court. This ramp was originally walled but the present bastions are later additions, as are the colonnaded porticos above – of which the one to the west has been restored. Proceeding up the ramp a short distance, you can take a staircase to the right that leads up to this portico and examine the reproduction of a bull in relief that was found here. Back on the ramp you proceed to the small stairway that takes you to the Central Court (**9**).

Central Court

Built on almost a perfect north–south axis, this great court is 60 by 28 m. in extent. In general, the official and ceremonial apartments are to the west of the court, while the private and domestic quarters lie to the east. The original Neolithic site of Knossos lies under this court; when the great palaces we know were built, the earlier buildings were simply levelled and covered over.

West Wing

Directly to your right (as you enter the court from the north) is the Throne Room (29) and its related chambers. First is the antechamber (30), with stone benches; then the Throne Room itself (29), with its gypsum throne, just where it was found. Facing the throne is a sunken lustral area – again, for purificatory, not functional, bathing. Beyond the Throne Room is a shrine and a room known as 'the kitchen'. Leaving the Throne Room you turn right as you come back on to the Central Court and pass a broad flight of steps (31) that leads up to the Piano Nobile. You then pass the foundations of a shrine (32) and beyond that you descend a few steps into a small open court, the Lobby of the Stone Seat (33). To the right of this is the room of the tall *pithos* (34); and beyond that the Temple Repositories (35). In this latter room were stored the treasures and offerings of the shrine, and in a crypt were found the Snake Goddesses and attendant statuettes now in the Iraklion museum. To the west of the lobby are two other rooms (36): note the double-axe signs scratched on each pillar, indicating that these pillar crypts had some special sacred character. Back in the Lobby of the Stone Seat (33), you leave by the double doors to the south and ascend the shallow flight of steps straight ahead to an open space (37) where was found a Greek temple – the only such late building found on the palace site itself. You leave this area at the far left and step on to the Central Court again and cross it to enter the Domestic Quarters in the East Wing.

East Wing: Domestic Quarters

You enter this wing by the Grand Staircase (38). Considered one of the major architectural achievements of antiquity (with five flights still preserved in situ), it was a grand setting for ceremonial processions. As you descend, you will see replicas of shields on the balcony of the first landing (Hall of the Royal Guard or Upper Hall of the Colonnades). You proceed directly to your left and down under the enclosed flight of stairs to enter the Hall of the Colonnades (**39**), with its typical light-well. Leaving this room by a door on the north-east corner, you go several steps along the lower east–west corridor, and then turn right into the King's Room or Hall of the Double Axes (**40**), named from the many such mason's marks on the wall blocks (right, as you enter). Off to the left is a second large room, which had partitions that could be closed separately. Back in the main part of the King's Room you leave by the door opposite from the one you entered and walk along a dog's-leg corridor into the Queen's Megaron (**41**), with its reproduction of the Dolphin Fresco. To the right is a small room, the bathroom (**42**). You leave the Queen's Megaron by the door to the right and pass along the enclosed corridor that leads into the Queen's toilet room (**43**), with the famous flush lavatory and drainage system. Taking a dark passage off this – with a closed room to its right (**44**), where tablets were stored – you go back into the Hall of the Colonnades (**39**). You leave this as though going back into the King's Room (**40**) but instead go straight ahead along the east–west corridor to its end, and then turn left for the Palace Workshops.

Palace Workshops and East Wing

Heading north along a short corridor, you first pass, on your right, some small workshops, the second one being known as the Lapidary's Workshop because of the basalt stones found there. You proceed on and enter the Potters' Workshop (**46**), once known as the Schoolroom, with its benches and receptacles. Going straight on through this you enter the Court of the Stone Spout (**47**), so named from the spout that drained water from the upper Great East Hall. You proceed on to the stairs and face the enclosed room with the giant *pithoi* (**48**). If you turn around and look back and up on to the Palace, at your right, you will see a large block of gypsum on a square pier; this protruded from the ground even before Evans began his excavations. You now descend the stairs to the East Bastion (**49**); you are advised to go all the way down to examine the ingenious system of checking the water flow. Evans suggested that the palace laundry was down here. He also suggested that the flat ground between the palace here and the Kairatos River below was the site of the arena where the famous bull-leaping ceremony was performed.

You turn back from the East Bastion and ascend all the way up until you come out on to the flat paved Corridor of the Draughts-board (50), so named from the gameboard found here and now in the Iraklion museum. Note the drain pipes beneath the grating; these survive from the first palace. To the left lies the North-east Hall (51), and on the right, below, a series of openings (52) that may have been kennels; beyond these, to the north-east, were the Royal Pottery Stores (53). You now turn and face south from where you can look at three sections: the left one is an open court; the centre one is the Magazine of the Medallion *Pithoi*; the right one, which you enter by a doorway, leads into the Corridor of the Bays (54). Its massive piers probably supported the Great East Hall, which was above, and in which, it is suggested, stood a giant statue of the Minoan goddess. You pass through the Corridor of the Bays and entering the Hall of the Royal Guard again, you are back on the upper floor of the Domestic Quarters.

South-east Wing

Entering the Hall of the Royal Guard, you immediately turn left and leave it along the east–west corridor. You then turn right into the now exposed Upper King's Room (above 40). Leaving this by the south-west corner, right, you proceed over to the Room with the Stone Seat; there are also the remains of a lavatory in the corner. Passing alongside this room, keeping it to your right, you wind down on to the roofed-over area. The first small room to the right is a bathroom, with a fine bathtub preserved there; behind it, around the corner, is a small room with three jars. Now proceeding south along the roofed passage, you cross over some stairs and turn right at the corridor and pass the small enclosed Shrine of the Double Axes, built after the destruction of the great Palace. You continue on around this corridor, passing a lustral basin at your left, to arrive at the south-east corner of the Palace. (On adjacent slopes are various houses which may be explored by those with more time. The totally enclosed one off to the left is the House of the Chancel Screen, so named for the dais with balustrade that was found here. Down below this house is the South-east House, with its pillar crypt and libation table.) You now have two choices in leaving the Palace. One is to turn right and proceed up the earthen ramp to the edge of the Central Court, turn left there, and make your way over to the south-west corner and the Corridor of the

Procession (5) where you entered the Palace. The other way is to proceed straight along and below the southern edge of the Palace and make your way to the narrow flight of stairs that leads up to the Corridor of the Procession and the way out. Alternatively, you may decide to turn south and investigate the South House and other palace dependencies described below.

Palace Dependencies

(*See plan opposite*)

The remains of several subsidiary structures lie around the palace – to remind us that Knossos was more than just a palace. Another hour or two might well be spent in climbing about the gentle slopes; we shall only attempt to call attention to the more obvious ones, referring more serious students to Pendlebury's handbook. (Ask at the entrance to the main palace which of these places may be locked at any given time.)

The South House (4), *the Stepped Portico* (5), *the Piers of the Minoan Viaduct* (6), *the Caravanserai and Spring Chamber* (7). These lie below the southern side of the palace. Their names identify their functions, a caravanserai being a sort of reception house for travellers and caravans.

Royal Villa (2). This is situated below the main palace, about 100 m. away to the north-east; it is best approached from the East Bastion (**49** on plan on pp. 146–7).

The Little Palace (1). This is off the main road from Iraklion to Knossos (p. 141), on the right, about 250 m. north-west from the palace; you leave the main road by a flight of steps over the bank and across a small bridge. It is the second largest building excavated at Knossos and is quite impressive in its own right.

Many other houses and tombs have also been excavated in the immediate neighbourhood of the palace, and digging continues to turn up still more remains attesting to the extent of the Knossos complex.

There is still one more point of interest in the area. If you stay on the main road, past Knossos, and follow its curves for about another kilometre you come to the head of the valley of Spilia. Arching across the gorge is an aqueduct, dating from about A.D. 1838; although the Egyptians were in control of Crete then, it is credited to a Cretan architect.

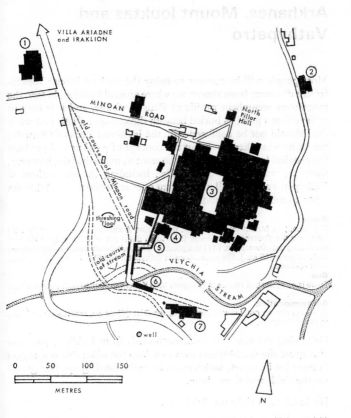

Knossos: Environs

1 Little Palace
2 Royal Villa
3 Palace of Knossos
4 South House

5 Stepped Portico
6 Piers of Minoan Viaduct
7 Caravanserai and Spring Chamber

Arkhanes, Mount Iouktas and Vathypetro

Most people will be content to enjoy the peak of Mount Iouktas from a distance; from almost anywhere around Iraklion, in fact, the monstrous recumbent profile of Zeus is visible, and it is easy to believe that a god lies buried beneath those slopes. (This god-who-died should not be confused with the immortal Zeus of Olympia; the name was taken over, but the concept of a dying god predates the classical image.) For those who want to make the trip, however, there are various 'fringe benefits', including the excavations at Vathypetro and the still more recent ones at Phourni near Arkhanes – not to mention the landscape.

Route
The ascent of Mount Iouktas is best made from Arkhanes, which is reached by following the Knossos road (Route B on town plan) out of Iraklion (p. 140) and continuing past Knossos (p. 141) to a point at 10 km. where you turn right for Patsides and Arkhanes [16 km.]. The excavations at Vathypetro and Phourni are also reached from Arkhanes.
Bus
There is a regular bus service to Arkhanes from Kallergon Square near El Greco Park in Iraklion.
Accommodation
Arkhanes has an hotel with a restaurant, the *Dias* (Class B), located about 1 km. south of the town.

Following the Knossos road southwards from Iraklion, you pass that great site (p. 140) and move on into the hills; this is a region famous for its wines, which come from the *rosaki* grape that grows on the fields and slopes here.

[10 km.] Turn right for Arkhanes.

[14 km.] **Kato Arkhanes.**

[16 km.] **Arkhanes.**

A relatively large and prosperous town, until recently Arkhanes had been known only for its vineyards; but in 1964 some new excavations began under the auspices of the Inspector of Antiquities for Crete and these have since revealed some remarkable and valuable finds. Some of the excavations are in the town itself and others are situated about 3 km. to the west on a hill known as

Phourni on the east slopes of Mt Iouktas. As these excavations are so recent the villagers know about them and will be able to provide a guide for a donkey-ride or walk out to them.

In the south part of Arkhanes a Minoan villa has been found, which is almost certainly of the sixteenth century B.C. – about contemporary with Kato Zakros. The building is of a size, construction and orientation that indicate that it must have been a palace; remains of paintings were even found on the massive walls, well preserved to a height of 3 m.

Some of the most interesting finds at Phourni are an ossuary of the third millennium B.C. and some later tombs of about 1400 B.C., all of which testify to a more extended and developed settlement here than had previously been suspected. In the ossuary, for instance, nearly two hundred human skulls and bones were found, along with several interesting carved seals – the first found in central Crete – and these indicate the existence of a flourishing, populous settlement from 2500 B.C. onwards. And in one of the two *tholos* tombs was found the first untouched royal burial excavated on Crete: a sealed *larnax*, which contained one woman – a queen or a princess, judging from the richness of the ornaments and household articles uncovered in and around it (more than 140 gold pieces of jewellery, pottery, fine bronze vessels, ivory pieces and necklaces of glass paste). The scenes and symbols represented on some gold signet rings, together with the presence of the skeleton of a bull – probably sacrificed to the deceased – show connections with archaeological evidence from other Minoan sites; they are not only of great immediate interest to the student of Minoan–Mycenaean religion but raise the hopes that other unplundered tombs may be found in this region.

'Modern' Arkhanes, for that matter, has had its own modest culture. As you drive through the town, after passing the attractive white Church of Pelayia and a clock tower on the right, down a side road to the right is the little *Church of Ayia Triadha* on the edge of the vineyards that encircle the town; a few fragmentary Byzantine frescoes have survived.

Church of Asomatoi

More interesting are the early fourteenth-century frescoes commissioned by Michael Patsidiotis in the Byzantine Church of Asomatoi: this is some 3 km. from the town, and before you set

F

out you should ask for the key at the open-air *taverna* in the square at the edge of Arkhanes where the buses wait. Follow the road that turns to the right after the Dias Hotel 1 km. south of the town (the same road as for Vathypetro – see below). About $\frac{1}{2}$ km. after the hotel, turn left across the vineyards along a rough track; bearing left after 1 km. continue for another $\frac{1}{2}$ km. until you come to the small church just below and to the left of the path, situated among vines and shady trees. The frescoes that remain include a striking Crucifixion and a figure of Christ dressed in full armour.

Mount Iouktas

If you intend to make a real ascent – it is only about an hour's climb – it is wisest to engage a guide in Arkhanes; but there is also a road along which cars can drive up to the peak. Once there, you will be shown the cave where Zeus was buried; no matter what you may believe, it has been used as a shrine over the centuries. In the middle and late Minoan periods there was quite an elaborate sanctuary on the summit; some fragments remain, and votive offerings of vases and figurines have been recovered. Evans was among the first to explore this site; the Greeks have continued the work. The Orthodox, not to be outdone, have built a Chapel to the Lord of the Transfiguration here; and the modern world has constructed *its* shrine – a radio transmitter. On August 6th, the whole town of Arkhanes turns out on foot and by car to celebrate the Feast of the Transfiguration on Iouktas.

Vathypetro

An interesting excursion can be made to this site, where after the Second World War the Greeks excavated a large Minoan *megaron*. The girl at the *taverna* referred to under the Church of Asomatoi (above) has been trained to act as a guide to the site. To get there, you follow the road southwards to the Dias Hotel; just past that, the road turns right and, becoming rather rough, continues up into the hills for about $3\frac{1}{2}$ km. until you see the site to your right across some vineyards. The remains themselves are on a domestic scale but their situation is impressive, overlooking a valley rich with vineyards. The excavations, which have been continued until now, have revealed a central court, a three-part sacred chamber, a main hall with columned façade, terraces and basement workrooms. In these latter were found several interesting objects, including storage vessels, a weaving-mill, a large oil press and – most impressive of all – a completely preserved wine press. (To visit these basement rooms you must be accompanied by a guide.)

Fodhele

People who come to Crete simply to see the home of the Minoans may be surprised at this excursion, for it is to the birthplace of Domenico Theotokopoulos, known as El Greco. Beyond that, Fodhele is an attractive village set among orange groves and there are several delightful bathing spots along the way.

Route
You leave Iraklion by the Rethymnon–Khania road (Route A on town plan) and at 8 km. turn right for Rogdhia, Akhlada and Fodhele [34 km.]. You can then either return to Iraklion by the same route or continue on through Fodhele for another 7 km. to pick up the main Iraklion–Rethymnon road just beyond Marathos [21 km. from Iraklion], from which point you could head either way. Obviously, too, this route via Marathos is another way to go to Fodhele.
Bus
There is a regular bus service from Iraklion to Fodhele, starting from the Khania Gate and taking the route via Rogdhia and Akhlada.

Leaving Iraklion by the Rethymnon–Khania road, you drive along the coastal plain.

[8 km.] Turn right for Rogdhia and Akhlada.

[10 km.] As you drive along you find yourself looking down a fairly sheer drop to the right. Below is an old mill, situated on the edge of a dark pond about 50 yards across. This is the *Almyrós of Malevizi* – the 'salt pond', one of three such brackish pools on the north coast; and as usual the natives claim that it is bottomless. What is left of the old mill dam may be Venetian masonry.

[17 km.] The village of **Rogdhia**, which is seen from Iraklion as a glimmer of white in the day and a sparkle of light at night. It is worth stopping here to look at the façade of a Venetian *palazzo* near the church. In the hills to the left is the *Convent of Savathiana*, where a few nuns still live and work.

[21 km.] A right turn leads to **Ayia Pelayia**, a place on the coast that takes its name from the monastery that was once here. There are some remains of a Venetian fortress near by, as well as a Byzantine kiln that is believed to have been used to fire the roofing for the fort. The beach is especially fine, and a new Tourist Pavilion is being built to provide refreshments and facilities for bathers; boat excursions often come here direct from Iraklion.

[24 km.] **Akhlada** is a lovely village with its white church and bell tower. From here the road descends in bends to the sea, passing several other bathing places before turning inland through orange and lemon groves.

[34 km.] **Fodhele.**

Fodhele is noted today for its orange groves and mild climate. There is a modest monument to El Greco, placed there in 1934 by the University of Valladolid in Spain. For the non-sceptics there is a Venetian-style house that is shown as his family's home, and a chapel with a much-treasured album of reproductions of his paintings. Those who insist on seeing his *real* birthplace will be taken through the village and across the fields to the ruins of an old house lying in a little gully – and imagination must do the rest.

That El Greco (1542–1614) came from Crete is not disputed, for he declared that he was a native of Candia. But the actual place of his birth was not known until this century, when research established that references to a family named Theotokopoulos living in Fodhele occurred in documents of the time; indeed, a family with a similar name still lives in the district. The region near Gortyna has also laid claim to being his birthplace, but on very slender evidence. In any case, Fodhele has been designated as El Greco's native village.

Little is known of El Greco until he arrived in Rome in 1570, when he was referred to as 'a pupil of Titian'. It is accepted that he worked under Titian in Venice; it is also claimed that he studied at the School of Mount Sinai in Iraklion, that he learned woodcarving at Vrondisi Monastery, that he painted at Valsamonero, but none of this is authenticated. He went to Italy in the 1560s and never returned to Crete. But El Greco carried the Byzantine style in his eye, and the island landscape in his mind; he was never to free himself entirely from their grip on his technique and imagination.

Lasithi Plain and Dhiktaion Cave

This excursion – which includes the birth-cave of Zeus and a plateau known as 'The Valley of the Windmills' as its destination – requires a full day, especially if any of the sites en route are taken in. The destination lies in Lasithi Nome and can be reached from either Neapolis (p. 247) or Ayios Nikolaos. Most people will make it as a round trip from Iraklion, however, so we describe the approach from there; those who are going on to the eastern sites might consider taking the alternative route when they do so.

Route
Follow the road out of Iraklion (Route C on town plan) described at the beginning of the route to Ayios Nikolaos (pp. 241–3) and turn right at 24 km.; then proceed up into the hills via Potamies, Avdou and Tzermiadhes to arrive at Psykhro [69 km.], the jumping-off point for the Dhiktaion Cave. From Psykhro you can either return to Iraklion by the same route or go on to Neapolis or Ayios Nikolaos; this latter route requires you to retrace the route from Psykhro for 8 km. and then take a right turn on to a winding road across the mountains.

Bus
There is a regular bus service from Beaufort Avenue in Iraklion to Psykhro and points en route.

Accommodation
Psykhro has a Class E hotel. *Dhiktaion*; the new Tourist Pavilion is due to open with eight beds; the Monastery of Panayia Kroustallenia (described below) has decent accommodation; and Tzermiadhes has an inn, *Tzermiadhon* (Class E).

[24 km.] Having taken the road eastwards out of Iraklion, as for Ayios Nikolaos (pp. 241–3), you turn off to the right; the sign directs you to Potamies/Kastelli/Lasithi. It is a good asphalt road leading through olive groves and climbing into the hills.

[29 km.] A right turn would take you in 10 km. to **Kastelli-Pedhiadhos** (p. 166), but for Lasithi keep left.

[33 km.] Just before the village of **Potamies** itself, across a field to the left, stands the little Byzantine *Church of Christos*, with fragmentary frescoes. A few hundred yards farther, a sign indicates another footpath to the left that leads you up a hill, about 5 minutes' climbing, to the *Church of Panayia Gouverniotisa*; this has fourteenth-century frescoes, including a Christ Pantocrator on the dome.

[38 km.] Just before the village of **Avdou**, a right-hand side road leads in ½ km. to the *Church of Ayios Konstantinos*, with much-damaged frescoes. A plaque commemorates that the chapel was restored in 1948 with money sent home by a villager who had made good in Egypt.

[39 km.] Off to the left in the village of **Avdou** itself, before the café, is the Byzantine *Church of Ayios Antonios*, with attractive fourteenth-century frescoes, including one of the Last Supper.

[40 km.] You pass through the village of **Gonies** and then on past the sign indicating a turn to the left for Mokhos; bearing to the right you begin a dramatic ascent of the Lasithi range.

[46 km.] The road passes the edge of the village of **Krasi**. Those who have the time should take a secondary road to the left and go on up through the village to see one of the more remarkable trees in the world: a gigantic plane tree that has been nourished by the endlessly gushing springs near by. You can sit under the tree and enjoy a glass of the water while watching the people come and go at the fountains.

[50 km.] Down to the right, just about 600 m. before the village of **Ano Kera**, lies the *Monastery of Kera*. Its once-famous icon of the Madonna of Perpetual Succour was taken in 1498 to the Church of St Alphonse in Rome. A small column in the churchyard is connected with the legend that the icon was three times taken away to Constantinople and each time miraculously returned. On one of these occasions the Madonna brought with her a chain and the column to which she could be bound to prevent her being removed. However, this was clearly not efficacious in preventing the icon's final removal.

[53 km.] Finally, just when you think the road cannot go any higher or farther, you find yourself going through a pass, with old stone windmill towers banked along the steep ridges. Ahead of you, spread out like some enormous Olympic Stadium, is the *Lasithi Plain*, with Mt Dhikti at its far end, and the slopes and peaks of the Lasithi range completely encircling it.

From 8 to 10 km. long and 4 to 7 km. wide, the plain appears almost symmetrical. After heavy spring rains or the thaw, the water may collect up to one metre in depth; this drains at the north-west entrance, forming a sizeable river as the water comes down on to the north coast. Thus the plateau is virtually an alluvial plain in that the run-off from the slopes has deposited a thick soil, making for some of the most productive land on Crete. Potatoes, apples and other fruit, and some grain are among the chief products. There are about eighteen villages, tucked away in the foot-hills both to avoid the floods and to free the land for cultivation. Because of its peculiar situation, this whole area has always been somewhat independent, yet it has never completely cut itself off from the culture of the rest of the island. Ancient sites and remains have been found all over the plain and its slopes: caves, buildings, forts, temples, tombs, with shards and artifacts of all sorts – with the British taking the lead in exploring and excavating these places. The history runs from Neolithic times to the Roman period, and to describe all these sites would require a book in itself. The Venetians, determined to do away with such an enclave, removed the inhabitants and prohibited farming and pasturing on the plain from 1362 to the end of the fifteenth century; but eventually its fertility could not be denied.

What makes it a spectacle today is not just the lush, flat farmland. Wherever you look there are windmills. Yes, windmills – some very slight and others quite ambitious, but when they all have their white sails unfurled it is a unique sight, best seen in mid-morning when the prevailing winds tend to sweep across the plateau. They are used to pump the water for irrigation. An actual count is said to have been taken some years ago, and it was claimed that there were some ten thousand windmills on this plain. It is said that a man's wealth here is measured by the number and size of his windmills – just like the Lapps with their reindeer.

[58 km.] Keeping to the left along the northern edge of the plain, you come to **Tzermiadhes**, the largest village on the plain (it has an inn). A little to the north-east of the village is the low plateau of Trapeza, where lies a famous cave. The *Cave of Trapeza* was discovered by Evans in 1896, but it was not until 1936 that the British got around to making thorough excavations. Many finds, including pottery, seals and figurines, were taken out of the cave, but they were so mixed up that it was hard to assign exact dates. It was definitely a dwelling in Neolithic times; human remains indicate that it was later a burial site. In Minoan times it became a cult shrine.

Another detour of interest to specialists involves an hour and a half's walk back in the direction of Kera to the post-Minoan city of *Karfi*, which was excavated by Pendlebury. Situated at about

1,100 m. above sea-level, it has a fine view, and it has been identified as one of several isolated and secure places that developed in the aftermath of the Minoans' decline.

[61 km.] Back on the main route, turn right off the Tzermiadhes–Neapolis road for Psykhro. To the right is the *Monastery of Panayia Kroustallenia*, which played an important part in Cretan revolutionary history, being twice destroyed by the Turks. It enjoys the singular, and rather un-monastic, luxury of its own generator, so that it has electricity. You can pass the night here in quite comfortable quarters.

[64 km.] The village of **Ayios Georgios** is recommended as the best jumping-off point for an ascent of *Mount Dhikti* (2,148 m.). Anyone who wants to make the climb must allow at least 5 hours by this route; the route to or from the south via Pefko or Ano Viannos (p. 166) takes about as long, as does the route to or from the west via Embaros (p. 167). There is no water to be had in the heights, and nights, even in summer, can be quite cold, but the view from the top is considered to be reward enough.

[65 km.] **Avrakontes.**

[69 km.] **Psykhro**: the starting-point for the climb to the Dhiktaion Cave, the birthplace of Zeus. The village is a popular spot for excursionists from all over Crete, with people coming to sit in the shade of the trees and enjoy the spring water after their climb to the cave. There is a Tourist Pavilion, a Class E hotel and light meals can be had in the village. Except for occasional week-ends, however, there are not likely to be many people going to the cave at any one time. It is strongly recommended that you arrange with one of the guides from the village to take you through the cave, both to avoid any risk and to be certain of seeing all the 'inner sanctums'. The usual fee is about Drs 30 to Drs 40, which may or may not include the candles he brings. The cave can be damp and slippery; rubber-soled shoes, or at least steady footage, are recommended. You can drive the 1 km. to the Tourist Pavilion and from there it is a steep $\frac{1}{2}$ hr climb up to the left to the cave. The visit in the cave itself takes about an hour.

Dhiktaion Cave

The cave, a gaping split in the mountain-side, was brought to light back in the 1880s by local men. Hadzidakis and Halbherr explored the exposed parts shortly afterwards, and Evans came there in 1894; but it was 1900 before the British, with the help of local people, undertook a thorough excavation, which was later continued by the French. Blasting was resorted to, and the unsuspected inner depths revealed, with local youths bringing up hundreds of votive offerings from the muddy depths. There are large stalagmites and stalactites; a huge stalactite, hidden in a chamber, is known as 'the mantle of Zeus' (i.e. his swaddling-clothes). There is a small underground pool, which runs dry in August and September. And in one tiny chamber – where there were particularly rich finds of votive offerings – it is claimed that the birth occurred.

The myth, briefly, is that Cronus, once the master-god of the earth, feared that he would be overthrown by his children, so ate all those that his wife Rhea bore him. After she bore Zeus she gave Cronus a stone to eat instead, and then left the baby to be raised by the goat Amaltheia and the bee Melissa. It must be recalled, too, that Zeus was no god for the Minoans; he was introduced into Crete by the later Greeks, and this story of his birth was evidently an attempt to relate the new god to the old mother, and to convert some Minoan deity into an acceptable Olympian figure. Hesiod is responsible for setting this down, and as noted elsewhere (p. 74) it is all further complicated by the question as to just where the Dhiktaion Cave should be located. In any case, this cave had a long history as a cult shrine from the middle Minoan period on. It would seem that the upper cave was used first; then the water receded and the lower cave was attended by votaries of the Mother Goddess. By 800 B.C. the cave's appeal was at its peak, and then it began to be superseded by the one on Mt Idha. But it is easy to see how such a cave would give rise to a cult and myths.

Ano Viannos and Arvi

A trip to the pretty village of Arvi on the south coast is a full day's excursion from Iraklion, especially if you include a visit to the Byzantine chapels around Kastelli-Pedhiadhos and the other sites en route. It is possible to continue along the rough roads to Ierapetra (p. 256), also on the south coast; but to appreciate the full charm of Arvi and to make the rather tiring drive really worth while we would recommend staying at least one night there to enjoy the delightful swimming and to explore the semi-tropical countryside.

Route

Take the Knossos road (Route B on town plan) out of Iraklion (p. 140), and continue past Knossos (p. 141) via Arkalokhorion to Ano Viannos and Arvi [85 km.]. From Arvi you can get to Ierapetra by returning along the coast out of the village for 2 km. and taking the first right turn northwards, which will bring you out on the Ano Viannos to Pefko road in about 15 km. From Pefko (a village, by the way, that can be used as a starting-point for climbing Mt Dhikti (p. 164), as can Ano Viannos) you make your way across the mountains via Mournies for about another 30 km. to Ierapetra.

Bus

There is a regular service from the Kainouryia Gate in Iraklion as far as Ano Viannos; from there you would have to engage a taxi. There is also a service from the same bus station to Kastelli-Pedhiadhos.

Accommodation

Simple accommodation can be had at the café in Arvi; Ierapetra has hotels (p. 256).

[10 km.] Having left Iraklion by the road to Knossos (p. 140), you pass the right fork to **Arkhanes** (p. 156).

[15 km.] **Kounavoi**.

[18 km.] **Peza**.

[20 km.] A turning to the left into the village of **Ayies Paraskies** leads off in 17 km. to **Kastelli-Pedhiadhos**. There are several small Byzantine churches in this area. Perhaps the most interesting is the *Church of Ayios Panteleimon of Vitzariano* in the village of **Pigi**. This is reached by taking the road to Kalo Khorio northwards out of Kastelli-Pedhiadhos and forking right after 1 km. on to a cart track, which brings you in another 2 km. to the church, situated among shady trees. (Ask at the café for the priest who has the key; he occasionally takes some finding – especially at siesta time.) The church was built in the Byzantine period from ancient materials, including four capitals decorated with acanthus leaves that have been stacked to form one of the columns.

Another church is *Ayios Georgios* near the village of **Xidas**, $6\frac{1}{2}$ km. to the east of Kastelli-Pedhiadhos; it involves about a ten minutes' walk below the village. And 3 km. beyond Xidas on the road to Aski to the east is the site of *Lyttos*, or Lyktos, which flourished in the classical and Hellenistic periods. It issued its own coins and had its port at Khersonisos (p. 243); it once even had a famous theatre, but nothing of any interest has survived. Just past the mound there is an extensive view over to the Lasithi mountains.

Back at Kastelli-Pedhiadhos you can either return as you came to the Ano Viannos road or continue southwards on a rough road to rejoin the Ano Viannos road farther down. This short cut would save some 28 km.; and on your right, 2 km. out of Kastelli-Pedhiadhos, you would pass the twelfth–thirteenth-century *Church of Ayios Ioannis*.

[33 km.] If you did not take the turning to Kastelli-Pedhiadhos but continued straight on along the Iraklion to Ano Viannos road, you will come to **Arkalokhorion**. In a near-by grotto there were valuable finds of bronze weapons and double axes. Some scholars suggest that this might well have been the cave either where Zeus was born or where he was brought to be raised; in any case, the finds indicate that it was the site of a *Curétes* cult (p. 171).

[43 km.] After **Panayia** the road begins to rise, goes through a pass, and then descends again.

[50 km.] Off the road to the left is **Embaros**. To the west lies *Arkadhia* (also Arkadhes), a site where extensive finds were made in tombs from the ninth and eighth centuries B.C. Embaros is another possible jumping-off point for the climb on *Mt Dhikti* (p. 164).

[66 km.] After emerging from a pass, from which you can see the Libyan Sea, and passing by Kato Viannos, you arrive at **Ano Viannos**. 'Upper Viannos' is the district's focal point, boasting a school and a fine plane tree. The village is delightfully situated on the mountain-side, surrounded by vineyards and olive groves. The frescoes and icons in the fourteenth-century *Church of Pelayia* up the hill are worth seeing; near by are the ruins of watermills and the fifteenth-century *Church of St George*.

For Arvi turn right out of Ano Viannos just before the church, keeping right after 1 km.

[70 km.] The *Monastery of Ayia Moni* is on the left. As you continue, off to the right rises the huge rock of *Keratokambos*, rising nearly 600 m. above the sea. On its summit are ruins of the Keratokastello ('castle of horn'), at its base remains of a post-Minoan village.

[78 km.] Keep left at the signpost to Arvi.

[85 km.] **Arvi**.

This tiny port-village lies on a small coastal plain, backed by high hills, and an almost tropical climate prevails; bananas grow here, as well as oranges. Behind the fruit groves is the gorge that has given Arvi its name and fame; legend has it that Zeus Arvios struck the rocky cliff, creating the cleft through which the irrigating waters flow. When the wind howls through the gorge or water rushes from the thousand-foot-high fissure, the noise is said to be like titanic thunder. When Pashley came here in the nineteenth century he found remains of what he decided was the Temple of Zeus Arvios; it is claimed that the present village church is built on the platform of that ancient temple. On the hillside to the right of the cleft is the now-crumbling *Monastery of St Anthony*, where a few monks eke out a bare existence.

In the village there is modest accommodation available and fine swimming. This would be an idyllic spot to stay for a restful few days – and after the precipitous last few miles of the drive down, that is just what you will feel like doing.

Mount Idha and Kamares Cave

Although no Alpine ascent, the climb to Mount Idha and a visit to the adjacent caves involves more than the casual traveller will be able to manage. There are alternative approaches, with various detours and diversions, but at least two or three days must be allowed. We shall describe the approach from Iraklion via the village of Kamares, not only because it offers convenient access to the summit and the caves but also because it provides an excursion with several interesting stops en route. Other approaches would be: from the north via the village of Anoyia (p. 171), from where there is a rough road which could be driven up to Idha Cave; from the west via the village of Fourfouras (p. 196) and from the south via the village of Voroi (p. 195).

All except the more experienced climbers and hikers should arrange for a guide; they can be picked up in the villages, but you would do well to consult the Iraklion office of the Tourist Organization. Here you can be put in touch with guides, consult more detailed maps or be introduced to the local Alpine and Touring Clubs who occasionally make ascents. Those who are determined to go alone will find the best available account in Robert Grantham's *Minotaur and Crete*.

Incidentally, so that no one goes to all this trouble by mistake, the Mount Idha in question is not the classically famous one of Homer and Aeschylus – that is near Troy. Crete's Mount Idha, in fact, is becoming more widely known today, at least among the natives, as Psiloritis.

Route
Follow the route from Iraklion to Phaestos (Route A on town plan) as far as Ayia Varvara (pp. 172–3), where you turn right along the mountain-sides to Zaros and Kamares [57 km.]. After making the climb you can continue walking northwards, returning to Iraklion via Anoyia and Tylissos (p. 198).
Bus
There is a daily bus service from the Khania Gate in Iraklion to Zaros and Kamares, as well as to Tylissos and Anoyia.
Accommodation
Simple overnight accommodation and meals can be had in Kamares and Anoyia.

[30 km.] Taking the Phaestos road out of Iraklion (pp. 172–3), you come to **Ayia Varvara**, at the end of which take a right turn that leads you westwards along the edge of the mountains and down into a lovely valley.

[40 km.] In the village of **Yeryeri** is the *Church of the Panayia* which has fifteenth-century frescoes.

[45 km.] **Zaros** seems cleaner and more prosperous than the average Cretan village; many of the doorways of the houses have carved lintels. It is also noted for its fine water, the same source that supplied ancient Gortyna (to the south, behind the mountains) and that still supplies Ayii Dheka. Remains of the ancient stonework are to be seen around the spring. Above this spring is the old *Church of Ayios Nikolaos*, with fifteenth-century icons and altar panels in early Renaissance style. Above this church, across a ravine and up the mountain-side, is a chapel in a cave. It dates from the fifteenth century, has frescoes, and takes its name from *St Efthimios* who lived and died as a hermit-ascetic in the cave.

[48 km.] Three kilometres out of Zaros, a right turn leads steeply up the hillside to the *Monastery of Vrondisi*. This is said to have been founded in the sixteenth century by pilgrims from Brindisi in Italy. It stands high on the hill, with a fine view, and there are large plane trees in the clearing before the walls. Here, too, is a sixteenth-century Italianate fountain, quite un-ascetic in its elegance and one of the finest in the Cretan countryside; between the two pilasters are badly mutilated statues of Adam and Eve. Notable frescoes in the Church of St Anthony and the fine overnight accommodation (with arrangements for meals) complete the attractions of the place. The six famed icons by Damaskinos, now in the Cathedral of Ayios Menas in Iraklion (p. 138), were once here at Vrondisi.

[52 km.] Back on the main road, a few kilometres farther on you will see off to the left, across a gentle ravine, a small isolated chapel: the *Church of Ayios Fanourios*, all that remains of the Monastery of Valsamonero.

[54 km.] Although it is possible to walk down across the ravine to the *Church of Ayios Fanourios*, most people will prefer to drive a couple of kilometres farther to the village of **Voriza**; from there you can take a small path that leads more easily and quickly to the church (a path that could, at a pinch, be used by a vehicle). Ayios Fanourios has two parallel naves, and a third at right angles to these, in place of a narthex; with its Gothic arches, decorated with leaves and palmettes, the exterior shows obvious Italian influence. The north nave was the original and is attributed to the fourteenth century; the other two are assigned, from the inscriptions of the donors, to the early fifteenth century. Within, a richly sculptured iconostasis, with delicate scallops on each niche, indicates more Italian Renaissance influence. The major attraction is the frescoes, considered among the most valuable on Crete. Those on the ceiling vaults portray the life of the Virgin in a naive style and date from the fourteenth century; along the walls are various saints, dating from the end of the fourteenth or early fifteenth century. Konstantinos Rikos is generally credited with these frescoes, although you may be told that Damaskinos and El Greco worked on them.

[57 km.] At the village of **Kamares** you can get modest accommodation and meals, rent mules, hire guides and generally prepare for the climb to the summit. The ascent and return via any of the possible routes requires a very long day, which means that you must either get a very early start or plan to stay overnight somewhere on the mountain (the latter course will be essential if you attempt to get to the caves as well as the summit). In any case, you are advised to bring your own water container and some warm clothing – and any camping gear you would want for the night.

There are three principal destinations on the mountain, the Cave of Kamares, the summit of Mount Idha (Psiloritis) and Idha Cave.

Cave of Kamares

This is about a four-hour climb. Discovered by local men in the 1890s, it was first explored by the Italians, and finally excavated by the British in 1913. Used in Neolithic times as shelter, it became a sacred cave for the Minoans; here were found some of the most eloquent witnesses to the Minoans' artistry – the thin, polychrome, delicately decorated pottery that is known as 'Kamares ware'.

Summit of Mount Idha

This is another six hours or so to the north-west from the Cave of Kamares. At 2,456 m. it is the highest point on Crete and there is snow here through most of the year: to see sunrise or sunset while standing here is a quite indescribable experience. A small cave lies about half an hour below the summit; but those who care to spend the night here should stay in the *Chapel of Stavros* at the peak itself. There is a cistern here, too, but it is usually dry in the summer.

Idha Cave

This is about four or five hours to the south-east from the summit, on the edge of the Nidha Plain. It was discovered and explored in the 1880s and yielded many rich finds, including bronze shields dating from the ninth and eighth centuries B.C. and showing Assyrian influence. These finds have been taken to indicate that there was a post-Minoan cult of the *Curétes*, who were worshipped at this cave. The Curétes were the warriors who danced round the cave where the baby Zeus was being nursed, covering his cries from his father Cronus by the clashing of their shields. Robert Graves claims that it was the son of Zeus, Zagreus, who was being protected at this cave.

From Idha Cave there is a descent of about six hours back to the villages of Kamares or Vorizas (p. 170). But it is also convenient to continue north above the Nidha Plain for about 20 km. to the mountain village of **Anoyia**. (There is a road just about good enough for a car leading from the cave to this village if you choose to come by this route.) During the last war, Anoyia was completely razed, except for the church, as a reprisal against the partisans who kidnapped the German commandant, but it is now rebuilt. The people live largely on their flocks, and are noted for their handicrafts. There are several lovely chapels in the neighbourhood, one built over an ancient mosaic.

About one hour's walk to the north-west of Anoyia is the site of *Axos*. It lies on the summit of a spur-end from the Idha range, and its steep slopes make it practically inaccessible. First settled late in Minoan times, it became an important site in the Archaic period. There are few remains except for cyclopean walls, but the view is impressive.

Heading east from Anoyia towards Iraklion, you might go on to visit *Tylissos* (p. 198). From there you descend to the main Rethymnon–Iraklion road for the last 11 km. to Iraklion.

ROUTE 1: IRAKLION TO PHAESTOS (VIA GORTYNA)

Here again is one of those excursions through history so peculiar to Crete. It can be managed in a day, but could just as profitably take three or four, depending on how many detours you make. Phaestos alone, as the second of the great Minoan palace-complexes, justifies a whole-day trip. Those with private transport will be able to set their own pace, but even those dependent on buses will find that the schedule allows Phaestos, Gortyna and Ayia Triadha to be included in a day's outing. And Phaestos, with its Tourist Pavilion, is ideal for an overnight stay.

Route
Leave Iraklion by the Khania Gate along the Rethymnon road (Route A on town plan). but after crossing the little bridge on the outskirts of the town turn sharply left away from the coast. You then climb up into the hills to Ayia Varvara [29 km.] and descend to Ayii Dheka [44 km.], Gortyna, and Phaestos [62 km.].
Bus
The Iraklion–Timbaki bus. which leaves from the Khania Gate, takes you all the way to Phaestos and will put you off at many points en route ; the tourist agencies arrange several guided bus tours, too.
Accommodation
The Tourist Pavilion at Phaestos is, one might even say, internationally famous for its hospitality and situation ; it is best to make reservations in advance, especially during the high season.

Leaving Iraklion by the Khania Gate as though heading for Rethymnon and Khania, you pass through the urban sprawl and litter of Iraklion and then cross a little bridge.

[2 km.] Turn sharp left off the Iraklion–Rethymnon road. From here you drive through the fertile central basin of Crete; during the Middle Ages the prized *malvasia* wine came from here, and today the celebrated *rosaki* grapes flourish. Then begins the long climb over the *Idha range*.

[27 km.] To the right you will see a naturally fortified hill, an almost vertical mass of stone that rises quite dramatically; this is considered by some scholars to have been the site of the acropolis of Rhizenia. The locale is now known as *Prinias*. There had been some settlement and structures here from Minoan times, but only in the post-Minoan period was the site fully exploited. The Italians, excavating in the first decade of this century, discovered the remains of two archaic temples (roughly seventh-century B.C.), including friezes depicting animals and warriors, and statues of two seated goddesses. The friezes are among the oldest Greek architectural sculptures and as such are considered an important example of the so-called Daedalic style (p. 95). They are now in the Archaic Room (XIX) of the Iraklion museum.

[29 km.] **Ayia Varvara** is a sizeable village and a centre for this region. As you enter the village you pass a huge rock on the right, topped by a chapel: the rock is called the *omphalos* – 'navel' – of Crete; popular lore claims that it is the island's geographical balancing-point.

[30 km.] At the end of the village a road to the right leads in 27 km. to **Kamares**, the starting point for the expedition to Kamares Cave and Mt Idha described on pp. 168–72.

[32 km.] Here you drive through the *Pass of Vourvoulitis,* at an altitude of about 2,000 ft. Then begins the long, winding descent to the Messara; with the mountains all about, and an occasional glimpse of the Libyan Sea in the distance, it is quite a spectacular experience to come down on to the plain.

Stretching some 40 km. back from the sea, and from 8 to 11 km. wide, the *Messara Plain* is Crete's largest flatland. You might think that this fertile plain would have ensured the island's prosperity and nourishment, but it has never been allowed to develop properly or peacefully. It is productive, but it will take more than fertilizer and tractors to make it flourish; the people of the Messara would have to want to change their way of life. It remains to be seen whether or when this will come about. For the time being, the Messara provides a modest living for the villages scattered around it, and a rich harvest of sites and pleasures for the traveller.

Water is a problem for the farmers on the Messara as elsewhere on Crete, but there are two major rivers that almost always have some water: to the east is the Anapodharis, while the Yerapotamos runs along the base of the Phaestos ridge, at the western end where you are entering.

[44 km.] As the road levels down on the plain, you arrive at the roadside village of **Ayii Dheka**. Ayii Dheka has been called a 'living museum', for the present village is all but built on and out of the remains of ancient Gortyna. Its name means 'the holy ten', alias the Ten Martyrs: in the third century A.D., ten of the inhabitants of this region refused to sacrifice to the gods of their Roman overlords, and were beheaded. There is a church in the village (off to the left), probably dating from early Byzantine times, but greatly restored, where the stone on which the Ten Martyrs are said to have been decapitated is kept in a glass case.

Just beyond the village a track to the left leads in about 200 m. to the attractive little *Church of Ayii Dheka* (see Gortyna plan), underneath which are the graves of the martyrs. On the right is the *'museum'*, a courtyard with a haphazard collection of headless statues, columns and inscriptions. (The best finds from Gortyna are in the Iraklion museum.) But it is a stroll through the village itself that reveals the museum: columns, statues, fragments of all kinds have been absorbed in constructing and patching up modern Ayii Dheka. If you go about it properly, you can usually get some of the local people to show choice pieces, built into courtyards, stairways and houses. There is nothing very dramatic, but it is sobering to consider how a once-great imperial city like Gortyna can be swallowed up by the sleepy routine of this village.

Striking across the fields from Ayii Dheka Church and the museum, you come to one group of the remains of *Gortyna*: these are the somewhat more recent Roman ruins (1 to 9 on Gortyna plan). A little farther on along the main road, the most interesting group of structures are on the right of the road, just behind the ruined Basilica of Ayios Titos: these are the older Roman, the Hellenistic and the Doric remains (10 to 16 on Gortyna plan).

HISTORY OF GORTYNA

First, a word about the various names of this site: in modern Greek it is called Gortys, but it is better known in literature by its Byzantine forms, Gortyna or Gortyn, so we have chosen to use the form Gortyna throughout.

If there was any settlement at Gortyna during the Minoan era, it was completely overshadowed by Phaestos. Not until the great Minoan centres declined and the Dorians took over did Gortyna come into its own; it began to compete as a commercial power from the eighth century B.C., eventually controlling the ports of Matala and Leben. During the eighth to fifth centuries B.C. Gortyna was advanced enough to be working out the society that developed its famous laws (see below). By 300 B.C. it probably had control of most of the Messara. But there was never much time for peaceful exploitation; there were, instead, continual wars with the other Cretan city-states and Mediterranean powers, until Gortyna fell to the Romans along with the rest of the island about 67 B.C. As part of Rome's imperial vision, Gortyna became the seat of a praetor, the capital of Crete and the Province of Cyrenaica. The Messara was to become a bread-basket for this empire, Gortyna to be turned into a splendid provincial city. Indeed, for a while, there was a period of prosperity and ambitious construction; irrigation helped the fields to flourish and brick-making allowed buildings to rise. When Byzantium replaced Rome, and Christianity the old idols, Gortyna managed to retain some of its prestige. But when it fell to the Moors in A.D. 824 it was partially destroyed and never again regained its stature.

Gortyna was among the first Cretan sites to be excavated – by Halbherr and the Italian mission, back in the 1880s. It took many decades, though, before all the ruins we see were exposed, for they spread over a considerable area. They are fairly difficult to find, but that is what makes this such a fascinating spot; you walk through dry fields, across crumbling walls, past gnarled olive trees, discovering the sunken foundations, columns, statues, arches and fragments – slowly piecing together the once-grand city of Gortyna.

DESCRIPTION OF SITE

Roman Remains

The group of ruins on the left of the road mostly date from the second century A.D., although there had been earlier structures in several cases and some were later adapted by the Byzantines. They include two Nymphaions (1) and (6), the Temple of Pythian Apollo (2), the Praetorium (3), the Sanctuary of Isis and Serapis (4), a theatre (5), an amphitheatre (7), a stadium (8) and the main gate (9). No one ruin is by itself very spectacular, but the total ensemble makes for an interesting stroll.

Basilica of Ayios Titos

Of the ruins farther down the road and to the right, the first structure to catch your eye is the high apse of the Basilica of Ayios Titos (10) – the Titus said to have been commissioned by Paul in person to convert the Cretans, and the first Bishop of Gortyna. It is claimed that he was buried here, but there is no way of proving this. The basilica dates from the sixth century A.D., with alterations up to the tenth century; eventually it fell to pieces, but enough remains to show the extent of the structure. One of the small side chapels is used as a shrine by the local people, and fragments of the original frescoes adhere to the walls. Outside stands an odd miscellany of remains in various architectural styles.

The Odeon and The Law Code

Walking into the fields by a path that runs on the right of the basilica past the Agora (11), you arrive at the ruins of the Roman Odeon (12). Originally there was a Hellenistic structure here; in the first to second centuries A.D. the Romans built this 'chamber theatre' whose ruins survive. Enough is preserved to give a good idea of its appearance. Behind the Odeon is the prize exhibit of Gortyna: the Law Code. Carved on stone blocks, it stands upright as it stood when the Romans came and incorporated it into their Odeon; it is sheltered under a modern brick gallery. The gallery is fenced in and locked, but a caretaker is usually about and will open it so that you can get a closer view of the code. (A small tip is expected.)

The stones you see are the originals, although when first inscribed by the Dorian Cretans of Gortyna – some time between 500 and 450 B.C. – they stood elsewhere, most likely in a more public

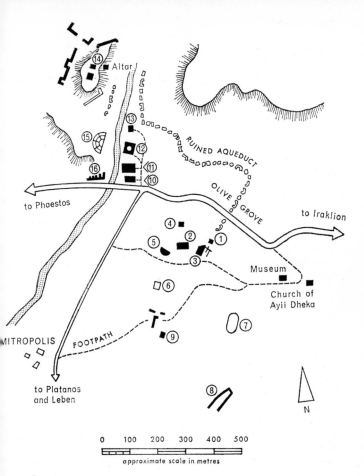

Gortyna

1 Nymphaion
2 Temple of Pythian Apollo
3 Praetorium
4 Sanctuary of Isis and Serapis
5 Theatre
6 Nymphaion
7 Amphitheatre
8 Stadium
9 Main Gate
10 Basilica of Ayios Titos
11 Agora
12 Odeon and Law Code
13 Mill
14 Acropolis
15 Hellenistic Theatre
16 Storage Chambers

place. The Romans, who may not even have been able to read the inscription, probably used it to decorate their wall. And there the stones stayed for many centuries, gradually forgotten, and finally submerged under the mill stream. It was not until 1884 that Halbherr, the Italian archaeologist, happened to be on the site when the water was drawn off from the stream. Now it is true that fragments of inscriptions found near by in 1857 and 1879 had alerted archaeologists. But no one would ever have dared dream that, when the water went down, there would stand a whole code, virtually intact.

It should be said, by the way, that there were actually two codes found at Gortyna. The other, dating from roughly the same period, was found in only a few scattered sections. To scholars, of course, these fragments are valuable supplements. But the twelve columns preserved in the Odeon make up what is commonly referred to as the Gortyna Code.

More than 17,000 characters are carved in the stones. The language is an archaic Doric dialect of Greek and most of its eighteen letters are recognizably Greek. The script has been set down in what is called the 'ox plough' manner, according to which the eye travels from right to left in one line and then left to right in the next, alternating continuously as a field is ploughed.

What was set down in the fifth century B.C. is not actually a complete code. It is, rather, largely a number of regulations amending earlier laws. These earlier laws probably date from a century or two earlier and were, in turn, based on a still more ancient oral tradition of law. The laws deal essentially with civil matters such as marriage, divorce, adultery, property rights, adoption, inheritance and mortgage of property. There is also some reference to trial procedure and, in general, the Gortyna Code gives a glimpse into early forms of Greek law. But beyond that it affords a good impression of the social structure and general affairs of Dorian Crete.

The Mill

Behind the Law Code gallery is a medieval mill (13), still used for grinding flour. If you are lucky enough to arrive when the miller is at home you may enjoy another unique experience, for he plays a primitive ancestor of the bagpipe. This is a goat's skin, turned inside out and sewn up, with small reeds inserted. The music may not be to everyone's taste, but it makes an unforgettable experience. The miller and his family also make and sell small reed flutes for a few drachmas.

Other Remains

On a hill to the right of the road and across a tributary of the Yeropotamos is the Acropolis (**14**) from the earlier post-Minoan period. Under the remains of the Greek and Roman times were found an Archaic altar, several religious shrines and a fortress. Important finds of Daedalic art have also been made on this site. Lower, towards the main road, on a terrace, are the remains of a Hellenistic theatre (**15**) that was later restored, while along the road itself are the remains of storage chambers (**16**).

[46 km.] Back on the main road, opposite the ruins, there is a turning to the left off the main road that leads to Mitropolis and Platanos and then on to the tombs of the Messara (p. 193) or to Leben (p. 190).

After passing the ruins of the storage chambers of Gortyna, you can see the *Agricultural School of the Messara*, housed in a former monastery. Here young Cretans are taught up-to-date methods of agriculture on a self-supporting farm that has become an integral part of the Messara farming community.

[53 km.] At the largish village of **Moires**, a bus junction, there are plenty of cafés for a refreshing pause. On Saturday mornings there is a lively market-bazaar, with dozens of mules carrying villagers and produce.

A few kilometres out of Moires you become aware of a low mountain ridge ahead and to the left: it breasts the Messara like the prow of a ship. On that spur is the site of Phaestos, some 250 ft above the plain.

[60 km.] The turn (left) for Phaestos is clearly marked. A new road crosses the Yeropotamos and winds up a steep ridge.

[62 km.] At the top of the hill is *Phaestos*, a spectacular combination of natural site and historic ruin.

PHAESTOS

Since Phaestos arouses as much enthusiasm by its situation as by its ruins, it is well to get oriented. As you stand looking down the long Messara Plain to the east, Mt Dhikti and the Lasithi range rise at the far end. To the right is the Asterousia range, bordering the south coast. To the north, is the Idha range. If you look carefully you will see a dark hole, at the extreme right of the saddle between two peaks on the Idha slopes: this is the Kamares Cave, where the famous pottery was found that has given its name to this type of delicate, black-based ceramics.

Accommodation
The Tourist Pavilion charges about Drs 50 per person for a room with four to six beds. Meals are available, and campers have been allowed to sleep on the roof. The atmosphere is more like a friendly inn than an official hostelry, and it makes a congenial starting-point for excursions to other sites in southern Crete.

HISTORY

The history of Phaestos is not so well known as that of Knossos, although recent excavations are bringing much to light. Among other discoveries are extensive remains of a Neolithic settlement, as well as various levels indicating continuous habitation of the site. It is said to have been founded by Minos, but it is traditionally associated with his brother Rhadamanthys – also a noted legislator. The weights and measures of Phaestos may have been accepted as standards throughout the Cretan 'empire'. Its people were known for their wit. The development of Phaestos, both political and architectural, seems to have paralleled that of Knossos, although it was never so extensive in power or so intricate in structure. The materials and workmanship at the palace of Phaestos were however at least as good as at Knossos. It passed through successive series of reconstructions and additions, and it fell to some natural disaster or to invaders – or both. The rise of near-by Gortyna denied it any later glory. How closely it was linked to Knossos in its heyday is in dispute; certainly there is a similarity in the design and structure of the palaces as well as in many of the artifacts found at both sites. Some scholars place great emphasis on masons' marks on stones which, they say, show that the palaces were probably built by the same men. Without having been a mere dependency, it would seem that Phaestos was closely associated with the achievements of Knossos.

Considering the height of the site, it is difficult now to understand how it ever came to be covered – but this happened. It was only after several experimental digs in the area that Halbherr located the exact site, in 1900. The great palace-complex was excavated over many years, largely by the Italians and the Greeks. Cemeteries and other remains were found outside the palace proper, indicating settlements from the Neolithic period through Minoan, Hellenic and still later ages. Phaestos, indeed, has been one of the most active sites on Crete in recent years, with many revealing finds – in particular, the pre-Minoan foundations and the Minoan city on the south side of the palace hill.

The Italians at Phaestos did not undertake as much reconstruction as Evans did at Knossos. There is a fair amount of buttressing and patching; walls, walks, cisterns, chambers, altars and urns are repaired in situ; otherwise the palace has been left pretty much as found. The current excavations serve still more graphically to expose the various strata of the site.

DESCRIPTION OF SITE

With the aid of a plan, as provided here, Phaestos is a relatively easy site to explore by oneself; if 'Mister Alexandros', the caretaker, is about, however, it is worth having one of his inimitable guided tours (described by, among other people, Henry Miller in his *Colossus of Maroussi*). You can orient yourself by standing near the Tourist Pavilion before setting out to stroll through the remains that lie spread out beneath you. We shall describe some of the major points of interest.

North-west Staircase (1) and West Court (2)

This is the staircase by which you enter the ruins; to the right are the raised steps – more than 20 m. long – that must have provided seats for spectators (3). It has been suggested that the West Court, also known as the Theatral Area, like the courts of Knossos and Mallia, was used for the bull sports. This is pure speculation, although it probably was used for ceremonies, sacred or otherwise. Whatever its function, this area survives from the earlier, Protopalatial period.

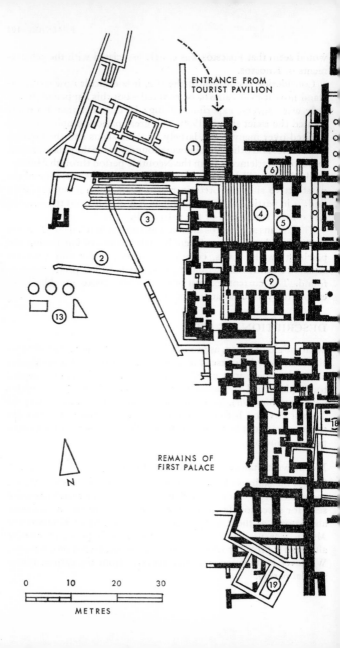

ENTRANCE FROM
TOURIST PAVILION

① ⑥ ③ ④ ⑤ ② ⑨ ⑬ ⑱ ⑲

REMAINS OF
FIRST PALACE

N

0   10   20   30

METRES

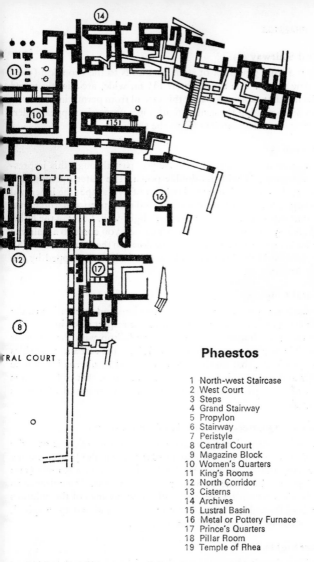

Phaestos

1 North-west Staircase
2 West Court
3 Steps
4 Grand Stairway
5 Propylon
6 Stairway
7 Peristyle
8 Central Court
9 Magazine Block
10 Women's Quarters
11 King's Rooms
12 North Corridor
13 Cisterns
14 Archives
15 Lustral Basin
16 Metal or Pottery Furnace
17 Prince's Quarters
18 Pillar Room
19 Temple of Rhea

Grand Stairway (4)

This is a truly grand set of stairs that leads to the Propylon (5) of the new palace. The steps, about 13½ m. wide, are slightly raised in the middle; explanations for this extend from permitting water to drain off to making the central figures in a procession appear taller. There is a smaller stairway (6) to the side.

Propylon (5)

After ascending the grand staircase you pass through this impressive entrance hall with its double porch. The outer opening was supported by a massive central column of oval shape; the inner had two large portals, without doors. Behind these porticoes, three oval columns supported the front of a large light-well. Leaving the light-well area by a door at the south-east corner, you come to a stairway that leads north to the Peristyle (7) or down to the Central Court (8). To the west is the Magazine Block (9), which was topped by the State Apartments.

Central Court (8)

Similar in size (46 m. by 22 m.), proportions and orientation to the great court of Knossos, this court is in one respect more impressive, because of its dramatic situation on the hilltop with the resultant view. The surface was flagstoned, and along the east and west sides were porticoes; that on the east was fronted by alternating square pillars and round columns. Keep in mind, too, that at least three sides of this great court had two- or three-storeyed structures rising above.

Women's Quarters (10) and King's Rooms (11)

Leaving the central court by the north corridor (12), you pass the area that is thought to have contained the Women's Quarters on the right (10) and move directly ahead into the King's Rooms (11); these got the best breezes during the hot months. The entrance to the north corridor, by the way, still shows remains of the columns that once framed it – a façade that resembled, and perhaps inspired, that of the great royal tombs at Mycenae.

Other Sights

We have described those areas that will be of greatest interest to most people. Other buildings noted on the plan are the Archives

(14), a lustral basin (15), a furnace that was used either for metal-work or pottery (16), the Princes' Quarters (17), the Pillar Room (18), a later Greek temple dedicated to Rhea (19) and cisterns (13). In addition, of course, there are the usual corridors, apartments, stairways and workrooms that distinguish a Minoan palace. Altars and other finds indicate that this palace, like the others, was used as a ceremonial 'temple'; storage jars and store-rooms indicate that it was also used as a palace workshop. Perhaps the single most distinctive find at Phaestos was the disc discovered in the Archives that is now in the Iraklion museum (p. 125). Around the hillsides of the palace are other remains, from graves to Minoan houses, but these are not very conveniently sited for the average traveller to visit.

EXCURSIONS FROM PHAESTOS
Ayia Triadha

One excursion that can conveniently be made from Phaestos, even by those who have only the time between buses, is to the Villa of Ayia Triadha, one of the miniature gems of the Minoan civilization.

Routes
There are three possible routes. Those who have their own transport should proceed along the new road from Phaestos for 3 km., which brings them out above the site, down on the left. Alternatively, the bus will drop you on the main road 2 km. past the turn to Phaestos, at another left turn: following this for about ½ km. you arrive at a river that can easily be forded; the site is reached after another few minutes' walk.
    The third route is for walkers. You pick up the trail by returning for 200 m. down from Phaestos towards the main road and then following a signposted footpath to the left, which you take along the northern side of the Phaestos ridge. It is easy to find your way, and it takes about 45 minutes to reach Ayia Triadha.

HISTORY OF AYIA TRIADHA

The ruins of Ayia Triadha lie at the western end of the Phaestos ridge; they were excavated by the Italians early in the century, after the discovery of Phaestos. The Idha range lies to the north; directly below, where the river meanders along the plain, is a lush, almost tropical region known as 'Paradise', where many fruit trees grow. To the west is the Bay of Messara, and it has been suggested that the sea once came much closer to the site, making Ayia Triadha a sort of seaside villa. Exactly what it was is not known. Some say that it was a summer palace for the Phaestos royalty; others think that it was a prince's residence; some see it as the home of a wealthy vassal-chieftain; still others think that it was a royal annexe, used for special ceremonial occasions. Certainly it must have been dependent on, if not actually subservient to, Phaestos; the trail still taken overland must have seen its share of messengers, functionaries and royal processions.

Just what this villa was called in Minoan times is also unknown. Its present name, which means 'Holy Trinity', comes from the little Byzantine chapel and village of this name, just beyond the site. There is a second chapel here, too, the fifteenth-century Church of Ayios Georgios Galatas ((**14**) on Ayia Triadha plan). This has frescoes and tombs of the Venetian period. ('Galatas', incidentally, means 'milkman'; it is not known which legend of St George this refers to.)

Many tombs have also been excavated in the vicinity of Ayia Triadha; in one, about 100 m. to the north-east, was found one of the most significant remains of Minoan culture – the painted sarcophagus now in the Iraklion museum (p. 129). There were other remarkable finds here; whatever the place was, it had a concentration of wealth and art that now figures among the greatest glories of Minoan times. These include some frescoes as well as the three steatite vases – the Harvesters' Vase, the Chieftain's Cup, and the Rhyton of Athletes, all now in the Iraklion museum (p. 127), Tablets inscribed with Linear A were also found; and, not least, the large 'talents' from the treasury of the sanctuary – weighing 29 kilos each, they must have been some official standard. Ayia Triadha, if hardly spectacular as a site, has its own appeal; and the value of the objects found here and now to be seen in the Iraklion museum makes it one of the most important pre-classical sites in the Mediterranean world.

DESCRIPTION OF SITE

Whoever lived here and whatever its original name, Ayia Triadha was a sort of 'vest-pocket' version of the grand Minoan palaces. There are the usual chambers, stairways, courtyards, terraces and

Ayia Triadha

1 Ramp
2 Men's Hall
3 Terrace
4 Queen's Hall
5 Storage Magazines
6 Central Corridor
7 Mycenaean Megaron
8 Drainage System
9 Minoan Road to Phaestos
10 Market
11 Steps
12 Storage Magazines
13 Remains of late Minoan Settlement
14 Church of Ayios Georgios Galatas

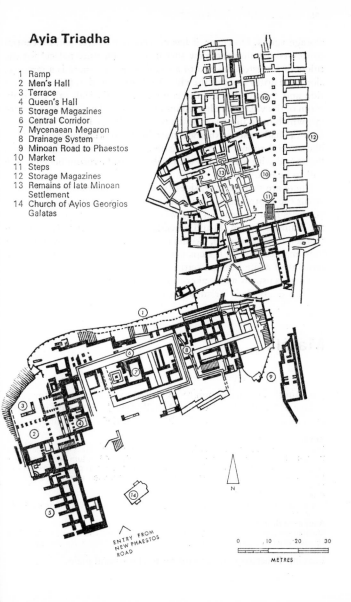

ENTRY FROM NEW PHAESTOS ROAD

N

0   10   20   30
METRES

storage vaults. However, it has no ceremonial area and no central court – confirming the view that it was a 'pleasure palace' for the rulers of Phaestos. Instead of a grand staircase, there is a ramp (1) along the north front of the villa that leads round to the north-west side and eventually into the columned Men's Hall (2), the main room of the villa with dimensions of 6 by 9 m. There is also a terrace (3), which has a fine view of the sea and Mount Idha. The Queen's Hall (4) had frescoes that are now in the Iraklion museum. This, like several rooms in Ayia Triadha, was decorated with gypsum floors and with walls lined with alabaster and gypsum benches – all still to be enjoyed.

There are storage magazines (5) and (12). Access to the latter is along the central corridor (6) that leads to the north-east section; you pass by a Mycenaean *megaron* (7) of a later date. Just beyond is the drainage system (8) and, outside, the traces of the Minoan road that led to Phaestos (9). To the north-east of this main wing is the long market (10) with steps (11), storage magazines (12), and the remains of a late Minoan settlement (13).

There is usually a caretaker-guide about the site, but even by one-self the site of Ayia Triadha can be enjoyed.

Matala

One unusual place that might be visited from Phaestos is the port-village of Matala, site of ancient Matallon; today it attracts people in increasing numbers mainly for its caves and the swimming.

Route
Leaving Phaestos by the new Ayia Triadha road, turn left almost immediately past the ruined Chapel of St George on to a rough road; at 4 km. turn right at an olive press. Some 3 km. farther fork right after a cemetery to by-pass part of the village of Pitsidia; when you reach the end of this village, continue down to the coast at Matala [12 km.].
Bus
There is a bus service to Matala from the Khania Gate in Iraklion, which can be picked up at Phaestos.
Accommodation
Matala now has its own Tourist Pavilion to provide rooms and meals, and the little village there can also provide both; some few may prefer the caves (see below).

Leaving Phaestos you descend on to the coastal plain.

[2 km.] On the left is a walled enclosure within which stands one of the more unique architectural forms on Crete. It is the little early-fourteenth-century rough-stone *Chapel of St Paul*, almost sinking into the ground. Burial plots lie round it, and the charnel-house is at one side; within are a few old frescoes and icons. But it is the structure that is so remarkable; it is almost as though you are witnessing the emergence of the Byzantine style out of some archaic form.

[4 km.] Here you come to the crossroads with an olive press across the road; turn sharply right and continue through olive groves.

[7 km.] After forking right to by-pass most of the straggling village of **Pitsidia**, you drive on through some fairly bleak landscape and gradually descend to the coast.

[12 km.] **Matala**.

The village of Matala is situated just above a striking circular cove with fine grey sand. The village is almost deserted in off-season, although there is always someone there to serve coffee.

The really unique aspect of Matala is the great promontory that forms the right arm of the cove – a high, sheer cliff of parched yellow earth that time has packed into a sort of rock. Into this cliff, across the centuries, men have carved caves. Some are little more than pockmarks, warrens barely able to shelter a few people; others are regular rooms, complete with benches carved out of the walls; and a few are quite elaborate apartments, with steps, vestibules, framed doors and windows, and fireplaces. The beds are reminiscent of Etruscan tombs, with their platforms for the dead, carved out of the natural stone. The left arm of the harbour also has a few caves; some people, too, have built houses on its gentler slopes, back against the caves.

It is difficult to find an authoritative statement as to what caused this unusual terrain. One theory is that forces of water, millions of years ago, built up great sand barriers, and when a stream cut through the compressed mound the cliffs were left on both sides. In any case, men came along and scratched out the caves, and these have been inhabited off and on for a few thousand years.

No one seems to know for certain who first dug out these holes. During the Minoan period, the main port of the Messara was actually north of Matala at a site called Komo (nothing much has yet

G

been excavated there). Matala only came into its own in post-Minoan times, when Gortyna had assumed power. Probably the caves were not dug out until the later Greek or Roman period, when they were used as tombs – as they were also used during the early Christian era. It has also been claimed that the caves were used by Gortyna as arsenal-magazines – again, not for the last time, as the Germans used them for this purpose during their occupation. Matala has also its share of myths and legends: here Zeus, disguised as a bull, came ashore bearing Europa (perhaps signifying the arrival of some Phoenician ship with the figurehead of a bull?); here some of Menelaus' vessels were driven ashore on their return from Troy (see the *Odyssey*, Book III).

For some centuries, too, it is safe to assume that local people at least occasionally made use of the caves; after all, they are as comfortable as many peasant dwellings – and cost nothing. In recent years the local summer visitors have been joined by an increasingly larger and more international set – mainly younger people seeking a cheap place in the sun. There are continual rumours that the Greek government is going to prohibit people from using the caves – on the grounds that their archaeological-historical value is endangered – but at present the caves are available on a first-come, first-served basis.

There are reputed to be some underwater remains at the edge of the cliffs as well as grottoes – an invitation to skin-divers – but most people who come to Matala are content to swim, to climb about and to enjoy the view. South from Matala, along the coast, are other more spectacular grottoes. You would have to get a local fisherman to take you in his boat; the trip takes about two hours. You could make a day of it by going on round Cape Lithinon to Kaloi Limenes, the little fishing village on the south coast (p. 192), and even on to Leben (below). Another possibility for ambitious walkers is to walk from Matala north to Timbaki (p. 196), and from there to Phaestos (p. 180) or west to Ayia Galini (p. 196).

Leben

Another interesting excursion from Phaestos, although a fairly demanding drive, is the seldom-visited site of ancient Leben – now known also as Lendas or Leda, the name of the near-by village.

It can also be combined with the trip to the Messara tombs (p. 193).

Route

From Phaestos you go back through Moires on the Iraklion road nearly to Ayii Dheka; just about opposite the main ruins of Gortyna (p. 179), turn right on to a small road for Mitropolis and Platanos. In Platanos turn left at the church for Plora, through which you continue eastwards along rough roads to Apesokarion. Then turn south for Miamou and the precipitous descent to the coast at Lendas [43 km.].

Bus

There is a service from the Khania Gate in Iraklion which goes as far as Platanos and Apesokarion. From there you would have to walk or hire a donkey to reach Lendas, which is a further 18 km. Alternatively, there is a bus from the same bus station to Antiskarion which is 5 km. overland from Lendas. All these buses could be picked up at Ayii Dheka.

Accommodation

Rooms and modest meals can be found at Lendas.

[9 km.] **Moires** (p. 179).

[16 km.] Here, opposite the ruins of *Gortyna* (p. 174), is the turn off to the right on to a small road for Mitropolis and Platanos.

[17 km.] **Mitropolis.**

[19 km.] **Koustouliana.**

[21 km.] **Platanos**: the starting-off place from which you can visit the tombs of the Messara (p. 193).

[23 km.] **Plora.**

[25 km.] **Apesokarion.**

[33 km.] **Miamou**; in a near-by cave (first explored by the Italians in 1894) important remains were found indicating that it was inhabited in the Neolithic period and later used for burials.

[43 km.] The village of **Lendas,** or Leda as it is sometimes known, is at the end of the road, with a cluster of houses and cafés and an attractive beach; you can get only the most modest of meals here, but the local people enjoy showing strangers about the ruins.

Leben

The remains – first excavated in the nineteenth century by the ubiquitous Italians, who returned to complete the work in 1910 – are quite impressive for such an isolated spot. They are situated on the hillside some five minutes' walk from the village and command a fine view across the Libyan Sea.

Leben seems to be derived from a Phoenician-Semitic word for 'lion' – referring to the promontory that juts out into the sea here like a crouching animal. This helps to form and protect the small harbour, enclosed to the east by Cape Psamidomouri, which must have once witnessed a fair amount of traffic. It was in the post-Minoan period that Leben came into its own, especially during the sixth and fifth centuries B.C., when Gortyna used it as a port, and it attracted people from some distance, thanks to the curative powers of its spring. Even today people come from as far away as the Greek mainland to drink the waters, which are especially recommended for ulcers. Leben is situated in such a favourable spot that tomatoes can be cultivated all the year round and swallows are said to winter there.

The major structure here was the *Temple of Asclepius* – as befits a site associated with curative waters. It dates from the third century B.C.; it may have been destroyed in an earthquake in A.D. 46 and then restored. Two columns are still in place. Marble steps lead down to an elegant Roman mosaic, depicting a prancing sea-horse; this is above the subterranean treasury-crypt. To the north of this are the remains of a portico. The wonderful well with the curative powers that still attract people lies to the south-east of the temple; a short distance to the south are large baths; and farther to the south-west are traces of structures that were probably the guest-houses for those who came to take the cure. Still farther to the east of these ancient remains is the eleventh-century *Church of Ayios Ioannis*, with frescoes of the fourteenth and fifteenth centuries. It stands in the ruins of the ninth-century basilica, which in turn was at least partly constructed out of ancient stones.

If you have a guide, you can go some 4 km. from the village to the remains of some Minoan circular tombs that have been discovered fairly recently. It has long been known that there was some Minoan settlement at the base of the 'Lion Cape', and now these tombs have yielded pottery, implements and jewellery – some of which confirms the early trade with Egypt. Dr Stylianos Alexiou of the Iraklion museum employed the most advanced methods of stratigraphic excavation to learn still more about the Minoan era from this relatively obscure site.

Kaloi Limenes

A possible excursion from Lendas is a walk overland (some 10 km.) westwards, to the little fishing village of Kaloi Limenes – the

'Fair Havens' mentioned in Acts xxvii 8. There is a small village here, with a nice sandy beach, situated against Cape Lithinon, on the other side of which is Matala (p. 188). Three rocky islets lie just off shore, one of which is called 'St Paul's Island'. There is a small chapel on the shore to mark the spot where St Paul is said to have preached when he put ashore in A.D. 46, on the way from Egypt to Rome.

If you have walked to this spot you will have a choice of going on to Matala or back to Lendas. It is also possible, though difficult, to drive here by going back to Platanos and then continuing on through Pombia and Pigaidakia to Kaloi Limenes.

Tombs of the Messara

This rather specialized excursion would take most of a day and is probably of interest only to fairly serious students of the period. In any case, private transport and a good guide are essential; arrangements can be made in Iraklion. This trip can also be combined with the excursion to Leben (p. 190).

Route
From Phaestos, you return along the Iraklion road through Moires to Gortyna and take the turn to the right that leads to Platanos, as described in the excursion to Leben (p. 190). This is then used as the starting-point for the various tombs described below.
Bus
There is a bus service to Platanos from the Khania Gate in Iraklion; it could be picked up in Ayii Dheka.
Accommodation
We assume that you will be using Phaestos as a base; at a pinch, you can always get simple accommodation in the villages of the Messara.

[9 km.] **Moires** (p. 179).

[16 km.] Turn right on to a small road that leads through **Mitropolis.**

[21 km.] **Platanos** is the starting-point for the tombs.

Tombs of the Messara

These tombs were among the earliest finds on Crete, as well as among the oldest remains, some having been excavated towards the end of the nineteenth century by local Cretan archaeologists and by the Italian mission. The tombs were free-standing, stone-walled structures, usually circular; the roofs may have been anything from thatch or wooden beams to real stone vaults. Although hardly as dramatic as the great beehive tombs of Mycenae (and by no means as high), these Messara tombs were considerably earlier and may well have had some influence on the builders of the mainland tombs. They were regarded as homes for the afterworld, and it is from them and their contents that we have learned practically all we know of the people who used them for burial. It was a Prepalatial culture, based on small tribes or clans. Existing well before the distinctive Minoan civilization, there were undoubtedly strong links with the Egyptian, Anatolian, Mesopotamian and Babylonian cultures, as the many finds testify. These finds – now in the Iraklion museum – include jewellery, amulets, pottery, idols, human and animal figurines, tools and weapons of all kinds. Some of the knives were made from obsidian, a stone found on the islands of Milo and Yali (south of Kos), and in Anatolia, a fact that opens up wide speculation about the trade and communications of the age.

The most revealing finds have been the sealstones – small, flat and oval-shaped. At first these were made of soft materials like ivory and steatite; later, harder semi-precious stones were used. They were carved intaglio-fashion (often on both sides) with representations of various forms including animals and, less frequently, human figures. They seem to have been something like 'totems', expressing the personality or ideal of the owners with whom they were interred, although most sealstones were probably used for the more prosaic purpose of identifying and protecting property. In any case, many are gems of artistry and revelations of a whole way of life.

Of course none of this is to be seen in situ, which is why most people will limit their examination of the Messara tombs to the artifacts now in the Iraklion museum. One of the most impressive tombs, however, is fairly accessible. From Platanos you continue straight on, keeping to the left of the church, and after 1 km. a track to the right brings you in 200 m. to the foundations of a tomb. It has a diameter of 13 m. with walls nearly 2½ m. thick, and was surrounded by fifteen chambers where many vases were found.

The next most interesting tombs are some distance to the east between Loukia and Koumasa, along the northern slopes of the

Asterousia Mountains; one is extremely well preserved. These
could be reached by driving over from Platanos via Plora, Apesokarion, Vasiliki and Vayionia. Still other tombs are located at
Kalathiana, Marathokephalo, Porti, Dhrakonas and Ayia Ireni, but
these would definitely require a guide and a specialist's concern.

ROUTE 2: PHAESTOS TO RETHYMNON

This is an alternative way back from Phaestos to the north coast for
those who have their own transport and some time to spare –
although you can make the trip by various buses. There is nothing
of major import en route, but it is a delightful trip through the
heart of Crete.

Route
Descending from Phaestos back to the main road, turn left for Timbaki and Ayia
Galini. After this turn inland to cross the island to Rethymnon [83 km.]. Alternatively,
you can turn off before Ayia Galini for Fourfouras in Amari Province and then con-
tinue to Rethymnon [77 km.].
Bus
You can catch the bus from Phaestos to Timbaki, where you can change to another
bus to Ayia Galini, and there get still a third bus to Rethymnon. There are also buses
from Rethymnon to Fourfouras and Amari, and to Lefkoyia for the Monastery of
Preveli (see below).
Accommodation
There are inns at Timbaki and Ayia Galini and you can probably find a bed in some
of the other larger villages; there are also rooms available at the Monastery of
Preveli.

[3 km.] Following the main road below Phaestos westwards to
Timbaki, bear left at a fork. The right branch would lead into
Voroi, which is one of the ways you could approach Kamares for
the climb of Mt Idha (p. 168).

[4 km.] Keeping on to Timbaki, you pass on the left a turning that
leads in about half a kilometre to *Ayia Triadha* (p. 185).

[6 km.] On the left, as you approach the outskirts of **Timbaki**, is one
of those incongruous features that crop up so often on Crete:
several hundred yards of asphalt spread over the landscape to form
an airstrip. Started by the Germans during their occupation in the

Second World War, it was expanded for strategic emergencies after the war and is now used by the Greek Air Force.

[7 km.] You arrive at **Timbaki,** the terminus for the Iraklion bus. This sleepy village has nothing of importance to offer, but there are two small inns, and a taxi can be hired for making other excursions.

[9 km.] On the left, 2 km. off the main road, is **Kokhinos Pyrgos,** with its tomato gardens, abandoned warehouses and Customs office – it was once a port for the African trade. Now it is of little interest except as a swimming place for the people of the district; a café serves basic drinks all year and a small restaurant provides light meals in the summer. Off shore are two islets known as *Paximadhia,* which is the word for the hard-baked bread, or toast, that you get in Cretan villages; to be eaten it must first be dipped in water or milk. These islets get this name for obvious reasons.

From Kokhinos Pyrgos you can rejoin the main road by a short cut to the north-west.

[16 km.] At a fork in the road a turn to the right leads up into the hills to **Apodhoulou** in 6 km. and then on to **Fourfouras** in another 12 km.; the latter village is the centre for *Amari Province,* noted for the scenic attractions of its hills and valleys. It also has many churches and chapels, some with first-rate Byzantine icons and frescoes. Wherever you choose to spend the night, you can be sure of finding some sort of accommodation. Fourfouras can also be used as a starting-point for the ascent of *Mt Idha* (p. 168). From Fourfouras you could go directly to **Rethymnon,** passing through the villages of **Apostoloi** and **Prasses** before striking the main Iraklion–Rethymnon road some 3 km. east of Rethymnon (the total journey from Phaestos to Rethymnon by this route is 77 km.). Incidentally, some 8 km. after Fourfouras you pass the *Monastery of Asomatos,* now used as an agricultural school; the Venetian influence in the architecture of its chapel is evident.

[21 km.] Having instead taken the left fork at 16 km., you arrive at another left fork that brings you in $1\frac{1}{2}$ km. down to **Ayia Galini.** This charming spot is, for those with a little extra time and curiosity, a picturesque corner of Crete. The name means 'holy serenity'. It is, essentially, a small fishing port clinging to the south coast – a cross between a pirates' cove and the Italian Riviera. Its main attraction are the grottoes that can only be approached from the sea. In addition to hiring a boat to see these, you might be able to get it to take you somewhere farther down the coast. There are four Class E hotels at Ayia Galini, the *Acropole, Lybia, Pantheon* and *Aktaion*; meals are available. A path leads from the main bay eastwards to a wide beach where there is fine swimming.

Ayia Galini might be taken as the starting-point – or end – of an ambitious walk along the south coast to Khora Sfakion and farther west. Leaving Ayia Galini on the Rethymnon road you pick up the trail westwards at the village of Melambes and continue along the southern slopes of Mt Sidherota. Eventually you come to Preveli (see below); pushing on via such villages as Mirthios, Selia, Rodakino, Patsianos and Vraskas, you finally arrive at the village of Khora Sfakion (p. 222) – a trip of some 60 km., and recommended only to experienced walkers.

[32 km.] Returning to the main road from Ayia Galini and heading north-west, you come to the village of **Melambes.**

[44 km.] **Akoumia.**

[53 km.] **Spili** is renowned for its cascades of water, an unusual fountain, and its shady trees; there are some pleasant eating-places.

[61 km.] A turning to the left to **Koxares** leads in another 16 km. to the *Monastery of Preveli*, near the south coast. After passing through Koxares, you drive through the gorge of Kourtaliotiko and on through the village of **Asomati**. About 10 km. after turning off the main road there is a fork: the right branch goes into **Lefkoyia**, where the bus from Rethymnon stops; the left fork brings you in a further 6 km. (bearing right before passing the deserted building of the old monastery) to the Monastery of Preveli, in its magnificent situation overlooking the sea. Founded in the seventeenth century in honour of Ayios Ioannis, Preveli was a centre of resistance against the Turks. It served as the same under the German occupation, when it became a 'waiting room' for the British soldiers and others who were to be picked up off shore by ships and taken to Egypt. Eventually, though, the Germans discovered this and put an end to such activities by the monastery. The monastery boasts a small museum of religious articles, priests' costumes and weapons, as well as a fragment of the True Cross; the icons and frescoes are of no special value. Rooms and meals are available for guests; a footpath leads in about 25 minutes to a fine bathing beach.

[73 km.] Back on the main road and continuing northwards you pass through **Armenoi.**

[83 km.] **Rethymnon** (p. 200).

ROUTE 3: IRAKLION TO RETHYMNON

This is a reasonably quick journey between two of Crete's major towns. Various excursions can be made, e.g. to Fodhele, Tylissos, the Melidhoni Cave and the Monastery of Arkadhi.

Route
Follow the main road to Khania, leaving Iraklion by the Khania Gate (Route A on town plan) and proceeding westwards along the coastal road. The road rises as it skirts the Idha range, and descends again to Perama and Rethymnon [78 km.].
Bus
There are several buses daily in each direction; they leave from near the Xenia Hotel in Iraklion. There are also services to Fodhele, Tylissos and Anoyia which leave from the Khania Gate. Buses run from Rethymnon to Melidhoni and to the Monastery of Arkadhi.

[2 km.] Here the Phaestos road (p. 173) branches off to the left.

[8 km.] If you are travelling in your own car you can turn right here for a trip of 26 km. to **Fodhele**, birthplace of El Greco (described as a separate excursion on pp. 159–60). If you take this as a detour en route to Rethymnon, you will rejoin the main road at a point 21 km. from Iraklion (see below).

[11 km.] Keeping on the main road, you come to a turning to the left that leads in another 3 km. to the village of **Tylissos**, where there is a site of the same name. To reach the excavations, turn left as you come into the village and then left again. The site is open during normal working hours. There is a small pavilion with two or three beds that are available for archaeologists and students who have some special concern with the site.

DESCRIPTION OF SITE

Although Tylissos can hardly compare with the major Minoan sites, it is still of considerable interest. Three Minoan houses and a *megaron* were excavated here by Hadzidakis after the First World War; Dr Platon has since done some valuable restoration work and now the remains offer a good glimpse into the architecture and living conditions of those Minoans one step removed from the great palaces. The most important structures date from approximately 1600 to 1450 B.C., but – as with most Minoan buildings – traces of both earlier and later structures also remain to complicate matters for the amateur visitor. Since only a lengthy, detailed description would be of real use, we have chosen to invite the casual visitor to walk about and recognize what he can of the Minoan architecture; more serious students will be able to get help at the Tourist Office or museum in Iraklion. Everyone will be interested to know, however, of the finds here: bits of frescoes, vases, figurines, bronze cauldrons; they testify to the level of culture even in such isolated spots. There was also a tomb that had been used for a cremation-burial, and since this does not seem to have been the customary mode of burial for the late Minoan period it has been suggested that this was the tomb of some distinguished foreigner.

Beyond Tylissos the road goes on to **Anoyia** (p. 168), one of the points from which *Mt Idha* can be climbed.

[20 km.] **Marathos.**

[21 km.] On the right is the turn leading in 7 km. to **Fodhele** (p. 159), past the *Monastery of Ayios Panteleimon.* From there you could return to Iraklion by reversing the route described on pp. 159–60.

[27 km.] **Dhamasta.**

[32 km.] **Geni Ghave** – a village noted for roast sucking pigs; if you pass through at noon, you might even get a taste of one. As you drive, the peaks of the White Mountains (*Lefka Ori*) rise ahead in the west; but it is the Idha range that dominates the surrounding landscape, with its waters accounting for its fertility. The most prominent river is the Mylopotamos, which winds about the valley on its way to the sea.

[54 km.] You arrive at **Perama**, to be noted solely for the turning to the *Melidhoni Cave*, which attracts many visitors both as a natural phenomenon and as an event in Crete's history. (It can also be visited by bus from Rethymnon.) The road to the Melidhoni Cave is a right turn out of Perama for **Panormos** – the site of a Hellen-istic–Byzantine port on the north coast. But, after crossing a bridge, you again fork right and reach, in 4 km., the village of **Melidhoni**. After driving through the village you take a road to the left that curves for some 2 km. up to a chapel. Here you must climb up to the left and then you immediately come to a small crater; the cave's entrance is down to the right.

The cave is quite large, with stalactites and chambers. At latest by the Hellenistic period there was a cult that worshipped Hermes here. The cave has also been claimed as the dwelling-place of Talos, the mythical bronze giant who went striding around Crete three times a day and hurled boulders at unwelcome strangers approach-ing the island. This story is part of the saga of the Argonauts; later Dante was to retell it in his vision of the *Inferno*. But it is its more recent historical associations that make the cave a shrine today. In 1824 several hundred Cretans from neighbouring villages had taken refuge here from a troop of Muslim soldiers ravaging the land. When the soldiers discovered that the Cretans were inside, they piled brushwood at the mouth of the cave and set fire to it. The Cretans within were suffocated. For decades afterwards, visitors to the cave reported seeing the bones and skulls in the crevices and corners where the people had scrambled for the last pockets of air. An altar in the first chamber commemorates this episode and, although not everyone will care to make such a pilgrimage, the cave and its surroundings are interesting and serve to round out the story of Crete.

[73 km.] Back on the main road, a turn here to the left at **Platanias** would lead to the historic *Monastery of Arkadhi* (p. 204), but, going straight on, you descend on to the flat and fertile coastal plain; to the left rises the Vrisinas range, source of Rethymnon's water.

[78 km.] **Rethymnon** lies sprawled along the coast.

RETHYMNON

Rethymnon, an attractive provincial town, is the centre of Rethym-non Nome. It has a distinctive air, reminiscent of its Venetian and

Turkish past; its minarets in particular give it an almost Oriental look.

Population 13,513.
Information
Tourist Police: Kefaloyianni Square (*Map* **6**).
Hotels
Class B: *Xenia* (*Map* **12**) (restaurant).
Class C: *Acropole*, Iroon Square.
    Valari, Kountouriotou Street.
Class D: *Emboron*, Ethnikis Antistaseos Street.
    Minoa, Arkadhiou Street.
Class E: *Akhilleion*, Arkadhiou Street.
    Arkadhi, Arkadhiou Street.
    Diethnes, M. Porta.
    Paradise, Hegoumenou Gabriel Street.
All of these are more or less centrally located, and, if not luxurious, they suffice; the new *Xenia*, on the beach, has the most modern facilities.
Camping
There is a camping site. 'Camping Elizabeth'. $2\frac{1}{2}$ km. east of the town along the beach (there are plans to have tents available for hire).
Restaurants
Rethymnon has the usual variety of eating-places and cafés, clustered around the squares and along the harbour.
Night life
In the summer there are popular eating–dancing spots such as the Romantzo and Trekhantiri as well as the usual selection of cinemas.
Clubs
There is an active branch of the Greek Touring Club, making excursions to the natural sites and antiquities of the nome. Foreigners are welcome to join in their activities; inquire at the Tourist Police.
Swimming
There are several good sandy beaches both west and east of the town.
Buses
There are regular services to Iraklion and Khania starting from near the Market. Buses to the Monastery of Arkadhi, Eleftherna, Melidhoni, Anoyia, Axos, Fourfouras and Amari all leave from Iroon Square. Buses for Lefkoyia, the nearest village to the Monastery of Preveli, Spili and Ayia Galini leave from outside the boys' high school (Gymnasion), a block to the south of the Church of the Four Martyrs.

HISTORY

Rethymnon is the third largest town of Crete and enjoys the reputation of being the 'intellectual capital' of the island (one of the modern classics of contemporary Greek writing is *Chronique d'une cité* – as it is known in its French translation – by Pandelis Prevelakis, a native of Rethymnon who wrote a tribute to his home town). But without getting too deeply involved in the town's claim, it can be said at least to be a source of pride for its citizens. Travellers in Rethymnon – both the city and nome – have claimed to see a little more pride in appearances, a little more order and cleanliness. In any case, Rethymnon has its own modest charms; it is a delightful place to pass a few days while taking excursions into the countryside. The nome lacks the extensive and spectacular sites of other parts of Crete, but there has been a fair amount of excavation of tombs, houses, minor settlements: the Germans, for instance, during the war, turned up quite an elaborate compound at Monastiraki, the westernmost Minoan ruins of any size. You need, however, a specialist's interest – and a guide – to find your way to these sites.

The city of Rethymnon is on the site of ancient Rethymna, but nothing of interest to the amateur remains and little is known of its history. In the medieval period Rethymnon is mentioned only in passing, with its fort and towers sketched as seen from afar. The town received its distinctive imprint from the Venetian period of the sixteenth and seventeenth centuries, with a slightly Turkish veneer to give it a special air: Venetian arches back up against wooden, overhanging Turkish balconies, creating a unique impression for the visitor strolling through the narrow streets.

PRINCIPAL SIGHTS

Loggia and Museum
Map 3

Hours
NOTE: The museum is closed on Monday afternoons and all day at Christmas, New Year, Greek Easter, March 25th and October 28th.
April 1st–Sept. 30th Weekdays 8–1, 3.30–6
                 Sundays and public holidays 10–1.
Oct. 1st–March 31st Weekdays 9–1, 3–5
                 Sundays and public holidays 10–1.
Entrance charge: Drs 5. Free on Thursdays and Sundays.

The principal architectural survival of the Venetian period is the elegant seventeenth-century Loggia where the civic museum is now housed. There is a small collection of finds from the nome – including Minoan, Hellenistic and Roman artifacts.

Venetian Fort
Map 1

The most impressive structure left by the Venetians is the great fortress surmounting the rocky promontory on the coast; the city proper is actually built on the isthmus connected to this citadel. The first fort on this site was ruined by marauding Turks in 1571; it was rebuilt and greatly enlarged, with the Cathedral of St Nicholas

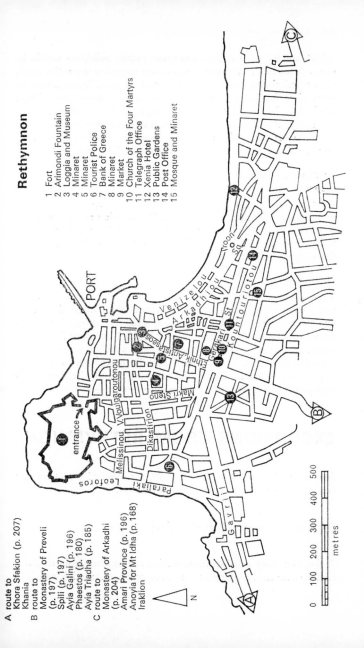

Rethymnon

1 Fort
2 Arimondi Fountain
3 Loggia and Museum
4 Minaret
5 Minaret
6 Tourist Police
7 Bank of Greece
8 Minaret
9 Market
10 Church of the Four Martyrs
11 Telegraph Office
12 Xenia Hotel
13 Public Gardens
14 Post Office
15 Mosque and Minaret

PORT

entrance

Leoforos

Paraliaki

Gavril

Melissinou

Dikastirion

Vouligaroutonou

Makti Steno

Venizelou

Ethnik Antistasseos

Arkadhiou

Gerakari St

Kountouriotou

Voon St

N

0   100   200   300   400   500

metres

(1585), the Rector's Palace, and other public buildings within its walls. After 1646, when the Turks finally occupied the entire place, the cathedral and other buildings went to ruin, intentionally or otherwise; the German bombardments of the Second World War finished the job. Its massive walls, though, are largely intact, and its main gate, as entered from the town, is most impressive. The outer ramparts survive, walls and arches stand here and there, and the remains of a great domed church dominate the scene.

Arimondi Fountain
Map **2**

Another surviving example of Venetian architecture is the Arimondi Fountain, dating from 1623. Alvise Arimondi was a Venetian Rector and built several fountains around Rethymnon; this one has four original Corinthian columns and a restored back wall from the Turkish period.

Other Sights

There are many churches around Rethymnon, some from the Venetian period, but none of any special value. (Rethymnon did have a fine clock tower from this period, but it fell into disrepair and was demolished after the Second World War.) The other interesting sights are the minarets; most were simply attached to 'converted' Venetian churches. And in a small park in the southern part of the city is a mosque with its minaret (*Map* **15**), dating from the early eighteenth century.

EXCURSIONS FROM RETHYMNON

See Chart of Excursions, facing p. 29, for other places of interest described on routes to and from Rethymnon.

Monastery of Arkadhi

A short but very worth-while excursion can be made from Rethymnon up into the mountains to the Monastery of Arkadhi, which of all Crete's religious foundations is the most famous for the part it played in the island's history.

Route
Follow the Iraklion road out of Rethymnon (Route C on town plan) for 5 km. to Platanias, where you turn right up into the hills. You pass through the villages of Adhele (home of Giamboudakis, who is sometimes credited with having set fire to the powder magazine at Arkadhi), Pigi and Kyriana before reaching the Monastery of Arkadhi [22 km.].

Bus
Buses run to the Monastery of Arkadhi and the village of Eleftherna from Iroon Square.

Accommodation
The monastery itself has a guest-house and there is a Tourist Pavilion near by that can handle some people on special occasions. Simple meals can be had.

The Monastery of Arkadhi

The Monastery of Arkadhi is the supreme symbol for Cretans of their ageless strife and dilemma: freedom or death. Like many other monasteries on the island – because of their isolated situations in the mountains – it has always served as a centre for resistance movements and revolts against foreign powers. Even under the German occupation, Arkadhi was used as a meeting-place for partisans.

It was during the revolution of 1866, however, that Arkadhi achieved its immortality. As usual, it had actively supported the uprising against the Turks; that autumn a sizeable group of Cretan fighters, as well as women and children, established themselves in the monastery. They were asked to surrender, but the abbot was the first to refuse. Thousands of troops were called in by the Turks, and when their overwhelming numbers made the fall of the monastery imminent the monastery's powder magazine blew up. Some said that the abbot himself gave the command to one Giamboudakis, and that is the story that has survived. Figures vary, too, but perhaps as many as 1,000 Cretans and 1,800 Turks perished. This was on November 8th, 1866, and the episode soon created reverberations around the world. The anniversary of the event attracts crowds and dignitaries from all over Crete and the mainland; it is marked by solemn ceremonies at Arkadhi, and in Rethymnon by athletic competitions, games, fireworks and dancing. But even if you cannot be there on that particular occasion, the monastery is something to see.

The church of the monastery, although still bearing scars of the assault of 1866, has been greatly restored. Its façade, however, is of intrinsic architectural interest, being the most ornate of the

Venetian structures on Crete. It dates from 1587, and is a mixture of styles: there are Corinthian columns, classical arches, Renaissance garlands, and baroque scrolls. Its light, almost fantastic appearance is somewhat incongruous in the wilds of Crete.

The stairs and portals of the church date from the seventeenth century. The main entrance and gallery to the monastery itself, although rebuilt after 1866, are worth inspecting. You may be shown the actual locale of the explosion – 'untouched'; also, some survivors were said to have been beheaded in the refectory, and the bloodstains may be displayed. There is also a small 'museum', with mementoes of Arkadhi's history, in the great hall. In the courtyard is a cypress, said to have been planted when the monastery was founded, and a laurel tree planted by Venizelos in 1905 when he was leading the struggle for Crete's freedom.

Eleftherna

About 6 km. north-east of Arkadhi is the post-Minoan site of Eleftherna. It can be reached by walking along a path that starts from the right of the Tourist Pavilion and continues round the walls of the monastery. You can also get to the site from the near-by village of Eleftherna, which is reached by taking a small right-hand turning off the main Iraklion–Rethymnon road some 10 km. after the turning to the Monastery of Arkhadi. By the eighth century B.C. Eleftherna seems to have been a prominent settlement, and remains of a bridge from the classical era testify to its endurance. It is chiefly known, though, for the Archaic statue – late seventh century B.C. – found here; this is one of the major specimens of Daedalic art.

ROUTE 4: RETHYMNON TO KHANIA

This is a pleasant trip of about 80 km., notable more for its sights than its sites, but with lovely landscape and several points of interest.

Route
Follow the main road west out of Rethymnon (Route A on town plan), which rises into the mountains and descends to the coast at Georgioupolis [32 km.], then rises and descends again, skirting Soudha Bay, and leads across the fertile plain to Khania [72 km.].
Bus
There are regular services between the two towns, starting from near the Market in Rethymnon and from 1897 Square in Khania. A bus also runs from Khania to Aptera (see below).

Leaving Rethymnon by the main road to the west, you pass through several villages such as **Prines** [7 km.] and **Ghonia** [10 km.].

[22 km.] **Episkopi** is the last village of any size in Rethymnon Nome.

[26 km.] The village of **Dhramia**, near which are fragmentary remains of the ancient Hellenistic site of *Idhramia*.

[31 km.] A turning to the left for **Kournas** leads in 3 km. to the only freshwater lake on Crete – *Lake Kournas* (the ancient Korion or Korisia). It is surprising to encounter such a lake on Crete, and travellers have always commented on its special atmosphere, tamer, lusher and more refreshing when compared with the island's usual rugged attractions. It is roughly 900 m. wide, and you may be told that it is bottomless. Other legends have grown up about it: if you shoot across it, the bullet will never reach the opposite shore; it was once the site of a village; and the ghost of a young girl who was raped on the spot by her father haunts the lake. The real mystery is just what such a body of water is doing here. If you were to go on to the village of Kournas, you might visit the *Church of St Irene* with its Byzantine frescoes.

[32 km.] **Georgioupolis** – on the coast – named after the Prince George who once served as High Commissioner of Crete (p. 87). Near by is the Hellenistic site of *Amfimalla*. After this the road passes through a well-wooded countryside, noted for its cypress trees; to the north extends the small Cape Dhrapanon, an especially fertile region.

[39 km.] **Vrises**, an attractive village with taverns along the road under large trees – a popular spot for excursions. There is an inn which serves excellent yoghurt and lamb roasted on skewers, especially at Easter time. There is a monument here to the Post-Constitutional Committee of 1897, and a road to the left leads to **Khora Sfakion** (p. 222).

[54 km.] **Kalives**, the first large village on Soudha Bay.

[58 km.] In **Kalamion** is the old Venetian fort of *Izzedine*, which the Turks used as a prison. Stretching before you now is a fine view of *Soudha Bay*, the largest and best-protected natural harbour of Crete, and possibly the most remarkable landlocked harbour of the entire Mediterranean. About 15 km. long, and 3 to 6 km. wide, its deep waters can take even today's great ships. In fact, it is a NATO naval base, and you are likely to see ships and sailors of several nations as you drive past the docks. More important than sheer size in ancient times was the fact that the entrance could be easily defended: the Akrotiri promontory is on the northern side, and there are three small islands – once known as the Lefkai Islands – at the narrows. The one that actually commands the bay is Soudha Island. Soudha means 'ditch', a translation of the Arabic name for the place – Khandax – most probably referring to the ditch round the fortifications. The Venetians built extensive fortifications; these still exist, along with the church, and give a good idea of the importance of this outpost. It was one of the last three forts held by the Venetians, only surrendering to the Turks in 1715. Eventually British troops were quartered there at the turn of the century when the Great Powers were running Crete.

[60 km.] A left turn signposted Aptera leads in 1 km. to another sharp left turn uphill; another 2 km. brings you to the ruins of *Aptera*, a Hellenistic city excavated early in the twentieth century. 'Aptera' means 'featherless'; it derived this name from a contest between the Muses and the Sirens at the Museion (a spot near the city); after the Muses triumphed with their music-making, the defeated Sirens plucked off their feathers and cast themselves into the sea, becoming the islands in the bay. From the fifth century B.C. onwards, Aptera was one of the chief commercial cities of Crete, and it was well known right into the early Christian era. There are fairly extensive remains, now in a ruinous condition, spreading over a large area to both sides of an abandoned church: cyclopean walls of an early settlement, a theatre, the Temple of Demeter, a Dorian temple, Roman cisterns, and other Roman and Byzantine remains including bas-reliefs and inscriptions. The view across Soudha Bay is one of the chief attractions of the spot; the best vantage-point is reached by taking the side road to the left just before reaching Aptera.

[66 km.] Back on the main coastal road you descend to the water's edge at **Soudha**, with its modern harbour installations. Soudha is the port of call for Khania and has grown rapidly since the last war; there is an hotel with a restaurant, the *Knossos* (Class D). The NATO operation has left its mark here – the great walls surrounding the facilities, the housing developments, and all the other paraphernalia of the contemporary situation. There is a large cemetery on the slopes for the Allied Forces – mostly British and Commonwealth troops – who lost their lives on Crete during the Second World War. The main square of Soudha is watched over by a statue of Prince George of Greece, who came ashore here in 1898 to take over as High Commissioner.

The road now crosses a fertile plain, with olive trees, vines, plane trees and orange trees making the landscape unusually green and lush. This is the chief orange-growing region of Crete, and Khania is the centre for export. (The orange, by the way, is called *portokálli* in Greek, as it was introduced here from Portugal.)

[70 km.] A left turn for **Malaxa** would bring you, after taking a right fork, in 4 km. to **Mournies** (p. 222).

[72 km.] The approach to **Khania** is by a shady street lined with trees and flowers – all quite suburban. On the outskirts of the town on the right is a domed building with a shop on the ground floor. This is the *Mausoleum of Hamit Bey* and the place is known as Koubes after the Turkish word 'koubes' meaning dome.

KHANIA

Khania is not only the capital of its nome but was also the former administrative capital of Crete, and has all the bustle befitting its position. At the same time, it has a rather more relaxed air than Iraklion – owing, perhaps, to the abundance of greenery and flowers in and about the town. And on an island noted for its hospitality, the people of Khania take a special pride in the gracious face and manner they offer strangers.

Population 38,268.
Air and sea connections
See pp. 32–5. Khania airport is near Sternes on the Akrotiri peninsula and the Olympic Airways terminal is in Karaiskaki Street (*Map* **22**). The port of Khania is

Soudha (p.209), where the regular mainland–Crete ships come in. For information and tickets apply to the Efthymiadis Lines office at 27 Kydonias Street near the Olympic Airways terminal.

Information
National Tourist Organization of Greece: Post Office Building, Tzanakaki Street (*Map 21*).
Tourist Police: Karaiskaki Street (*Map 24*).

Hotels
Class B: *Kydon*, 1897 Square (restaurant).
       Lissos, King Constantine Street.
       Minoa, Tzanakaki Street.
       Xenia (*Map 2*) (restaurant).
Class C: *Canea*, 1866 Square.
       Cyprus (Kipros), Tzanakaki Street.
       Elyros, Mylonoyianni Street.
       Plaza, Tombasi Street (above Kavouria restaurant on harbour).
Class D: *Hellas*, Mylonoyianni Street.
       Hermes, Hadzimikhali Yiannari Street.
       Nea Ionia, Verovits Pasha Street.
Class E: *Achilleion*, Skalidi Street.
       Arkadhi, 1866 Square.
       Averof, 1866 Square.
       Bristol, Tzanakaki Street.
       Europe, Venizelou Street.
       Piraeus, Zambeliou Street.
       Psiloritis, Tzanakaki Street.

Near Khania
Class C: *Aptera Beach*, 2 km. west of Khania (bungalows, restaurant).

Boarding houses
Inquire at the Tourist Office for information about these (see p. 46).

Youth hostel
There is a youth hostel in Hadzidaki Street, near Dhikastirion Square. See note on p. 48 for regulations.

Camping
There is a public camping-site 3 km. out on the road to Rethymnon. The address is Shell Station Camping, Khania.

Restaurants
Apart from the hotels with restaurants there are numerous restaurants and cafés in Khania; some of the best are near the harbour and round the Public Market. At the moment the *Kavouria*, Tombasi Street, on the harbour, has the best reputation. Other restaurants are the *Pharos*, Tombasi Street, near the Janissaries' Mosque, *Kontosouvli*, Tombasi Street, *Nylon*, Kotzambasi Square, *Rex* and *Panellinion*, 1897 Square, and *Caprice*, 1866 Square. In addition there are many *tavernas*, especially in the area to the west of the harbour; also the *Annitsaki*, Hadzimikhali Yiannari Street and the *Brokali*, Syntrivani Square. There is also a large café, the *Kipos*, in the Public Gardens.

Dining and dancing
Some eating-places which feature music and dancing are *Prasini Paparouna* ('Green Poppy'), King George Street, and *Honolulu*, Venizelou Street. Outside the town are the *Kri-Kri*, *Milos* and *Riviera*, on the coast road west to Platanias (p. 237); and the *Neraida* and *Nykterida* on the Akrotiri, the former of which is about 3 km. out of Khania and the latter at Korakies (p. 220).

Cinemas
There are several cinemas; some are open-air in summer.

Consulates
Only France, Germany and Sweden now maintain consulates in Khania.

Churches
Roman Catholic services are held at the Catholic Church in Khalidon Street (*Map* 17).

Clubs and Institutes
There is a library, a music conservatory and a broadcasting station. The local branch of the Greek-American Cultural Institute – a private organization – teaches English and welcomes visitors. The French Institute teaches French.

There are many professional associations in Khania, involving everyone from doctors and pharmacists to raisin-growers and fishermen. There are several intellectual and artistic organizations. Anyone desiring to contact any of these groups could get help at the Tourist Office. For clubs concerned with mountain climbing and expeditions, see under Sport and Swimming below.

Hospital
The Government Hospital where foreigners can be treated is located in Dragoumi Street.

Shops and Souvenirs
The shops of Khania offer a complete line of goods and services and can handle all normal needs of the tourist; there is not the selection of Iraklion, however. There are several banks, including the Bank of Greece, to handle any special transactions.

Khania offers a fine selection of native handicrafts in many shops: textiles, jewellery, costumes, needlework, embroidery, wood carving and musical instruments are among the items. Travellers are reminded that handwork may occasionally be bought in the villages.

Sport and Swimming
For information about sporting events in Khania, contact the office of the National Stadium on King Constantine Street.

There is good hunting – hares and partridges – and fishing in the region; inquire at the Tourist Police about seasons and regulations (p. 58) and for information about the local associations devoted to these sports.

Khania is the centre of much activity in the field of mountain climbing and excursions. There are three groups that go on excursions to visit antiquities or to make ascents of near-by mountains: the Greek Mountain Climbing Association, the Alpine and Nature Worshippers' Union and the Touring Club of Khania. Foreigners are welcome on any of their trips. The Tourist Office can provide more detailed information.

There are several fine beaches to the west of Khania: two favourites are Galatas and Platanias, the former about 4 km. and the latter about 11 km. along the road to Kastelli-Kissamou. Buses leave from 1866 Square. There is also a beach and amusement centre off Venizelou Street on the way to the Khalepa quarter.

Buses
Khania is the terminal for all buses within the nome as well as for those for Rethymnon and Iraklion. The bus stations for the principal destinations are as follows:

1897 *Square*: Rethymnon, Iraklion.

Area around Public Market: City buses for Khalepa quarter, Akrotiri (Kounoupidiana and Korakies), Soudha, Mournies; also buses for Khora Sfakion, Aptera.

Venizelou Street: Country buses for Akrotiri villages, Sternes, Monastery of Ayia Triadha.

1866 *Square* (also known as Neon Katastimaton Square): Galatas and Platanias beaches, Theriso, Alikianos, Meskla, Lakkoi (for Gorge of Samaria), Kandanos, Palaiokhora, Souyia, Rodovani, Kolymvarion, Rodhopou, Kastelli-Kissamou, Platanos.

Taxis and Car Hire
The main taxi ranks are round the Public Market and 1866 Square (for charges, etc., see p. 40). The tourist agencies can arrange private excursions and it is possible to hire cars (see p. 41).

HISTORY

Khania is the descendant of ancient Kydonia – home of the Kydon-
ians, one of the early peoples of Crete, who took their name from
King Kydon, son of Apollo. (The Greek word for 'quince' is also
derived from this name; Crete is credited as the homeland of this
fruit.) Recent excavations in the Kastelli quarter of the town have
shown that Kydonia was inhabited from the end of the Neolithic
period and was an important centre during Minoan times. It later
played a prominent role in the various inter-island wars and alliances
during the post-Minoan era and led the fight against the Romans.
After the Romans took over, and on into the Byzantine period,
Kydonia continued to be of some importance, but by the seventh
century A.D. it had declined along with the rest of the island. From
the time of the first brief Arab occupation in the ninth century –
when the city got its modern name – up to the coming of the
Venetians, Khania was a small town, noted for little else than its
cheese. But when the Venetians chose to rebuild the city, naming it
La Canea in 1252, a new era of prosperity began. The Genoese
seized it from 1267 to 1290, but the Venetians took it back and
turned it into a centre for the whole western end of Crete. By the
sixteenth century, the Venetians had constructed the Kastelli – the
old city on the hill above the harbour – the outer fortifications and
harbour installations, and many churches and other public and
private structures. La Canea briefly enjoyed the reputation of being
'the Venice of the East'. But after a two-month siege it fell to the
Turks in 1645. They converted the churches into mosques, repaired
the fortifications, and settled in; in the nineteenth century they
made the former Venetian Kastelli the capital of the whole island.
The Pasha's seraglio was also here. And travellers in the nineteenth
century report a whole community of Africans and Arabs en-
camped at the edge of Khania, which must have added to its exotic
atmosphere. In 1898 the Turkish troops had to withdraw, and
international forces moved in under the aegis of the Great Powers.
Prince George came as the High Commissioner, and Khania was
kept as the island's capital – an honour it retained when Crete was
united with Greece in 1913.

MUSEUMS

Archaeological Museum
Map **14**

Hours
NOTE: The museum is closed all day on Mondays and at Christmas, New Year
Greek Easter, March 25th and October 28th.
April 1st–Sept. 30th Weekdays 8–1, 3–6.
                Sundays and public holidays 10–1, 3–6.
Oct. 1st–March 31st Weekdays 9–1, 2.30–5.
                Sundays and public holidays 10–1, 2.30–5.
Entrance charge: Drs 5. Free on Thursdays and Sundays.
Fee for taking photographs: Drs 5.
Director: J. G. Tzedakis.

Although it can hardly rival the great Minoan collection of Iraklion,
the Khania museum has an interesting collection of art and artifacts
from western Crete, including pottery, sculpture, coins, mosaics,
inscriptions, utensils and armaments. An intensified series of
excavations in recent years is adding considerably to the museum's
collection, which has also been newly organized and displayed. The
new exhibits include some finds from the recent excavations of
ancient Kydonia in Khania itself. Of these, the most interesting are
the Neolithic and Minoan pottery, some imported Cypriot pottery
of the late Minoan period, and some pottery inscribed with Linear
B. There is also a collection of early Minoan stone and pottery
vases from Platyvola Cave. The museum is installed in the Church
of St Francis, itself of some historical interest (p. 216).

Historical Museum
Map **25**

Hours
Weekdays 8–1.30.
Mondays and Wednesdays 5–8 (only on Monday afternoons in summer).
Closed on Sundays and public holidays.
Entrance free.

This is considered one of the major archives of all Greece, with its
many rare documents and books from the late-Byzantine, Venetian
and Turkish periods as well as from modern Crete. There are also
other items of historical interest – armaments, flags and pictures.

PRINCIPAL SIGHTS

Remains of ancient Kydonia have recently been excavated in the
Kastelli quarter and many relics turned up over the years attest to

the history of the site. Most of these finds are now on exhibition in the Archaeological Museum (p. 213).

Although the once magnificent Venetian structures have largely disappeared, the main historical interest of a tour through Khania is to see how much does remain from this period. Enough survives to hint at what must have been its days of glory.

Khania may be divided into two parts – the new town and the old. The new Khania has grown up along the plain behind the harbour, gradually absorbing the suburbs such as Khalepa (p. 218). This new town has most of the facilities for the tourist, although the cafés and restaurants by the old harbour are the most popular. The new town has the bus termini, for example, and the Public Market (*Map* 19); this is a large structure in the shape of a cross, modelled after the great market at Marseilles. Here is brought the produce of the region, and it can be quite a heady experience to stroll through the crowded lanes. More restful are the Public Gardens, in the heart of the town (*Map* 23); a bandstand, cinema and café add to the attractions of these gardens – at least for the native Khaniots.

The old town of Khania lies clustered around the harbour and spreads back through the narrow streets where the Venetians erected their town houses and churches. It is divided into five

---

Khania

'quarters' (in Greek, *synoikía*): Kastelli in the centre, Evraiki and Tophanas in the west and Splanzia and Chiones in the east. We shall describe the principal points of interest that might be investigated on a quarter-by-quarter tour of the city.

Kastelli Quarter

This name is applied to the actual fortifications above the harbour (the *Inner Wall*) as well as to the quarter of the city. The Venetians started constructing in the thirteenth century, erecting the walls on the older Byzantine foundations and probably using materials from the ancient ruins of the acropolis of Kydonia. Not much has survived of the fortress proper except for fragments of the bastions. Within the Kastelli there were once a palace, a cathedral and a monastery; little remains. There was also the *Venetian Archive* (*Map* 6); a fine portal survives in Lithinon Street, with an inscription dated 1623. The columns and pilasters are side by side, with the orders superimposed. Also within the Kastelli quarter are the remains of the *Arcade of St Mark* (*Map* 7).

And as a sign of the 'changing of the guard', near the harbour stands the *Mosque of Djamissi*, or *Mosque of the Janissaries* (*Map* 8), erected in 1645 after the Turks had conquered the city. The original dome survives, but it is supported by exterior arches of a later period. The graves of some Mohammedan priests are at one side.

Finally, recent excavations have uncovered evidence of ancient Kydonia: notably remains of a late Minoan megaron with paved floors and parts of storage rooms which can be seen on Kanevaro Street.

Outer Venetian Wall

The Kastelli quarter was the original Venetian city and lay within its own inner wall. But during the fifteenth and sixteenth centuries the Venetians erected a much more ambitious wall to embrace the large city that had grown up. The total circumference is some 3,000 m.; alongside it was a moat, 50 m. wide and 10 m. deep in places. Much of the wall, especially on the eastern and western sides, is intact; there are also remains of the *Lando Bastion* (*Map* 18).

Evraiki Quarter

West of Kastelli quarter, this was once the Jewish quarter. Its most important structure is the *Church of St Francis* (*Map* 14) (also known by its other name, Idhaon Andron), which now houses the Archaeological Museum (p. 213). It is one of the finest of the Venetian buildings on Crete, and the largest of the twenty-three Venetian churches in Khania. It has three vaulted naves, with Gothic windows; its façade is somewhat disfigured, but it is otherwise well preserved. The Turks converted it into a mosque, naming it after the Youssouf Pasha who conquered Khania; they left a legacy, too – a lovely Turkish fountain in the inner court. The church is on Khalidon Street, near Syntrivani Square – 'syntrivani' being the Turkish word for 'fountain'.

On the edge of this quarter is the *Cathedral of Our Lady (Map* **15**), built in 1864 from the remains of an earlier church.

Tophanas Quarter

The westernmost quarter of the old city, its prize possession is the *Renieri Gate (Map* **11**), off Zambeliou Street. The portals bear an inscription from 1608 and the escutcheon of the Renieri family. Beyond, to the left, is a small Venetian chapel; past this are some old powder magazines and a house that probably served as headquarters for the arsenal. At the end of Theotokopoulou Street is the Venetian *Church of San Salvatore (Map* **3**), which the Turks used as a mosque and which is now a warehouse. There are also some Venetian portals with a balcony within the enclosure of *Firka Tower (Map* **4**) behind a closed gate. And on Zambeliou and Angelou Streets are some Venetian mansions with architectural details worth noting; also on Zambeliou Street is the ruined *Venetian Club Loggia* which has a Latin inscription.

Splanzia Quarter

Situated to the south-east of Kastelli quarter, this quarter's finest attraction is the *Church of St Nicholas (Map* **10**). Built under the Venetians, it served as a Dominican monastery and took its name from the famed Bishop of Myra. The Turks converted it into the Imperial Mosque of Sultan Ibrahim, which it remained until 1912, when it became a Greek Orthodox church. As a result of its various conversions, its tower now looks, as you might expect, like a cross between a minaret and a campanile; indeed it is the tallest minaret in Khania. The church is on Splanzia Square, a delightful place to sit and enjoy a cool drink under the shade of a giant plane tree. On the same square is the *Venetian Church of San Rocco (Map* **9**) with a Latin inscription from 1630.

A few streets away to the south-east, embedded in narrow lanes, is the *Church of Ayii Anargyri (Map* **12**), dedicated to the martyrs Kosmas and Damianos. This was a Greek Orthodox church, built in the sixteenth century, and the only Orthodox church in Khania allowed to hold services under the Venetians and the Turks. Its icons are of considerable age and artistry.

There are several other interesting sights in this old quarter, with its picturesque narrow lanes. On Hadzimikhali Daliani Street there is a *Venetian Portal (Map* **13**) and a fine *Minaret (Map* **16**). At 30 Rianou Street there is a Venetian mansion.

Chiones Quarter

This quarter lies to the north of Splanzia around the harbour. The Venetians had great plans for La Canea, but, no matter how much they dredged, the harbour was never really successful. They built a breakwater (*Map* **1**) by rafting out rocks and dumping them. In the middle of the breakwater they erected a small Church of St Nicholas and a fort; the latter was used by both the Venetians and the Turks as a place to execute convicts (no remains are now left). Along the harbour the Venetians also constructed great *arsenali* (*Map* **5**) – large domed dockyards for shipbuilding and storage. There were two main projects, one in the fifteenth and one in the seventeenth century, but of the two dozen *arsenali* only seven remain. The tops of the arches were once covered by lead, but the Turks removed this.

Khalepa Quarter

This is not in the old city, but it is still another, modern quarter of Khania that should be seen – a pleasant, hilly suburb on the sea at the base of the Akrotiri. You leave the town by Venizelou Street and continue on after crossing King George Street; there are frequent buses from near the Public Market and Khalepa might be combined with an excursion to the Akrotiri.

When Prince George moved to Crete, he settled in Khalepa, and his mansion and the former Palace of the Governors are to be seen. Khalepa has always been something of a prosperous residential section, and it has many fine villas, some of which have served as national consulates. There is also the Convent of the Sisters of St Joseph, French nuns who have been influential in keeping French culture alive in Khania. The Church of St Mary Magdalene was built by Prince George's sister, the Grand Duchess Maria; it is in the Russian manner, a sort of Gothic–Byzantine style. The famous Cretan–Greek statesman, Eleftherios Venizelos, built a house here too; it is kept by his family, and near by is a small park with his statue.

EXCURSIONS FROM KHANIA

The main points of interest are described in some detail here; for a few other places that might be reached from Khania see the Chart of Excursions, facing p. 29.

The Akrotiri

Akrotiri means 'the promontory', and a glance at the map reveals how it acquired this name. It is a region rich in history, from earliest times to contemporary Crete, and is visited every year by thousands of people, from native Cretans to international travellers. There are two main destinations for most visitors: the Hill of the Prophet Elias (only a few kilometres outside Khania) and the Monastery of Ayia Triadha (some 17 km. into the hills). Buses take you to both places, as well as to one or two other sites on Akrotiri; only feet will take you to some parts. And many people will get a glimpse of the Akrotiri en route to or from Khania's airport, which is located near Sternes on the south-east corner.

Route
Leave Khania by Venizelou Street (Route C on town plan), passing through the suburb of Khalepa (p. 218). Continue until in about 6 km. you come to a left turn off to the Hill of the Prophet Elias. Almost immediately there is another fork, the left branch of which leads to the Monastery of Ayia Triadha [17 km.] while the right-hand branch goes to Korakies [8 km.].
Bus
The city buses for Kounoupidiana and Korakies leave from near the Public Market. The country buses which go to the various villages on the peninsula, including the Monastery of Ayia Triadha and Sternes, leave from Venizelou Street near the junction with Nikiphorou Phoka Street.

[6 km.] A left turn brings you straight on to the *Hill of the Prophet Elias*, with its superb view across the water and down on to Khania. This hill is a symbolic peak of Crete's long struggle for freedom, and a statue to Eleftheria, Goddess of Liberty, commemorates this. For it was here, in 1897, that Cretan insurgents raised the flag of Greece, despite the injunctions of all the Great Powers and the Turks. When the flagpole was broken by the subsequent bombardment from the fleet off shore, a Cretan stood up and held the flag in his own hands. Many legends have accrued to this incident: one is that the sailors of the fleet stopped firing and cheered the valiant Cretans; another claims that an explosion occurred in one of the Russian ships taking part in the shelling – and this was attributed to divine anger, because the shells were destroying the Church of the Prophet Elias. If any further associations with Cretan aspirations are needed, there is the grave of Eleftherios Venizelos close to the statue. He has recently been joined by his son Sophocles.

Just beyond the turn-off to the monument, you come to a fork in the road. If you take the right branch, it leads in 2 km. to **Korakies,** which has two or three restaurants overlooking a fine view of Soudha Bay – favourite gathering-places in the evening. There is also a convent here, noted for its embroideries.

For Ayia Triadha take the left turn at the fork.

[8 km.] After passing a new road coming in on your right, bear right into the village of **Kounoupidiana.**

[15 km.] After joining another road coming in from the right, in about ¼ km. you drive down a side road to the left.

[17 km.] Monastery of Ayia Triadha

This is one of the most important monasteries of Crete, although like all of them it has declined since the nineteenth century. It is situated in the centre of the promontory in a sheltered position at the foot of limestone hills. Founded in the seventeenth century by Jeremiah Zangarola, a Venetian convert to Greek Orthodoxy, it shows a strong Venetian influence in its architecture. A monumental entrance in the classic style dates from 1632 and the campanile from 1650. It has an especially rich treasury. Today Ayia Triadha is a school for Cretan boys from all over the island; they come here on scholarships to be trained for service in the Orthodox Church, particularly in the music.

Gouverneto Monastery and Katholiko Cave

This is a somewhat more ambitious excursion for those who have the extra time and energy. It means setting off on foot for about a two hours' walk overland to the north, taking the path to the left from Ayia Triadha, to arrive at the Monastery of St John of Gouverneto, a local hermit-saint who lived and died in a cave near Katholiko (below). The monastery, situated in its isolated mountain landscape, shows Venetian influence in its architecture. Above it rises Mt Sloka, with an excellent view.

Still another hour's walk is required to reach Katholiko. You set off behind Gouverneto Monastery and the path leads eventually down to a narrow gorge; there, wedged between rocky precipices, are the remains of the deserted Monastery of Katholiko and cave-dwellings of early Christian hermits. It was one of the older monasteries on Crete, but in the late sixteenth century it was pillaged by pirates from Africa; the monks began to abandon it, moving to Gouverneto. In a near-by cave, which you pass on the left before reaching the ruined monastery, St John the hermit died. Inside there is a large chamber – some 150 m. wide and up to 20 m. high – with many stalactites. It is all quite spectacular.

The saint's day is observed every October 7th, when hundreds of pilgrims and visitors come to Gouverneto and Katholiko.

Other Remains

The Akrotiri has still other remains, but they are of little concern except to specialists. At **Sternes**, for instance, the modern village near the airport, there are the remains of the old *Church of Ayii Pantes* on the right as you enter the village; in the centre of the village, next to the *Church of the Annunciation*, are remains of structures and catacombs from the early Christian era.

The Akrotiri is also especially rich in caves, many of which have yielded important finds to archaeologists and anthropologists during the twentieth century. To name only a few: in the *Koumarospilion* the German Jantzen discovered human skulls at least 5,000 years old; above the beach at **Stavros** is the *Cave of Lera*; and west of **Rizoskloko,** opposite the military airport, is the *Cave of St Spyridon*, with a church dedicated to this saint.

H

Theriso and Mournies

These two villages are of interest only to those intent on pursuing the career of Eleftherios Venizelos. Theriso is his mother's home village. Having formed a party in 1901 with the pledge to seek union with Greece, he convened a Revolutionary Assembly at Theriso in 1905 and ended up by resorting to armed rebellion. The village is some 17 km. south of Khania and can be reached by taking a left fork off the road to Kastelli-Kissamou on the outskirts of the town – the bus leaves from 1866 Square. The road goes through an impressive ravine; 2 km. outside Theriso, located in the ravine, is *Sarakina Cave*, where Neolithic finds have been made.

Mournies, meanwhile, contains what is called 'the house where Venizelos was born'. In any case, it is a pleasant enough village with its trees and springs; it can be reached by taking a turning to the right just outside Khania on the road back to Rethymnon; Mournies lies some 4 km. down this road. The bus for Mournies leaves from near the Public Market.

Khora Sfakion and Sfakia Province

On an island where nature and history have conspired to create a tangle of legends and mysteries, perhaps no part of Crete has quite such an aura of myth as the province of Sfakia of which Khora Sfakion is the centre. Among those who know, the very word 'Sfakia' conjures up visions of almost superhuman mountain-men – staunch fighters for their independence, marauding brigands, clambering over stark gorges, tending their flocks, hunting the wild goat, striking down their enemies. Inevitably, too, Sfakia prompts visitors and writers to superlatives: the land is the most rugged, the people are the most fearless (or lawless!), the flora and fauna are unique. In brief, it is a region that will attract some and repel many.

How much time is required for a trip through these parts? Well, the village of Khora Sfakion can be reached in a few hours by bus or car. But to explore the region thoroughly – going from site to site and taking things as they come – would require several days. Most of the possibilities are described below.

Route

Follow the main Rethymnon road (Route B on town plan) east out of Khania (pp. 207–9), turning right at Vrises [33 km.] to cross the island to Khora Sfakion [74 km.]. NOTE: The road from Vrises to Khora Sfakion is often blocked by snow in winter.

As an alternative return trip you could drive overland from Khora Sfakion to Rethymnon via Komitadhes, Patsianos, Skaloti, Rodakino, Selia and Ayios Ioannis, joining the Timbaki–Rethymnon road just above the turning to the Monastery of Preveli. This drive along rough roads through some wild scenery would allow you to take in excursions to Frangokastello (p. 226) and the Monastery of Preveli (p. 197) – the latter by turning right after Selia at 43 km. for Mirthios and Lefkoyia; after Lefkoyia you bear right and the monastery is another 6 km. farther on. You could then come back to join the Timbaki–Rethymnon road via Asomati and Koxares and continue either to Rethymnon or to Phaestos (pp. 195–8).

Bus

There are regular services to Khora Sfakion and the surrounding region from near the Public Market in Khania.

Accommodation

Vrises, en route, has an inn and several other eating-places. Khora Sfakion has a Tourist Pavilion.

For the reverse route from Khania to Vrises see pp. 207–9.

[33 km.] **Vrises** (p. 207) is where you turn right and head inland. Climbing up into the mountains you pass the ravine of *Katrai,* named after a son of Minos and the scene of two bloody massacres: in 1812 thousands of Turks were trapped and slain here; and some 44 years later the troops that had occupied Arkadhi were destroyed here.

[52 km.] The *Plain of Askifou* opens up before you; situated about 730 m. above sea-level, it is surrounded by hills and villages, of which **Amoudarion** is the most important.

[55 km.] A left turn off the main road would bring you in 6 km. to **Asphendou,** in the middle of another small plain on a hilly site. There are several interesting old churches here, including that of *St George.* Near by is the ravine of *Kapni* and the *Cave of Falangari,* with stalactites and water. Farther to the west, overland across the mountains, is **Kalikratis,** noted for its spring with curative waters and a subterranean brook.

[58 km.] Continuing south on the main road you pass through the village of **Imbros.** Then you wind through a lovely pine forest and descend through a ravine with a dramatic view of the barren landscape and the rugged coast of the Libyan Sea.

[71 km.] A turning on the left leads in 1 km. to **Komitadhes** (p. 226).

[74 km.] You come down to the coast at **Khora Sfakion,** with its imposing sheer cliffs giving it the air of a pirates' nest.

Khora Sfakion and Sfakia Province

In its heyday, during the sixteenth century, Khora Sfakion was the largest town on the southern coast, with some three thousand inhabitants, a thriving commercial life and – it is claimed – one hundred chapels and churches. These were built by individual benefactors and neighbouring villages; most of them are now gone or in ruins. Today it is a sleepy little village with only a few hundred inhabitants (and a Tourist Pavilion); you could almost believe that the town had tumbled into the sea down the rocky slopes.

Nevertheless, it is still the centre of Sfakia Province, home of the Sfakians. It is hard to say whether the land made the men, or the men chose the land. Now they are inseparable in their rugged isolation. Although the population has declined drastically, this cannot really be blamed on the terrain. One theory has it that the Sfakians are pure descendants of the Dorians who moved into Crete after the break-up of the Minoan–Mycenaean empire; other theories claim them as Achaeans, as the Eteocretans – as Saracens, even! Whatever their origin, the Sfakians were left to their own resources, and over the centuries came to be feared by native Cretans as well as by invading foreigners. The Venetians had the intention of subduing the Sfakians and built the impressive Frango-kastello on the coast (p. 226), but little came of this. When the Turks divided up the island among the Pashas at the end of the seventeenth century, the Sfakians still held their own. They not only continued their autonomous affairs, but actively harassed the Turks – again, to the great discomfort of their less belligerent fellow-Cretans, who lay exposed to the vengeance of the Turks after the Sfakians withdrew to their mountain stronghold. By the end of the nineteenth century there was hardly a patch of Sfakian soil that was not coloured by the blood of some incident. During the German occupation this region once more became the centre of resistance. It is fair to say that Sfakians have remained a law unto themselves throughout their history.

Then, too, they have this not entirely undeserved reputation of being lawless – pirates, smugglers, brigands, revolutionaries, brawlers, what you will. That day is largely past, except for a bit of sheep-stealing or petty smuggling. And to give them their due, they have always fought and killed as much among themselves as against outsiders; vendettas have taken the lives of many Sfakians. As with those other island outposts, Sicily and Corsica, family blood runs thick, passions run high and quarters are close. But none of this involves the visitor to Sfakia. What the visitor notes, rather, is a land inhabited by mere hundreds, where once thousands lived and worked and fought. Ports lie idle. Flocks and trade have dwindled. Decimated by rebellions and vendettas, bypassed by history, many Sfakians have emigrated in search of a livelihood. The people remaining still hold to the old ways – in fact, Sfakia is noted for the pure tradition of its handicrafts. There are the ruins and sites of its past that may yet draw tourists. There will always be the spectacle of the land. But Sfakia's energy is slipping. Perhaps it is because there is no longer any serious challenge to their existence, no tension in their lives; Sfakia thrived on resistance. A bastion of independence, Sfakia is now independent – and ignored.

You will still hear Sfakia and its people described as 'dangerous' or something to that effect, but this is not true. Certainly the foreigner need not fear for his safety or property. They are a rugged, proud people, and if you go there with respect for their integrity, they will respect yours.

Churches and Caves

As Khora Sfakion has always been a rallying-point for revolutionaries, the whole area has many sites associated with various historical episodes. In Khora Sfakion itself – up on the hill to the right as you descend into the village – is the *Church of the Holy Apostle*; several others have frescoes of the Byzantine period. Near by, on the left after you have taken the turning to Komitadhes village, is the *Thymniani Panayia Church*, where the self-governing Sfakians held their assemblies during the years before 1821.

There are also several caves in the region, the most famous one being the *Cave of Daskaloyiannis* – 'John the Clerk' or 'John the Educated'. It is reached by sea, some ten minutes to the west. Daskaloyiannis is one of the best known of the many revolutionary leaders of Crete, thanks largely to the ballad, *The Song of Daskaloyiannis*, set down some sixteen years after his death and recounting his bloody fate. He had taken the lead in the uprising of 1770 and, when he finally delivered himself over to the Turks to discuss surrender terms, they disagreed and he was seized, tortured in the fort at Iraklion and then skinned alive. (His bust is now in the square in Iraklion named after him.) It was in this cave that the revolutionaries of 1770 established their own mint.

Frangokastello

An interesting excursion from Khora Sfakion is to Frangokastello, about 15 km. to the east; you can pick up a bus from Khora Sfakion which will drop you at Patsianos within walking distance of the castle. To get there you return along the main road out of Khora Sfakion; after 3 km. turn right and continue a further 1 km. into **Komitadhes**. There is a *Church of St George* about ten minutes' walk down from this village which dates from the early fourteenth century and has some fine frescoes.

Then you pass on through the villages of **Vraskas** and **Vouvas** until you arrive at **Patsianos**. From here there is a footpath running down to the coast which brings you in about half an hour's walk to the castle. Alternatively, if you continue about 4 km. beyond Patsianos, a track (which will take a car) leads across to the isolated point on the coast where this old Venetian fort is situated.

The Venetians thought they could subdue the Sfakians, so in the fourteenth century they erected this impressive fort, using, in part, stone from some ancient site. It is a sizeable, square fortress, with four corner towers – and still fairly well preserved, with the Lion of St Mark on guard. But the Venetians never really succeeded in taming the Sfakians, despite the many bloody battles fought in this area. It is said that the Cretans used to dance on the flat land by the castle – doing the *Pyrrikhios*, the soldiers' dance of war, as taught by Rhea to the *Curétes* who had protected the young Zeus. Nowadays, in place of battles and dances, the Cretans claim to see the ghosts of the hundreds of Sfakians who died defending the fort against the Turks in 1828. Only in early May, at dawn, do these *drossoulítes* – 'dew shades' – appear; evidently a mirage of some sort, due to peculiar weather conditions.

Returning to the Patsianos road, you could continue on eastwards and northwards to Rethymnon by the route described on p. 223.

Ayia Roumeli

This is another possible excursion: to the village to the west that lies at the end of the Gorge of Samaria expedition described on pp. 228–33. You can either take a boat or walk overland to Ayia Roumeli, from which point you could walk up through the gorge to the north – although most people will prefer the north-to-south walk to avoid having to climb uphill. Either way, the local boats make frequent trips between Khora Sfakion and Ayia Roumeli; the fare depends on the number of passengers, but it comes to about Drs 300 for four people. The journey takes about 2 hours in good weather.

For those wanting to walk overland to Ayia Roumeli – a long day's trip – the following is the route. The first stretch to **Anopolis** can actually be done by bus from Khora Sfakion (although the bus does not return to Khora Sfakion until the next morning); walking this bit takes a good two hours. Because of its position and the near-by harbour of Phoenix, Anopolis flourished under the Romans and into the Byzantine period; with its suburbs and dependencies, it is claimed to have numbered seventy thousand inhabitants at its peak. It was an autonomous city, with its own mint. There are some ruins to be seen, including cyclopean walls. There are also remains of a house, said to have been the residence of Daskaloyiannis, which the local people are very willing to show.

Below Anopolis, on the coast, is **Loutro**, where *Phoenix*, an ancient port mentioned by Strabo, was situated. (This village can also be reached by walking directly from Khora Sfakion – or by boat in about ½ hour.) Loutro stands on a steep, bare hillside on a peculiar promontory; it is shaped like a spade, with shelter on both sides. There are subterranean vaults – Venetian structures – indicating that it was once a thriving port. There are only a few scattered remains from the Roman period, as well as early Byzantine ruins. During early Christian times it was the see of a bishop. The *Church of the Transfiguration of Christ* has frescoes from later Byzantine times. There is also a building, in a fair state of preservation, where the first government of the revolution of 1821 met: it is called the *Kangelaria Kivernion* – 'the chancellery'.

Another two-hour walk overland, north-west from the coast and across a ravine, brings you to the village of **Aradena**. Its *Church of the Archangel Michael* dates from the Byzantine period, although it is probably built with material from ancient ruins; the frescoes are worth examining. Near by is the site of ancient *Aradin*; its name is Phoenician, and it is mentioned in an ancient military alliance with the King of Pergamon in Asia Minor. The ruins include a structure called 'the dance of the Hellenes' and prehistoric dwellings carved in the rocks. There are several caves in the vicinity: the most elaborate one is *Dhrakolakoi* (*dhrako* means 'dragon'), quite large, with water and sandy ground; no one is advised to explore unless properly equipped.

A few kilometres farther on is the deserted *Monastery of Ayios Ioannis*, from where the trail descends to the sea coast, passes the *Chapel of St Paul* (p. 233) and arrives at Ayia Roumeli.

Gorge of Samaria

Probably the most spectacular adventure that Crete offers is a trip through the Gorge of Samaria. People who have made the excursion – and there have not been very many apart from natives of the area – resort to all sorts of extravagances in their descriptions, and, even allowing for travellers' tales, it is a moving experience. To do it properly you must allow from two to four days, starting from Khania, not because it takes so long just to walk through the gorge – if you press, you can get through in six hours – but because the whole excursion (the approach, the gorge, adjoining sites and the return) takes up the time. And if you were to combine several of the sites along the south coast then still more time could be profitably spent.

Although it is not really necessary, it would be possible to arrange for a guide, either in Khania or at one of the villages at the edge of the Omalos Plain. Even experienced walkers are advised not to go alone. It is not that there is any threat from local people – the fact is, you are not likely to see anyone during the passage except a stray shepherd. But it is rocky terrain and there are usually some patches of water; if you twisted your ankle it might be some time before anyone came by. Otherwise there is no risk involved. You can walk the 18 km. in a long day, but spending a night in the gorge is considered a unique adventure. Take warm clothing for evenings, and light camping gear if you plan to spend any time there; be prepared to feed yourself for the hours you will pass in the gorge. And note: the gorge is completely blocked during the winter by torrents and snow.

Route
Follow the Kastelli road westwards out of Khania (Route A on town plan) and after 2 km. turn south for Alikianos and Lakkoi. Continue on to the Omalos Plain, at the farther edge of which is the Xyloskalon (or 'wooden steps') that leads down to the gorge [44 km.]. For the actual walk through the gorge, see p. 231 for sketch map. If you are driving you will have to leave your car at the entrance to the gorge; you can then either walk back up through the gorge to fetch it or go all the way round via Khania by one of the ways suggested under Bus and Boat.

Bus and Boat
Regular buses go from 1866 Square in Khania only as far as Lakkoi; from there you would have to take a taxi, a donkey, or walk the 19 km. up to and across the Omalos Plain to the beginning of the gorge. (Sometimes you can get a lift on the back of a lorry taking workmen up into the mountains.) In summer there is an early morning bus on Sundays from 1866 Square all the way to the entrance of the gorge.

Once you arrive at Ayia Roumeli after walking through the gorge, you can get the café to telephone to Khora Sfakion for a boat to come and fetch you if none is on hand; this journey takes about 2 hours in good weather; a fair price would be about Drs 300 for four people. Another possibility is to walk overland to Khora Sfakion by reversing the route described on p. 227. From Khora Sfakion, of course, you can get a bus back to Khania. Or you might get a boat or walk overland to Palaiokhora to the west (p. 235), which also has bus connections with Khania. Still another possibility is to walk back up through the gorge from south to north, but this is rather harder going; you must take especial care to bear to the left after the village of Samaria to avoid getting on to the mountain of Mavri.

Accommodation
There is a new Tourist Pavilion, which at present has no beds, at the top of the gorge; cheap beds and meals are obtainable at the cafés on Omalos Plain [3 km. from the entrance to the gorge]. There is another Tourist Pavilion at Khora Sfakion and, at a pinch, you could put up at Ayia Roumeli.

[2 km.] Turn left for Alikianos.

[12 km.] After driving through lush and fertile scenery, with many orange groves, you come to a fork where there is a war memorial to the people of the surrounding villages. The right-hand branch leads in 1 km. to the attractive village of **Alikianos**; but you take the left branch for Fournes.

[15 km.] At the end of the village of **Fournes** you have to fork right to Lakkoi. If you were to take the left fork, however, you would come in 5 km. to **Meskla**, known as Crete's 'Garden of Green' (there is a bus to Meskla from 1866 Square in Khania). Thanks to its well-watered orange groves and fine trees it is a prosperous village. The Venetians used Meskla as an administrative centre; it was also the headquarters of Kantanoleon, a native leader in the struggle against the Venetians. The *Church of the Transfiguration of the Saviour*, just off the road up to the left before crossing the bridge, has fourteenth-century frescoes of some note. Near by is the site of what scholars think may be the ancient settlement of *Keraia*; little is known about it but, judging from its cyclopean walls and chambers carved out of rocks, it must have been settled fairly early. It is on the Kerides river at the foot of a mountain.

From Meskla you could walk overland to the east to **Theriso** (p. 222). You could also climb for about 4 km. over steep hills south-west from Meskla to Lakkoi; but most people will have taken the right fork back at Fournes.

[20 km.] 5 km. from Fournes you take a left fork.

[25 km.] **Lakkoi,** the end of the line for the bus, is another of the more idyllic mountain villages of Crete, surrounded by green slopes and fields.

[39 km.] The road continues across the *Omalos Plain*. At over 1,000 m. elevation and covering some 25 square km., the Omalos is one of the most impressive of the Cretan upland plains; it almost seems to be a great drained lake – and indeed gets quite marshy in the centre. It is not nearly as thickly populated as the Lasithi Plain, but it is very fertile and produces potatoes and cereals.

Soon after reaching the plain you pass the house and grave of Hadzimikhali Yiannari, one of the leaders in the rebellions against the Turks in the late nineteenth century; he later wrote his memoirs.

[41 km.] About halfway across the plain are a couple of cafés where you can get cheap meals and beds.

[44 km.] At the far edge of the plain is the actual entry-way to the gorge – the *Xyloskalon*, or 'wooden steps'. There is a Tourist Pavilion here; and an impressive view out across the mountains.

Gorge of Samaria

The Gorge of Samaria, one of the largest in Europe, is 18 km. long and varies in width from 3 to 40 m. The steep walls rise from 300 to 600 m., at some points so sheer that there is barely any sunlight, and at the *sideroportes* ('iron gates') you walk through a narrow pass of steep rock. Thousands of years of torrents have eaten away the rocks, creating such a gorge. Even now there is a sizeable stream during the rainy season and after the thaw; in 1955 Ayia Roumeli was inundated, owing to unusually heavy rains in the White Mountains. Throughout the trip you will see flowers, herbs and shrubs

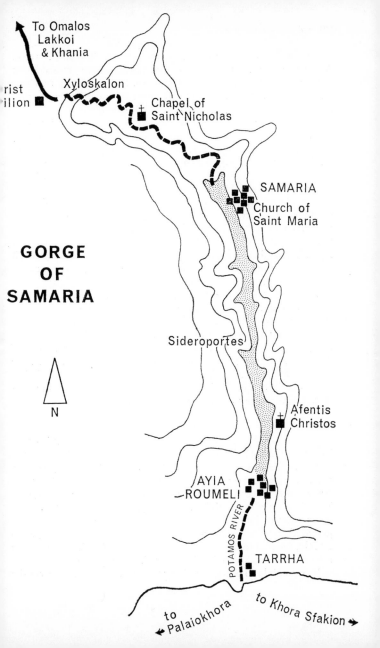

To Omalos
Lakkoi
& Khania

rist
ilion

Xyloskalon

✝ Chapel of
Saint Nicholas

SAMARIA

Church of
Saint Maria

**GORGE
OF
SAMARIA**

Sideroportes

△
N

✝ Afentis
Christos

AYIA
ROUMELI

TARRHA

POTAMOS RIVER

to
← Palaiokhora

to Khora Sfakion →

clinging to the crevices; dittany and cypress are especially notable. And if you are really lucky you may see the famous Cretan wild goat – the *agrími*, now confined to this gorge. It is so elusive that it is unlikely that the casual visitor will spot it; but those who have confirm the tales of its prodigious leaps and agility.

You set out, zigzagging down the Xyloskalon, descending into the gorge. After some kilometres you pass, standing in a lovely grove of pines and cypresses, the little *Chapel of St Nicholas*. Continuing down, you pass on your left the village of **Samaria** with its stone huts; its Venetian *Church of Saint Maria* (1379) has given its name to the gorge. Pashley, the famous nineteenth-century classicist-traveller, placed the site of the ancient Dorian city of *Kaino* near Samaria. There was an Oracle of Apollo; here, too, according to myth, was born the nymph Britomartis, daughter of Zeus – the Cretan Artemis or Dictynna. And the nereid Acacallis, wife of Apollo, was said to have been worshipped in this region. All in all, it is most atmospheric; it is easy to believe in the gods and goddesses of nature as you pass through such a gorge.

The gorge begins in earnest after Samaria, and you will do best to follow the river; it will be dried out in the summer, and you can make your way along the rocky river-bed. The river disappears underground at times, and bubbles forth in springs elsewhere. Eventually you come to a widened valley where are the houses of Ayia Roumeli; you proceed through this somewhat deserted village and continue another 2 km. to arrive at the coast itself. This is a small alluvial plain, and since there is a sudden drop at the shore, no delta forms where the river enters the sea.

Ayia Roumeli

The hamlet of Ayia Roumeli offers nothing spectacular; it is noted largely for its inhabitants, Sfakians who make their living tending flocks, hunting game and otherwise subsisting off the gorge and the land. There are the remains of a *Venetian Castle* above Ayia Roumeli. And there is one church of note: *Our Lady of St Roumeli*, built by the Venetians early in the sixteenth century. In the pavement round it are mosaics dating from the pre-Christian era, and it has been suggested that the church was built over the ruins of a temple to Apollo, a sacred spot for the ancient city of Tarrha, situated on what are now the outskirts of Ayia Roumeli.

It is possible to get something to eat at the little tavern on the coast; and there is good swimming here. There are several possibilities for getting out of Ayia Roumeli – all mentioned in the Route Directions for this excursion, p. 229.

Tarrha

Tarrha was settled from at least the fifth century B.C., through the Roman period, and on to the fifth century A.D. It was probably abandoned because of the decline of the trade routes and attacks by pirates. A few Hellenic remains have been turned up in recent years, as well as some Roman structures and fortifications. Tarrha was important enough to have its own coinage; it is also surmised that there was a glass factory, as a distinctive type of glass has been found only in this part of Crete. The latest excavations have turned up tombs with jewellery and pottery. Tarrha was particularly noted as the site of a temple-sanctuary of Tarrhanean Apollo. Its inhabitants had a flourishing religion and mythology, involving not only Apollo but Acacallis (daughter of Minos and wife of Apollo) and the Cretan virgin-goddess Britomartis.

Chapel of St Paul

Just a few kilometres to the east of Ayia Roumeli is a delightful chapel on a little clearing some ten feet above the shore. It is known as the Chapel of St Paul, for he is said to have come ashore here and christened converts in a near-by spring (now only a trickle). The chapel is in the free cross form; its façade has an arcade of the Byzantine style from the twelfth century. It is not particularly spectacular, but is well worth a detour from Ayia Roumeli, and could be taken in on a walk down the coast to the east – a trip described in some detail, starting from Khora Sfakion (p. 227).

Selinou Province

Tucked away in the south-west corner of Crete is the province of Selinou, probably the least visited area of the island. Today it is noted for its fine olives and oil, but it has many ancient sites and historical monuments that deserve to be better known. None of them is very spectacular in itself, but taken as a whole they provide an interesting glimpse into the post-Minoan, Byzantine and Venetian periods of Crete. It is difficult to imagine that such isolated settlements could ever have 'made' history, but in their time they were involved in the power struggles of the Mediterranean. In the third century B.C., for instance, several of them – Elyros, Lissos, Hyrtakina, Syia and Poikilassos – formed the Confederation of Oreioi, allying with Gortyna and Cyrenaica under King Magus (p. 83). Under the Romans, some of these prospered; in the early Christian centuries, still others – Syia, in particular – came into their own. Later, many Byzantine churches and frescoes flowered, and the Venetians saw fit to develop some of the sites. What remains today is fragmentary and only partially explored; the definitive excavations and identifications have yet to be made. For the average traveller these remains will be too specialized; but anyone wishing to explore the area will find one generally available source to be *The Tourist's Guide to Khania* by Anestis Makridakis, which gives an impression of the history and remains of the region.

Route

Taking the Kastelli road westwards out of Khania (Route A on town plan), you follow that route for 19 km. to Tavronitis (pp. 236–7); there you turn left and continue to Kandanos [58 km.] and on to Palaiokhora [77 km.]. Alternatively, you could walk overland from Ayia Roumeli (p. 232), following the trails along and above the coast and visiting sites en route; but, although this is only about 25 km. as the crow flies, at least two or three days would have to be allowed, for the distance walked would come to at least twice that.

Bus

The buses for Kandanos, Palaiokhora and other places in Selinou Province leave from 1866 Square in Khania.

Accommodation

There are an hotel, the *Livikon* (Class D), and restaurants at Palaiokhora, with the possibility of light refreshments en route.

Follow the road westwards out of Khania as described on the excursion to Kastelli-Kissamou (pp. 236–7).

[19 km.] At **Tavronitis** turn left and south, passing along by the river through cultivated land and starting to climb slowly.

[28 km.] **Voukolies** is notable for its Byzantine *Church of Ayios Konstantinos in Nembros*, on the left just before reaching the village, and for the market, or bazaar, that draws many visitors on Saturday.

[42 km.] Soon after **Mesavlia** you enter the province of Selinou.

[48 km.] **Floria** has two fifteenth-century Byzantine churches with frescoes: the *Church of Ayii Pateres* in Epano (Higher) Floria and the *Church of Ayios Georgios* in Kato (Lower) Floria.

[58 km.] **Kandanos**. During the Second World War this village won such a reputation as a centre of resistance against the Germans that they destroyed it, but today it has largely been rebuilt. This whole region is noted for its Byzantine churches and their frescoes. In Kandanos itself there is the *Church of Ayia Paraskevi*; and in the hamlet of **Anisaraki**, a few kilometres to the north-east of Kandanos, are the *Churches of Ayia Ana, Panayia, Ayia Paraskevi* and *Ayios Georgios*, all with fine wall-paintings.

[64 km.] **Kakodiki** is also known for its Byzantine remains, including a wall-painting in the fourteenth-century *Church of the Archangel Michael*, just before you enter the village.

[77 km.] At the crossroads on the edge of **Palaiokhora** a left turn leads down into the harbour; the right turn takes you into the town.

Palaiokhora

Palaiokhora is a small place, once known locally as 'the bride of the Libyan Sea'. It is also known as Selinou Kastelli, after the Venetian fort on its promontory. As it has an hotel and several eating-places, it makes a convenient spot to spend some days while making excursions in the region. There is good bathing from a sandy beach on the west side of the peninsula.

As mentioned above, it would be possible to walk overland to Ayia Roumeli, taking two to three days to visit the sites en route – *Hyrtakina* and *Elyros* inland to the north-east of Palaiokhora and *Lissos* and *Syia* on the coast, and then on via *Poikilassos*. Incidentally, there is a bus from 1866 Square in Khania to the modern village of **Souyia** where the site of Syia is located; Lissos is a fifteen-minute boat trip from Souyia to the west. There is also a bus from 1866 Square to **Rodovani**, which is the nearest large village to Elyros and Hyrtakina. Both these services do not return to Khania until the following morning.

Gavdhos Island

A more interesting possibility for most tourists would be an excursion to the island of Gavdhos, some 50 km. off shore from Palaiokhora. It has the distinction of being the southernmost territory of Europe – once you concede that Crete belongs to Greece and Greece belongs to Europe. A boat leaves once a week from

Palaiokhora, but with luck you might catch a *caique* at any time. You might also catch a ride from one of the other ports along the south coast – Ayia Roumeli, Khora Sfakion or Ayia Galini.

Little is known about the island's exact history. There are some ruins to be seen, but although surface finds from Neolithic times have been claimed, it was most probably not settled until post-Minoan times. Some have claimed it as Calypso's island; if so, it is not hard to see why Odysseus kept moving. In Acts xxvii 16 it is mentioned by its Roman name, Clauda. It was also known as Kaudos. By the Middle Ages, it was actually the see of a bishop. It has probably seen its share of pirates come and go, too. Today less than two hundred people live there, supporting themselves by the flocks of sheep. The village of **Kastri** passes as its capital, but the general impression of the island is of a desolate landscape and deserted houses. A few kilometres north-west of Gavdhos is the islet of *Gavdhopoula*, a deserted spot used for pasturing sheep.

Kastelli-Kissamou and North-west Crete

This region of Crete reveals still another practically unknown island: rough terrain; a primitive landscape of valleys, mountains and isolated villages; unexplored ruins. For the traveller with two or three days to spare, an excursion into this region can be a unique experience.

Route
Take the road west out of Khania (Route A on town plan) and drive along the coast to Kastelli-Kissamou [42 km.].
Bus
Buses from 1866 Square in Khania run to Kastelli-Kissamou, Rodhopou and Platanos (for Phalasarna, see below; this bus does not return until the following morning).
Accommodation
There are three hotels in Kastelli-Kissamou: the *Kastelli* (Class C) and the *Kissamos* and the *Morfes* (both Class E). There are several possible eating-places.

[3 km.] On the left is an imposing eagle. It had been erected by the Germans as a memorial to their parachute assault on Crete in the Second World War; the Cretans have chosen to leave it there – as their own memorial.

[11 km.] The village of **Platanias** straggles along the road surrounded by bamboo and banana groves. At several little restaurants here you can eat delicious *dolmadákia* and *souvlákia* (p. 113); one of them, the *Milos*, is enhanced by its situation – beside the mill stream of a mill that is still used. On the opposite side of the road fine sandy beaches run along the coast. Off shore you should note the *Island of Ayios Theodhoros*, the ancient Akytos. It has a cave that seems to have been used as a place of worship around 2000 b.c.; its mouth looks like the gaping jaws of some beast, and legend has it that the island was once a wild animal that tried to devour Crete but was petrified by the gods. The Venetians and Turks used the island as a fortress, and now it is a sanctuary for the *agrími*. There are two or three dozen of these wild goats there at present.

[18 km.] **Maleme** is the site of the airport where the decisive battle for Crete was fought by the invading German airborne forces (p. 88).

[19 km.] Driving along through the valley of the Tavronitis river (from *távros* = 'bull') you come to the village of **Tavronitis**. This is where a turn to the south inland would take you to **Kandanos** and **Palaiokhora** in *Selinou Province* (p. 233).

[23 km.] Keeping along the coast road, a right fork brings you almost immediately into the village of **Kolymvarion**, situated just within the curve of the Rodhopou Peninsula. Kolymvarion has an inn and a restaurant and is noted for its wines.

Rodhopou Peninsula was known in ancient times as Cape Tityros; today it is sometimes called Cape Spatha, after its outermost point. It is one of two peninsulas that crown this end of Crete like bulls' horns; the western peninsula is *Cape Vouxa*, and between them lies the Gulf of Kissamos. At its widest part, Rodhopou Peninsula is only some 8 km. across, but its central ridge rises to 750 m.

If you proceed on to the peninsula, about 1 km. past Kolymvarion you will come to the *Monastery of Ghonia*, overlooking the coast and the Gulf of Khania. Also known as Odhiyitrias, the monastery was founded in 1618, burnt down by the Turks in 1645, re-erected in 1662, restored in 1798 and raised by another storey in 1874–84. Although it has a fort-like appearance, the Venetian influence is evident, especially with the baroque decoration of the refectory door. It counts among its attractions a handsome main gate, a rich treasury and several fine icons of the sixteenth and seventeenth centuries – particularly a crucifixion by Paleokapas. The monastery observes its main feast-day on August 15th. A new Orthodox Academy has recently been built just beyond the monastery for international theological conferences.

Continuing past the monastery, the road ends in another 3 km. at **Afrata**, from where it is about an hour's walk to the *Cave of Helleno-spilios*. The cave is quite long, with many corridors and pools, stalactites and stalagmites; many archaeological finds, including some from Neolithic times, have been made here.

Still another $3\frac{1}{2}$ to 4 hours' walk would bring you to the little port of **Ayios Georgios Kanzilieris**, near where is located the site of *Dhiktinaia*, named after the goddess Dictynna. It was from this spot that the nymph Dictynna (alias Britomartis, alias Artemis) threw herself to escape from the lustful Minos. She was saved by the nets of fishermen – her name is derived from 'net' – and has since been venerated in western Crete as everything from a goddess of nets to a moon-goddess. At times the whole peninsula was called after her – Dhiktinaion. There was a Hellenistic temple to her on the site; this was replaced by a Roman temple in the second century A.D., and it is mainly the remains of this that are to be seen.

Back on the main road to Kastelli-Kissamou, and opposite the turning to the Monastery of Ghonia and the Rodhopou peninsula, a road to the left brings you in 3 km. to **Spilia**, noted for its Byzantine art. Just through the village (turn right) are two churches: *Our Lady*, higher up and reached by a path, has fourteenth-century frescoes, superb examples of the Cretan school; while the *Church of Michael Arkhangelos* has a fine altar-piece. Above the village is a cave with a natural interior amphitheatre.

[26 km.] Continuing westwards along the main road, you come to a right turn that leads on to the Rodhopou peninsula again and arrives in 6 km. at the village of **Rodhopou**. If you drove on another 15 km. inland, and then walked for about 10 minutes, you would come to the *Church of St John Giona*, where a festival is held each August 28th and 29th. It is probably the largest religious festival in the entire nome of Khania, and crowds from the whole western part of Crete gather here.

Back on the main road, you continue driving through a distinctive landscape of dry earth, limestone slopes, olive trees and vines.

[42 km.] **Kastelli-Kissamou.**

This is the site of the ancient Kissamos, port for Polyrhinia (see below). Kissamos was an autonomous post-Minoan settlement; the Romans took it over – remains of their aqueduct are still to be seen; and in the early Christian era it became an episcopal seat. The Venetians chose to develop the site; they made it the see of a Catholic bishop, encouraged trade and constructed walls in the mid-sixteenth century (of which vestiges remain), doubtless using material from ancient Kissamos. A Venetian church survives, and there is a little collection of archaeological finds from the region in the central square (the key is with the schoolteacher). Present-day Kastelli is quite rural in appearance, but it is the centre for the production and trade of the wines of the district; and there are hotels (p. 236). On Sundays a delicious garlic roast pork is said to be available in town. A near-by nunnery, Parthenonas, is noted for its woven fabrics.

Polyrhinia

In Kastelli-Kissamou a sharp left fork leads in 7 km. to the village of Polyrhinia. Then a 10 minutes' walk up the hill brings you to the scattered remains of ancient Polyrhinia – 'town of many flocks'. At some 275 m. above sea-level, it enjoys an excellent view over the Gulf of Kissamos. Founded during the eighth century B.C., Polyrhinia was one of the chief settlements of Archaic Crete. Statues, bas-reliefs and coins contribute to the image of a once-influential city that probably dominated much of the area because of its strategic position. The worship of such familiar gods as Apollo, Hermes, Dionysus, Dictynna-Artemis and Zeus is indicated by the coins. The foundations of cyclopean walls, aqueducts, reservoirs, temples and some graves carved in rock-caves are to be seen, but the inhabitants of the area have used much of the material over the centuries. The near-by *Church of the Ninety-nine Holy Fathers*, for instance, has probably utilized parts of older temples.

Phalasarna

If you proceed westwards along the main coast road from Kastelli, the road turns to the south after about 4 km., and then after another 7 km. reaches **Platanos**, where there is a frescoed church of uncertain date; the bus stops here. In this village, a right fork takes you along a bad road, bearing left in **Kavousion** over the hill and down to the sea. Continuing northwards along the coast you come eventually to the fragmentary remains of the post-Minoan city of Phalasarna (some 20 km. from Kastelli).

The site of Phalasarna was first explored early in this century, but not much in the way of a conclusive history has yet been provided. It probably served as a port for Polyrhinia. It seems to have had its temple to Dictynna-Artemis, but no particular palace – although there is a so-called throne carved out of the rock. The bulk of the remains – remnants of walls, reservoirs, quarries, houses, storage rooms and tombs – probably date from the Hellenic and Roman periods. With the great shifting of Crete – placed in the sixth century A.D. – Phalasarna's port installations were left high and dry and are now some metres inland. Phalasarna sits on its promontory, in all its megalithic, isolated splendour, looking out across the Mediterranean to the west.

Above Phalasarna protrudes *Cape Vouxa*, the ancient peninsula of Korykia, now virtually deserted. Off the tip of the peninsula are two islets: the one to the north is *Agria* ('wild') *Gramvousa*, and the other *Imeri* ('tame') *Gramvousa*. The latter is a precipitous, almost unassailable islet that is probably one of the oldest Mediterranean pirate lairs. The Venetians constructed a fortress here and it was one of the last three hold-outs against the Turks, capitulating only in 1692. Eventually the Christian Cretans managed to get it back, and marauders operating from there became a nuisance to all parties. The fort is in fair condition and there are caves, a frescoed Byzantine church and some Venetian structures to be explored if you can find a *caique* to take you out.

At the northern end of the cape, on the east coast, is the Doric site of *Agneion*, with its shrine to Apollo. It is one of many little-known sites in western Crete that are being investigated by archaeologists.

Nunnery of Khrysoskalitisa

This is an excursion that would appeal only to a few who would like to explore the remotest parts of Crete. It is a nunnery down on the south-west corner of the province of Kissamou, and the road is not very good, although it can be driven along. You start by driving out of Kastelli-Kissamou back towards Khania; then turn right on to a side road in the village of **Kaloudiana**, 5 km. out from Kastelli-Kissamou. This road passes through such villages as **Potamida**,

Topolia (beyond this village can be seen on the right the large *Cave of Ayia Sophia*), **Elos**, **Kouneni** and **Stomion** before reaching the nunnery – a distance of some 36 km. from the main road. The road curves and climbs through the mountain landscape that the local people call 'the Switzerland of Crete'; it is quite lush, almost tropical, and is especially noted for its chestnut trees. The nunnery sits on a rocky promontory above the sea; if you have come as far as this you can count on the usual Cretan hospitality, and there is a beach near by.

ROUTE 5: IRAKLION TO AYIOS NIKOLAOS (VIA MALLIA)

This is one of those unique excursions through time that Crete offers; to take advantage of the many points of interest en route, you should have your own transport and a long day. The palace of Mallia – contemporary with those at Knossos and Phaestos – is merely the chief attraction of the trip; the other sights will come more as surprises.

Route
Leaving Iraklion by the St George Gate (Route C on town plan), you descend sharply round a corner. Continue through the fairly modern suburb of Poros and then along the coast road for Mallia [35 km.], Neapolis [55 km.] and Ayios Nikolaos [70 km.].

Bus
There are frequent buses to Ayios Nikolaos via Mallia; they depart from Beaufort Avenue in Iraklion and the trip takes about 2 to 2½ hours. Careful planning should allow a person to get an early bus, visit Mallia and pick up a later bus to go on from there.

Accommodation
There are several hotels along the north coast; some near Iraklion (p. 120) and others at Stalis, Mallia and Neapolis.

[3 km.] You come down to sea-level at *Katsamba*, at the mouth of the Kairatos river and once a harbour town serving Knossos. The river is still here, but dries up for much of the year. Excavations have turned up remains of houses and tombs, some yielding rich artifacts and testifying to the continuous habitation of the site from Neolithic through late Minoan times.

[4 km.] Climbing slightly, you emerge on a flat stretch where, to the right, is a Greek Army Officers' Training School.

[5 km.] Iraklion Airport.

[6 km.] Swinging down through a gully, you pass a small wayside chapel on the right, and then, to the left, *Karteros Beach* – known as 'Florida Beach' – a popular swimming spot.

[8 km.] There is a turning to the right signposted Episkopi; if you take this, you wind up a road about 1½ km. to where there is a small sign on the left of the roadside, indicating the *Cave of Eileithyia*. The fig tree that marks the cave's entrance, several yards down the slope, is most suitable for this 'womb of the earth', the fig being an ancient symbol of fertility. The cave itself offers a glimpse into the truly primitive side of Cretan culture. It was first explored in the 1880s by Hadzidakis and Halbherr, although the local people had never really 'lost' it. It is known that the cave was a shrine and habitation in the Neolithic era, well before 3000 B.C. and the later Minoan civilization. Through Minoan times it was revered as a sacred spot, dedicated to manifestations of the Nature Goddess in general and to Eileithyia the 'liberator', goddess of childbirth, in particular. It retained its prestige throughout Crete's history, and is mentioned in the *Odyssey* (Book XIX), when Odysseus, disguised as a beggar, lies to Penelope and claims that Odysseus put in at Amnisos, 'where the Cave of Eileithyia is'.

You can walk about 50 m. into the cave; burning rolled news-paper or brushwood is more impressive than a **flash**light. It can be slippery. There is a sacred stalagmite, or lingam, and always the possibility of finding a shard of pottery from some ancient votive offering.

Back on the main Iraklion to Ayios Nikolaos road, almost immediately after the turning to the Cave of Eileithyia, there is a sign to Amnisos beach on the left. Down this turning, before you reach the beach, just off to the left are the remains of *Amnisos*, surrounded by barbed wire. Amnisos was a Minoan settlement, sometimes referred to as the port or 'naval headquarters' of Knos-sos. It was from here that Idomeneus and his ships left for the Trojan War. Vestiges of several buildings have been discovered here, including the Altar of Zeus Thenatas and the Villa of the Lilies. It has been suggested that this villa was the home of the port commander.

Continuing east on the main road, you follow the shore round the flank of *Kakon Oros*, the mountains that descend sharply to the sea here – a delightful drive. Off shore is the islet of *Dia*, another of the island refuges for the wild goats of Crete.

[13 km.] After swinging around a curve you pass on the left a small house with a well and a tree. Opposite are the remains of the Minoan *megaron* of *Nirou Khani*, excavated by Evans and Xanthoudides in 1919. The remains are not spectacular, but important finds were made there: great bronze double axes, oil lamps, vases, tripod altars – all to be seen now in the Iraklion museum. They were found in such concentration that it is thought that this was the dwelling of some high functionary of the Minoan state religion, who may have acted as a 'distributor' of these religious objects through the small port at this spot. Evans reported sighting a sub-merged quarry and column bases in the harbour here.

[16 km.] Just past the little village of **Gournes** on the slopes to the right, you come across on the left one of the most unexpected sights in Crete – an American Air Force Station. It is virtually a pocket of the twentieth century, and, although it has acted as a great stimulus to the local economy, it is surely one of the strangest labyrinths ever erected on this island.

[24 km.] To the right is the side road that leads up into the mountains to the *Lasithi Plain* and the *Dhiktaian Cave* (p. 161).

[27 km.] Driving on into the village of **Limin Khersonisou**, a turning to the left – to the sea – brings you to a curious *Roman fountain* with fragmentary mosaics and gutters for the water to run through. Farther along at the end of the promontory is the little *Church of St Nicholas*, on the site of a sixth-century basilica. Kherso-nisos is said to have been the trading port for the city of Lyttos (p. 166) and Evans reported seeing submerged house walls along the shore here.

[31 km.] Proceeding along the main road, you reach the village of **Stalis**; it has a fine beach with palm trees. There is comfortable accommodation and a restaurant at the *Blue Sea Motel* (Class B), as well as *tavernas* that provide simple meals.

As you continue along the road you find yourself entering the bay and plain of Mallia, spread out at the foot of the Lasithi Mountains. Hundreds of windmills can be seen; they pump water for the farm-ing carried on here, which includes banana-growing.

[35 km.] You arrive in the village of **Mallia**, with its cafés, *tavernas* and a beach that is reputed to be the finest on Crete. This is reached by taking the road to the left out of the centre of the village and then winding through the fields and groves to the sea. With its clean white sand, and its little off-shore islet and chapel, this beach makes a perfect retreat. There is a delightful hotel that provides full pension, the *Grammatikakis* (Class B), and a new hotel, the *Mallia Beach* (also Class B). You could also find cheaper accommodation in the village.

[38 km.] Proceeding eastwards on the main road out of Mallia village, you come to a side road to the left, signposted to Mallia Palace. You take this road and head towards the sea; on the right, you pass the ruins of a *megaron*, of interest mainly to specialists. A short way farther on is the small house used by the caretaker and the French Archaeological School. Hadzidakis had made the initial excavations during the Second World War, but the French eventually took over the site and have continued to make important finds here.

MALLIA PALACE

Although not as dramatic as those of Knossos or Phaestos, the remains of the palace of Mallia are relatively well preserved, with a minimum of restoration. There is no better way to feel the authenticity and delights of a Minoan palace than to stroll through this site on a good day, when Mallia seems to hover between the mountains and the sea. Although the original name of the palace site is still unknown, the history of the structures is generally analogous to those of Knossos and Phaestos. After a first Neolithic settlement on the site, which was relatively small and short-lived, the first palace was begun about 2000 B.C., a new and more splendid palace was built around 1700–1650 B.C., and both of these were destroyed by the great catastrophe of about 1450 B.C. (now accepted by some scholars to have been the eruption and tidal wave from Santorini, the volcanic island to the north). What we see today are principally the remains of the splendid second palace, traditionally associated with King Sarpedon, brother of Minos and Rhadamanthys. And like its history, the basic pattern of the palace here resembles that familiar from Knossos and Phaestos: the large central court, the various corridors, chambers and stairways, the storage magazines, the royal quarters, the signs of religious life, etc.

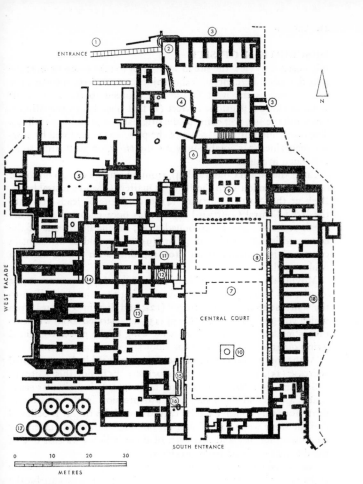

Mallia

1 Flagstoned Street
2 Main Entrance Hall
3 Storage Magazines
4 North Courtyard
5 King's Quarters
6 Corridor
7 Central Court
8 Colonnades
9 Pillared Hall

10 Sacrificial Pit
11 Throne Room
12 Staircase
13 Pillar Crypt
14 West Corridor
15 Ceremonial Staircase
16 Kernos
17 Cisterns or Storage Silos
18 Storage Magazines and Museum

DESCRIPTION OF SITE

It is possible to view the site in an hour or to take much longer; the tour described here includes the major features. You approach the palace towards the west façade and proceed to the north end; walking along a flagstoned street (1) that once led to the Minoan town and the sea, you come to the original main Entrance Hall (2). The north and north-east sides of the palace were enclosed by storage magazines (3); notable now are the *pithoi*, or giant urns, some decorated in relief.

Enter the North Courtyard (4), from which you can go on to the north-west section with the King's Quarters (5) and a lustral basin. Back at the North Courtyard (4), a corridor (6) leads you into the large Central Courtyard (7). It was once enclosed along the north and east sides by colonnades (8); on the north side of the courtyard is a fine hall with pillars (9). In the middle of the main courtyard is a sacrificial pit (10), the only such one found in a Minoan palace.

Moving down the west side of the courtyard, you come first to a loggia, the 'throne room'(11), overlooking the courtyard; then to the staircase to the second storey (12); and then into an area from which you go into the Pillar Crypt (13), a flagstoned room with two pillars marked with signs. The west wing of the palace contained living quarters and the West Corridor storage rooms (14).

At the south-west corner of the main courtyard is the ceremonial staircase (15), which led to the upper storey. Beside this staircase, still in situ, is a *kernos*, or offering table (16). It is a circular stone nearly a metre in diameter, with a depression in the centre and thirty-four tiny concave circles carved round the rim. It is believed that the stone was a sort of altar for offering thanks and prayers for continuing fertility and that each of these hollows was for one of the different seeds or crops produced on Crete.

Just outside the palace at the extreme south-west corner are eight cisterns or storage silos (17) – usually conceded to be the former, since Mallia Palace has yielded no other waterworks. Along the east side of the main courtyard are storage magazines (18); with their rebuilt walls and reconstructed roof, they now serve as a museum for the various artifacts found on the site. Of special interest is the ingenious way of storing wine and oil; all in all, this little display offers a glimpse into the domestic, commercial and ceremonial life of a Minoan palace.

In the area surrounding the palace, particularly to the north, excavations have revealed various houses, tombs and connecting roads. The only one of real interest to the amateur is the *Khrysolakkos* – 'pit of gold' – close to the sea. About 40 m. long and 30 m. wide, it contained many burial chambers, a columned hall and a sanctuary with an altar. It must have served as a communal tomb for the royal family. It was plundered long ago, but random surface finds of gold gained it its name; and when it finally was excavated it did yield several treasures (now in the Iraklion museum), including the exquisite honeybee pendant.

[45 km.] Having returned to the main road to Ayios Nikolaos, you climb up from the coastal plain and continue driving through a dramatic ravine. Where the road widens, on the right stands the *Monastery of Selinaris*, now a home for the elderly. Its chapel is dedicated to St George, and it is customary for travellers – including buses – to stop here and say a few prayers for a safe journey. In the chapel is a rather incongruous, if typically Greek, scene: an impressive modern safe to hold the offerings and, alongside, the little silver simulacra, or *támata*, of the various parts of the human anatomy that people want cured or blessed – arms, heads, eyes, torsos, moulded in metal and crowding round the altar. Outside the chapel is a tree that has lovely flowers in early summer. Fresh spring water is to be had, and across the road is a small inn with more elaborate refreshments. The monastery is the place for one of the largest festivals on the name-day of St George, April 23rd.

[48 km.] Still climbing along a narrow curved road, you come to the mountain town of **Vrakhasi**. From here you go through a pass and descend.

[55 km.] **Neapolis**, the central town for this region, with its leisurely, provincial air, yet just enough bustle of buses and markets. It is the judicial capital of Lasithi Nome, so it gets the court traffic. The people of Neapolis pride themselves on their intellectual traditions: their schools, library, and even a small collection of antiquities from the region, displayed in the *museum* just off the central square, which is a fine shaded park. (You may have to ask for the museum key from the teacher at the local school in the square.) It was on the outskirts of Neapolis, too, in the village of Kares, that Peter Philargis was born in 1340 – the man who became Pope Alexander V (p. 99).

Neapolis has one main hotel, the *Vassilikon* (Class C); the Tourist Police could make other arrangements. There are several eating-places; one of the local specialities is *soumádha*, a milky drink made from almonds.

There is a fairly good road that climbs south from Neapolis and across the mountains to the *Lasithi Plain* and *Dhiktaian Cave* (p. 161).

[57 km.] But proceeding eastwards, just outside Neapolis, you approach a row of turret-like structures on the left that turn out to be old windmills placed so as to catch the winds. At the village of **Nikithiano** by these mills there is a side road to the left. If you are serious about examining all the sites, you can take this turning and at about 4 km. you will come to the outskirts of the village of **Kastelli**; there another turning on to a track up to the left would allow you to drive for another 1½ km. At a white chapel you must get out and walk up over the fields for another 2 km. to reach the remains of *Dreros*. You are advised to get someone from one of the villages to guide you, as the site needs some searching out – and a bit of climbing. Dreros was an Archaic settlement, with an acropolis that dominated the passes and plains of the vicinity. Its harbour was Olous (p. 255) and together these two cities were said to have counted many thousands of inhabitants. The French, excavating here in the 1930s, found the remains of a small temple of Apollo Delphinios; they also found some small bronze idols, made by hammering the metal over a wooden core – a technique for which the Cretans were famed. In addition, they found two bilingual Eteocretan-Greek inscriptions that will undoubtedly prove crucial in the final decipherment of the Eteocretan language (p. 270).

If you choose to go on from Dreros down to Elounda, a village on the coast which can easily be reached from Ayios Nikolaos, you return to the road just before the village of Kastelli and continue through that village and those of **Phourni** and **Pines**. You will wonder how anyone makes a living from such miserable ground, but perhaps the people are compensated by the wonderful view over the Gulf of Merabello and the Sitia mountains. From **Elounda** (p. 254), there is a good asphalt road into Ayios 'Nikolaos; but this road over the mountains via Kastelli to Elounda is extremely rough and the whole expedition is recommended only for the most persistent.

[70 km.] Most people will have stayed on the main road to **Ayios Nikolaos**, and after some hairpin bends and a fine view of the Gulf of Merabello and the mountains of Sitia in the distance, you descend to **Ayios Nikolaos**. For the harbour keep left at a fork as you enter the town. Along the coast to the left is the Minos Beach Hotel.

AYIOS NIKOLAOS

This little port has now become something of a tourist centre as a result of the Minos Beach Hotel. Besides its own attractions it is the point from which one can visit the sites of eastern Crete.

Population 3,665.
Sea connections
See p. 34.
Information
The Tourist Office is at present being run from the headquarters of the Tourist Police, which is near the bottomless pool (*Map* **5**).
Hotels
Luxury: *Minos Beach* (bungalows; restaurant in attractive central building; luxury amenities, including water-skiing, etc.).
Class C: *Hotel du Lac*.
Class D: *Lato* (overlooking harbour).
Class E: *Aegeon*.
　　　　Athinai.
At least two new hotels are being built at Ayios Nikolaos and there are several pensions; including the *Delphini* near the Minos Beach.
Youth hostel
There is a youth hostel in the town (*Map* **1**). See p. 48 for regulations.
Restaurants
There is the usual choice of restaurants, *tavernas* and cafés.
Swimming
There are several fine beaches on the outskirts of Ayios Nikolaos. One in particular is on the road that goes from the harbour to the Minos Beach bungalows.
Buses
There are services to Iraklion (and places en route, including Mallia); to Sitia (and places en route, including Gournia); to Ierapetra (also via Gournia); to Kritsa; to Elounda; and to Psykhro (for the Dhiktaian Cave). There is a list of times and destinations outside the bus station (*Map* **4**).

HISTORY

Ayios Nikolaos is a quiet little port-town, noted for its healthy climate and fine beaches. Although it is officially the capital of

I

Lasithi Nome, the town and its people seem unimpressed by this. It is an especially neat and clean town: shady trees, whitewashed kerbs, everything well tended – down by the harbour you could almost believe you were in a Dutch or Scandinavian village. But it pays a price for all this: it has no ruins or buildings of any interest to the traveller!

The town of Ayios Nikolaos is comparatively new – largely built since 1870 – and somewhat artificial: a small creek was made into the harbour when it was decided to establish the town on the hillside. During the nineteenth century many Sfakians seeking employment and a new lease of life settled here. The chief attraction of the town is the harbour, with its nonchalant activity: a naval patrol keeps guard, an occasional fishing boat puts in, and the cafés create what excitement there is. On the promontory that forms the southern side of the harbour, and up near the modern Prefecture, was the site of some ancient acropolis, as well as the Venetians' Castle of Merabello (there are only a few remains).

PRINCIPAL SIGHTS

Museum

This contains a small collection of antiquities from eastern Crete. In 1968 the museum was temporarily closed; inquire at the Tourist Office whether it has re-opened.

'Bottomless Pool'

Perhaps the most spectacular attraction of the town is the dark, so-called 'bottomless pool', Lake Voulismeni, situated some yards to the west of the harbour. It is not volcanic in origin; more probably it is the aperture of some subterranean river that comes out here after draining down from the mountains. It is known by some as 'the bath of Athena'; there is also the legend that a secret passage connects it to Santorini, the volcanic island north of Crete. The pond's diameter is about 60 m., and despite its reputation for being bottomless, certain sceptics have claimed that the water gets quite solid about 64 m. down.

Almyros

To the north of Ayios Nikolaos, a few hundred metres from the sea, is one of the three brackish springs to be found along the north

Ayios Nikolaos

1 Youth Hostel
2 'Bottomless Pool'
3 Post Office
4 Bus station
5 Tourist Police

A route to
    Minos Beach Hotel
    Elounda and Spinalonga (p. 254)

B route to
    Lasithi Plain and Dhiktaian Cave
    (p. 161)
    Mallia (p. 244)
    Iraklion
C route to
    Kritsa and Lato (p. 252)
    Gournia (p. 258)
    Ierapetra (p. 256)
    Sitia and Eastern Crete (including
    Kato Zakros) (p. 258)

coast. On Ascension Day the people of Ayios Nikolaos gather at the church here for a festival with dances and fireworks.

EXCURSIONS FROM AYIOS NIKOLAOS

See Chart of Excursions, facing p. 29, for other places of interest described on routes to and from Ayios Nikolaos.

Kritsa and Lato

Kritsa, one of the largest and most attractive villages in this part of Crete, is principally known for its Byzantine chapels. Lato is another of those minor sites that, while not comparable with the great palaces, reward those who are willing to explore Crete.

Route
Take the road out of Ayios Nikolaos as for Ierapetra and Sitia (Route C on town plan), but just outside the town turn sharp right and continue up into the hills as far as Kritsa [12 km.].
Bus
There are daily buses to and from Kritsa: to reach Lato you must either have your own transport, hire a taxi in the village or be prepared for a walk of about one hour.

[2 km.] Take the right-hand side turning for Kritsa.

[10 km.] A short track to the right, signposted *Pros Cèran*, leads to a white church standing in the middle of an olive grove and surrounded by white walls. This is the chief glory of Kritsa and one of the jewels of Byzantine art: the fourteenth-century *Church of Panayia Kera* (All-Holy Lady). There are three naves, with corresponding apses, of which the south nave is the oldest; tambour and buttresses were added considerably later. The frescoes, dating from the fourteenth and fifteenth centuries, are accepted as one of the major triumphs of Byzantine art. They have been partly restored, but their strength and art derive from the originals. Scenes from the life of the Virgin are depicted on the vaults with some realism; saints and evangelists are portrayed along the walls and, with their rich gowns, muscular lineaments and intense eyes, they make an overpowering impact. Frescoes such as these would make the fortune of a town on the main route; here in Kritsa they go almost unnoticed (although many people have now had a glimpse of them through the Walt Disney film of *The Moonspinners*).

[12 km.] **Kritsa.**

The main asphalt road leads on to become the narrow, winding main street of Kritsa and eventually opens up to become its main square. The village has a spectacular position, clinging to the steep mountain-side and with a superb view over the Gulf of Merabello – especially from all those balconied houses that crowd the slopes. The people of this region have kept up the traditional handicrafts, particularly in textiles, and the villagers are very willing to show their work to anyone who may be interested in buying. It was in Kritsa, incidentally, that the film version of the Kazantzakis novel *The Greek Passion* (or *Christ Recrucified*) was made; it was called *He Who Must Die*. The director was the American Jules Dassin (later known for his *Never on Sunday*); the principal actors were French and Greek, and many of the local people appeared. Although the setting of the novel was Anatolia, both history and the film make the Cretan setting quite legitimate.

A left fork off the main street brings you, after a five-minute walk out of the village, to the little *Church of Ayios Georgios Kavousiotis* on the left of the road; it contains some Byzantine frescoes. There are several other attractive small churches in the neighbourhood of Kritsa.

Lato

Just before entering Kritsa, a signpost to the right directs you along a dirt road that passes the cemetery; after 3½ km. the road ends just below the remains of Lato; the site is reached by a footpath up the hillside to the right. The road as far as this footpath can just be travelled by car; walking the total distance from the asphalt road takes about an hour.

Lato was originally explored by Evans, but the French took charge of the excavations there early in the twentieth century. Founded in the seventh century B.C., probably as a Doric settlement, most of the remains date from later, Hellenistic times – mainly the third century B.C. The extensive remains rise in banks or tiers, with two acropolises, fortifications, houses, shops, cisterns and roads. The market-place, the magistrate's house and a temple have also been identified. In its day, Lato must have been a fairly strong and prosperous city. Among its curiosities is a circle of stones – a rotunda of some kind, perhaps a ceremonial area – and recent excavations are turning up still more structures. But it is the setting of Lato that is its principal charm: the fine view down across the almond and olive trees to the coast and the Gulf of Merabello.

Elounda and Spinalonga

The little fishing village of Elounda is an ideal place to spend a quiet evening – rather like being on some calm fiord. Although seldom visited and insignificant now, Elounda has seen its share of history. The near-by site of Olous was originally a Minoan settlement, and since then the inlet has witnessed the comings and goings of Greeks, Romans, Venetians, Turks, French, English, Italians and Germans. Under the Venetians it was an important trading port and even now largish merchant ships lie off shore; during the 1930s English hydroplanes used the bay.

Route
A decent asphalt road leads from Ayios Nikolaos (Route A on town plan), past Minos Beach and along the coast to Elounda [11 km.]. (This road was laid down to facilitate the filming of *The Moonspinners* (p. 253).) It is also possible to drive to Elounda from the site of Dreros (p. 248).
Bus
There is a bus service from Ayios Nikolaos to Elounda.
Sea
You can hire a boat in Ayios Nikolaos to take you direct to Elounda; the Tourist Police will help you to do this. The fare should be about Drs 30 per person (round trip), with a maximum of about Drs 120 for a party of reasonable size.
Accommodation
At Elounda there is a modest little hotel, the *Nea Elounda* (Class E) where you can get meals.

[11 km.] Just before reaching the village of **Elounda**, a track, sign-posted Olous, forks sharply backwards to the right. A fifteen-minute walk takes you along a built-up causeway across the salt flats, and over a small bridge across the channel between the large peninsula of Spinalonga and the isthmus linking it to the mainland. The French are credited with these constructions during the occupation by the Great Powers at the end of the nineteenth century. There are also old abandoned mills to be seen. The salt flats – which are still operated as a state monopoly – are filled with sea water; the dykes are then blocked and the water evaporates, leaving the salt.

Olous

The ancient part of the remains of Olous are along the edge of the peninsula, to the right; they are now sunk beneath the water, owing to the island's shifting in the sixth century A.D. What you see is not very impressive, but skin-divers might find it worth exploring further. Ship-berths are clearly visible; Olous was the port for Dreros. There were once structures on land, including temples to Zeus and Britomartis, but the stone was carried off and used in walls and other buildings. The most interesting survival here is the *mosaic floor*, most likely the remains of an early Christian basilica. It is situated in a field about 100 m. from the shore; its fenced enclosure can be seen as you cross the bridge, to the right between two abandoned mills. The mosaic depicts some lively fishes and is worth crossing the field to see.

Spinalonga Island

Just to the north of the peninsula of Spinalonga is an islet of the same name; it can be seen across the bay from Elounda. The Venetians constructed a most impressive fortress here, and it became one of their last outposts on Crete; it was 1714 before the Venetians finally surrendered this fort to the Turks. The Turks held it until early in the twentieth century, when, under the administration of Prince George, it was converted into a leper colony. This has long since been dispersed and now the island is abandoned except for caretakers. A boat from Ayios Nikolaos or Elounda will take you round the island; if you want to go ashore, there is no risk of getting leprosy.

Psira and Mokhlos Islands

You can hire a boat from Ayios Nikolaos to take you to both these islands in the eastern reaches of the Gulf of Merabello; or it is possible to arrange a trip from the village of Mokhlos (p. 261), farther along the coast. The ideal way would be a cruise round the entire gulf, to include Elounda, Gournia and even Sitia.

The islands, which were excavated by Richard Seager during 1907–8, are barren now and without water, yet at one time they were active settlements for trade in eastern Crete. Psira, about 2 miles off shore, must once have had a spring to support its prosperous Minoan community. Finds from Psira indicate close relations with Egypt, Syria and Palestine. Houses contemporary with those of Gournia have been found, yielding stone and pottery vases as well as fragments of painted relief.

Mokhlos is only about 200 m. from the shore and was probably once a peninsula. An early Minoan necropolis was excavated here, and vases of alabaster, marble, breccia and steatite, some as thin as porcelain, were brought to light from a settlement that flourished in the Minoan Neo-palatial period.

Ierapetra

This is the largest town on the south coast of Crete, although it has long since lost whatever importance it enjoyed as a port of trade with Africa and Asia Minor. Today it is noted largely for its sandy beaches, rich vegetation, wine and hospitality – enough to entice many people for a visit.

Route
Follow the Sitia road (Route C on town plan) out of Ayios Nikolaos (pp. 258–261); after passing Gournia (p. 258), turn right at Pakhia Ammos [22 km.] to cross the island to Ierapetra [38 km.].

From Ierapetra you can recross the island to the main road along the north coast and then go either on to Sitia or back to Ayios Nikolaos. It is also possible to take an extremely poor road west to Ano Viannos, via Mournies and Pefko, with a detour to Arvi (p. 165). For the adventurous there is a route to the north-east, via Koutsouras on the coast and up through the mountains via Stavrokhorion to Sitia; this could take in visits to sites such as Praisos and Akhlada (p. 269).

Bus
There are regular services from Ayios Nikolaos to Ierapetra, taking about 1 hour. You could get the bus to drop you off at Gournia.

Accommodation
There are five hotels at Ierapetra: *Creta* and *Alkion* (Class C), *Alete* and *Arkhadi* (Class D) and *Venizelos* (Class E). There are plans to build a bungalow development on the coast near Ierapetra.

For the route as far as Gournia and Pakhia Ammos [22 km.], where you turn inland, see pp. 258–61.

[25 km.] Continuing southwards across the island, on your right is a knoll where the early Minoan settlement of *Vasiliki* was excavated by Seager early in this century. The site is about 1 km. to the right of the main road. (Incidentally, it can also be reached direct from the village of Pakhia Ammos by a track to the village of Vasiliki, which is near the excavations.) Dating from as early as 2500 B.C., the remains are of little interest to most people. What does concern us, though, is the extraordinary pottery found in graves around Vasiliki. This mottled red-and-black pottery is found elsewhere around the Mediterranean, but nowhere with such a brilliant quality as here; as a result, it has given its name to a basic pottery type, the 'Vasiliki flameware'.

[30 km.] Proceeding along the road to Ierapetra, you come to the village of **Episkopi**. Just to the left and below the road opposite the church square is a tiny *Byzantine Church* with a fine altar-piece.

[38 km.] **Ierapetra**.

Ierapetra offers fine swimming, and a small collection of antiquities in the *Town Hall*, just beyond the square with a statue. The prosperity of the town now rests on olive oil and tomatoes. It is also known for its local wine, which has been compared to everything from sparkling Burgundy to sweet port. There are hotels (opposite) and several decent eating-places, particularly around the central square and down along the beach.

The modern town is on an alluvial plain, with the town protruding into the sea. It is situated on the site of ancient Ierapytna, a Minoan harbour-town that grew to importance as a junction for trade between Crete and the African and Asian ports to the south and east. It must have been linked with Gournia as part of an overland route. The post-Minoan peoples kept up the port, and it is said to have been the last Cretan city to fall to the Romans under the Roman consul Metellus. It once had fine Roman buildings, including theatres, but little remains from that period. Later came the Venetians and the Turks. From this period survives the *Venetian Fort* to the west along the coast; four of the square towers are well preserved. Also in the western part of the town are a *Turkish Minaret* and *Fountain*. You may also be shown a house where it is claimed Napoleon passed a night, on his way either to or from Egypt; there is no evidence to support the claim, but it adds to the charm of the town.

ROUTE 6: AYIOS NIKOLAOS TO SITIA (VIA GOURNIA)

The drive to Sitia starts along a pleasant, although extremely winding, road, with the Gulf of Merabello off to the left, the sheer vertical rise of Mount Thrifti in the middle distance and the Sitia range in the far distance. There are a few straggling villages en route, in addition to the great site of Gournia, but it is the dramatic landscape that makes the trip – inlets, promontories, beaches and green slopes. You could also make a detour across the island to Ierapetra on the south coast (p. 256).

Route
Follow the road out of Ayios Nikolaos (Route C on town plan) and continue eastwards along the coast to Sitia [74 km.].
Bus
Bus services run from Ayios Nikolaos to Sitia (about 2½ hours); also to Ierapetra (about 1 hour); both these buses will drop or pick up passengers at Gournia.
Accommodation
You can stay at the Monastery of Faneromeni near Gournia; Ierapetra has hotels (p. 256); otherwise you will have to rely on village inns.

[2 km.] A right turn leads in 10 km. to **Kritsa** (p. 252).

[18 km.] A branch road to the right leads up to the *Monastery of Faneromeni*; it is not especially notable, but it can provide overnight accommodation for 5–6 people.

[19 km.] Proceeding to the flat land beside a small bay, the new road has a small sign to the right that points directly to *Gournia*, just beside the old road. Gournia deserves to be better known as one of the wonders of the archaeological world; here was uncovered not another Minoan palace but the almost complete remains of a Minoan town. It is a sort of 'poor man's Pompeii', and, although lacking the glamour of some of the great Mediterranean sites, should be visited by anyone who intends to go home feeling that he has seen Minoan civilization. There is a caretaker who may happen to be on the site; his English is adequate and with a little imagination you will understand his explanations of the site and its finds.

HISTORY OF GOURNIA

The name 'Gournia' is topographical: *gourni* is the trough from which barnyard animals drink, and the valley formed here as the land comes down to the sea resembles this trough. At this little bay on the narrowest section of Crete, sailors and traders of old probably beached their craft in order to take their cargo overland, thus avoiding the rough passage round the eastern end of the island. Ierapetra (p. 256) was at the other end of this commercial route. A settlement grew up and prospered, and by 1600 B.C. it must have been a flourishing town, self-supporting if not self-governing. Little is known of its exact relationship with the great Minoan powers to the west; certainly Gournia had some sort of ruler, whether an independent prince or a dependent governor. Undoubtedly its prosperity was linked with the wealth and influence of the great Minoan palace centres. But Gournia grew and functioned on its own terms, as a self-contained town with many of the features that we see in Greek towns today. It made no impact on the times, and when Minoan power declined Gournia declined. Probably it fell to marauders, was destroyed in a conflagration and then abandoned; this would have happened around 1500–1450 B.C. It was forgotten, and eventually disappeared from men's sight and minds. When the great age of Cretan excavation began, Gournia's whereabouts were not only unknown, its very existence was unsuspected. There were no traditions, no classical references, no remains.

Evans must be credited with arousing interest in discovering Gournia. It was his finds in the region which suggested that there was probably some sort of settlement. An American archaeologist, Miss Harriet Boyd, inspired by the find of a sealstone brought to her by a local Cretan, decided that the hypothetical settlement might be on the ridge where many potsherds had been discovered. Digging began in 1901, and by 1904 virtually the whole town had been unearthed: the answer to an archaeologist's dream. Miss Boyd (who married the English scholar Hawes and so is often referred to as Boyd-Hawes) was assisted by her American colleagues, Miss Hall and Richard Seager – not to mention the local people who did the actual digging.

DESCRIPTION OF SITE

The site is a limestone ridge, and the town – its streets and structures – was built to conform to the lie of the land, so that Gournia sprawls rather gracelessly over the hillside. It was never fortified, and it was quite exposed except for what protection the sea afforded.

On top of the hill – we hesitate to call such an unclassical place the 'acropolis' – was the 'palace': a miniature Minoan palace, even less ambitious than Ayia Triadha. There were stairways, pillars, courts and the usual apartments; but nothing is particularly grand in comparison with the rest of the town nor is the palace particularly isolated from the community. There was an *agora*, or public market-place, and a small sanctuary where cult objects were found, showing that the Mother Goddess was worshipped here: terracotta images twined with snakes, doves, tripods, the double axe. But none of these really add to our knowledge of Minoan rituals. It is as a revelation of domestic economy that Gournia is valuable, for within and around the houses and shops were found objects invaluable for the study of the life of the 'middle' and 'lower' classes: vats for washing oil; a forge with a mould for casting chisels, awls and nails; loom weights; a carpenter's kit, including saws, files, axes, chisels and nails; and many other artifacts now in the Archaeological Museum in Iraklion.

Up and down the streets you may walk, stepping in and out of the houses. Stairways are still in place; the low doorways and second storeys of the houses are clearly indicated. It is all very familiar to anyone who has strolled through a contemporary Greek mountain village; some of these houses at Gournia would need little except roofs to be habitable as modern peasants' homes. More than one visitor to Gournia has commented on how small the houses are; but think of other primitive settlements of this era and then look at Gournia as a whole. Here are block after block of dwellings where men lived and worked, roads and steps that they climbed, urns and implements that they used, a square where they gathered to conduct their affairs, altars where they worshipped. True, it is all rather crude and cramped. But it is basically familiar: Gournia is the prototype of European civic life.

For a last striking impression of Gournia, continue along the main road to the east some few hundred metres to where the road begins to climb up to a pass; if you halt about halfway up and look back, you will see Gournia spread out like a great spider's web across the slopes.

[21 km.] After going through this narrow pass you emerge to look down at the harbour of the little port of Pakhia Ammos. To your right as you descend is a large stone villa. This was constructed earlier this century by Richard Seager, when he was excavating in eastern Crete. An American of independent means, there are tales of grand parties which he gave in his villa with dozens of distinguished guests. At the news of still greater 'finds' in Egypt he went there to dig, caught some disease and died in 1925, still in his prime, shortly after his return to Crete. The Germans occupied the villa during the war; you can still see signs of their occupation.

[22 km.] **Pakhia Ammos** is a port of call for local coastal shipping. Tomatoes and olives are cultivated on the rich plain behind the harbour. Minoan cemeteries were found scattered over the plain, but there is nothing of interest to the non-specialist. In the town are several eating-places, as well as inns where you can get a bed for around Drs 20 a night.

Just outside Pakhia Ammos, you could take a road south across the island for 16 km. to **Ierapetra** (p. 256).

[28 km.] Continuing along the Sitia road you come to the village of **Kavousi**, set in a valley with the peak of Mount Thrifti rising above. There is a small site dating from post-Minoan times near Kavousi, but it is of interest only to experts.

The next stretch of road – from Kavousi to Sitia – has been called the 'Riviera of Crete', with its slopes and tiers of orchards and the villages clinging to the hills. The road, too, certainly reminds one of a 'Corniche' with its everlasting twists and turns.

[39 km.] The mountain village of **Lastros**.

[44 km.] At the village of **Sfaka** there is a side road to the left leading north in 7 km. to the village of **Mokhlos** on the coast; off shore are the islands of *Mokhlos* and *Psira* (p. 255), and a boat can usually be hired in the village to take you to them.

[47 km.] **Tourloti**, another mountain village.

[56 km.] **Mesa Mouliana.**

[58 km.] **Exo Mouliana.** This area is famous for its red wine. There are also some beehive tombs where finds were made of swords and bronze objects.

[64 km.] At **Khamezi** the remains of an oval house from the middle Minoan period were found. As this is the only oval-shaped Minoan structure that has been found, some scholars think that it may have been some sort of sanctuary rather than a house. Khamezi is also the village where it is believed that the seventeenth-century poet Cornaros may have been born, since his family are known to have lived there.

After passing Khamezi you see the Bay of Sitia spread out before you: in the distance stretches the north-east extremity of Crete – Cape Sidheros – with the islands known as the Dionysiadhes to the north-west of the cape.

[74 km.] You descend to the coast at **Sitia**.

SITIA

Sitia is a travel-poster version of a quiet little Mediterranean port, with cafés along the harbour and the air of an isolated terminal. It is also a jumping-off point for several interesting excursions into the easternmost reaches of Crete.

Population 5,521.
Sea connections
See p. 34.
Hotels
Class C : *Crystal.*
Class D : *Mysson.*
          Praisos.
Restaurants
The usual collection of eating-places.
Swimming
There is a sandy beach, with cabins, just east of the town.
Buses
There is a regular service westwards to Iraklion via Gournia and Ayios Nikolaos. There are also buses to Ierapetra and to villages in the district, including Palaikastro, Ano Zakros and Maronia (for Praisos) ; a list is posted outside the bus office opposite the port. There is also a summer service to Toplou Monastery, Itanos and Vai.

PRINCIPAL SIGHTS

Gently sloping to the sea, crowned by a few remains of the Venetian fort, Sitia has little of the glory that the Venetians projected for it : Sitia was to be the fourth of the great coastal cities but never quite became one. The Venetians themselves recognized its failings and dismantled much of the fort, carrying the cannons off to other cities. There was a small castle and a rector's palace, but when the Turks took over these fell into decay along with the fort. Two churches remain, one in the form of a Greek cross and the other in

Venetian style, with three naves. Perhaps Sitia's greatest claim to fame is as the home of Vincenzo Cornaros, the seventeenth-century author of the master-works of the Cretan literary renaissance (p. 97).

Today the chief source of income for the region is the *sultanina* – the raisin. The people are mild and genial – a far cry from their brawling relatives in Sfakia. Incidentally, this part of Crete was occupied by the Italians during the Second World War.

Sitia has provided the name of this region and nome: 'Lasithi' is a corruption of La Sitia, the Venetians' name for their settlement. Before the coming of the Venetians, this eastern region had the reputation of being the home of the 'Eteocretans' – the 'true' or indigenous Cretans. It is claimed that with the arrival of the Dorians after the break-up of the Minoan–Mycenaean civilization, some native Cretans retired to these eastern hills where they preserved their language and culture in some 'pure' form. As we shall see when we discuss some of these eastern sites, some traditional modes survived; but in general no modern scholars really believe that the 'pure Minoans' – whoever they would be – linger on in Lasithi.

EXCURSIONS FROM SITIA

Kato Zakros

The discovery of a Minoan palace at Zakros is one of the most exciting archaeological finds in recent years. Owing to the condition of the roads in this part of Crete it is a long day's trip from Sitia. However, if you were prepared to camp or to trust to local hospitality, you could combine it with visits to the Monastery of Toplou and other sights described below (p. 266).

Route
Following the coast road eastwards out of Sitia, after 19 km. you arrive at Palaikastro (p. 267); here you turn south, winding up through a pass and through several villages such as Khokhlakes and Kellaria until you come to Ano Zakros [39 km.]. The road continues descending to the coast at Kato Zakros [48 km.], where the site is located.

Bus
There is a bus from Sitia to Ano Zakros, which would still leave a 9 km. walk down to the site.
Accommodation
You can get simple overnight accommodation in the villages of Ano and Kato Zakros.

[15 km.] A turning to the left leads up in 4 km. to the *Monastery of Toplou* (p. 267).

[19 km.] **Palaikastro** (p. 267). Take a right turn at the centre of the village.

[39 km.] Having turned south, after driving through the mountains you arrive at the village of **Ano Zakros** (*ano* = upper; *kato* = lower); this is the end of the bus line and has good spring water and a Class E hotel as well as an inn. From this village a small road leads down to the coast; it passes through fertile fields and olive groves and another mountain pass. Then, to the left, you see the rocky cliffs that have now come to be known as 'The Valley of the Dead' because of the ancient tombs and burials discovered there. The road descends in curves to the sea, with the Bay of Kato Zakros in the distance and bananas and olives growing on the flat coastal plain.

[48 km.] You arrive at the little village of **Kato Zakros**. Here you can get simple meals and beds, and enjoy the fine bathing as well as the excavations. These are just to the left of the road into the village, a few hundred metres back from the coast.

HISTORY OF KATO ZAKROS

Kato Zakros was first explored in 1901 under the direction of the British archaeologist D. G. Hogarth. He turned up some small houses, with finds of potsherds and seal impressions, but concluded that it had been little more than a Minoan port of call for ships between Crete and Africa and Asia Minor. That seemed to dispose of the site. Then, just before the Second World War, some gold objects found their way into the collection of Dr Giamalakis; they were said to have been hoarded by a peasant who had worked on the original dig under Hogarth. In 1945 the Greeks supported an archaeological survey of the sites in eastern Crete, and Nicholas Platon took a special interest in Kato Zakros. In subsequent years several finds of stone and other objects convinced Dr Platon that there must have been more than a little port here. In 1961 he sank a trial trench and turned up still more evidence of an ambitious settlement. Meanwhile, Leon Pomerance, an American with an interest in ancient art and archaeology, came across Platon's statement in the museum guide that there were still important Minoan remains to be dug on Crete. He confronted Platon, who countered with Kato Zakros; Pomerance offered to help finance the project and digging began in the autumn of 1962. Excavations have continued each autumn since then, financed by the Greek government as well as by Pomerance, and the result has been the unearthing of the fourth great Minoan palace and all its treasures.

DESCRIPTION OF SITE

The ruins visible date from the period between 1600 and 1500 B.C., and it is now clear that this site – whatever its name at that time – was a prosperous and important 'royal' centre as well as an important trading centre. As such it must have been the major transmitter and sustainer of the high Minoan culture in eastern Crete and it would seem to have been the peer of Phaestos and Mallia. Dr Platon estimates that the total complex covered at least 8,000 square m., with anywhere from 200 to 300 rooms on two to three storeys. Excavations so far have revealed that it conforms to all the other features of the Minoan palace-sites – the large main court, the various chambers, the cult and religious rooms, the royal areas, the stairways, the workrooms and store-rooms. Unfortunately most of this must be imagined by the average visitor, since only the lower parts of the structure are being found intact, and it seems unlikely that it can ever be 'restored', even to the extent that Phaestos is.

However, the reason for its levelling is also the cause of our great gain from the site. It was destroyed in a sudden catastrophe – possibly an earthquake followed by fire, possibly the eruption of Santorini and the resultant tidal wave (now credited by many scholars with the destruction of Knossos and the other centres about 1450 B.C.). Whatever happened, it must have driven away any people whom it did not trap; the complete destruction, possibly together with the site's isolation, meant that it alone of the great Minoan palaces remained unreconstructed – and, more important, unplundered. And this has meant that treasures are being found at Kato Zakros in an unusual number, condition and value. In one store-room some five hundred large *pithoi* were found, many painted; in the 'archives' were found clay tablets with Linear A script (one of the few such finds outside Ayia Triadha); and in the treasure room, or cult repository, some fifty-five stone vessels – quite incredible in the diversity of their forms and decorations – were found, along with an equal number of ceramic pieces. Also found here were many metal artifacts, including a large saw used for cutting stone, cast-iron tools and some fine swords; a dark stone capital of a column, the first such to be found except for the representations in frescoes; large copper ingots and ivory tusks, indicative of trade; traces of frescoes; and quantities of vases, pitchers, pots, jugs and other vessels. All these things may now be seen in the Iraklion museum (p. 127). In general, it might be said that, although individual pieces have their intrinsic aesthetic value or add to our knowledge, the site and finds at Kato Zakros are serving to confirm, rather than change, our previous image of Minoan Crete.

There was a city settlement around this palace, too, and excavations may ultimately turn up still more from the site. Interestingly, the surrounding area was occupied for some thousand years after the catastrophe, which makes it still more of a mystery why the palace was not plundered. As it was, the palace lay under only a relatively shallow cover of earth. All in all, Kato Zakros has been further evidence that Crete is a place where legends are born – and there is no reason why excavations in the years to come should not produce still more.

Toplou, Palaikastro, Vai and Itanos

This expedition takes in the isolated Monastery of Toplou and minor remains at Palaikastro and Itanos (known as Erimoupolis, the deserted city). For many people the greatest attraction will be the beautiful palm-fringed beach at Vai. Some of these places could be included in an expedition to Kato Zakros (p. 263).

Route
Follow the coast road eastwards out of Sitia, arriving after 15 km. at a left fork for the Monastery of Toplou. If instead you proceed straight on for a further 4 km. you arrive at Palaikastro, from where a road leads north in about 10 km. to Itanos and Vai.
Bus
There is a bus service to Palaikastro from Sitia; you could get off at the turning to Toplou (4 km. walk). There is a summer bus service to Toplou, Vai and Itanos.
Sea
Another way to get round to these sites would be to hire a boat at Sitia and put in at various coves, from which you would then have to make some overland treks.

[15 km.] Following the coast road eastwards out of Sitia, you arrive at a fork to the left which takes you up a track in about 4 km. to the *Monastery of Toplou.*

Founded some time in the fourteenth to fifteenth centuries, the original building was burnt down; it was rebuilt in 1718 and named Toplou by the Turks – their word for 'cannon', since, it is said, the monastery was armed with one. It has the appearance of a fortified castle and has indeed been an important centre for resistance and refugees from the occupation of the Turks to the Second World War. The Panayia Akrotiriani – 'Virgin of the Cape' – is worshipped here. On the façade of the chapel is an ancient plaque commemorating a treaty between Egypt and the Cretan realm of Itanos-Ierapytna (circa 70 B.C.). Within are some valuable icons: one in particular, by Ioannis Cornaros, dating from the eighteenth century, depicts the creation of the world and scenes from the Bible – a masterpiece of miniature work, crowded with figures and scenes.

What makes a visit to Toplou really worth while, besides the distinctive architecture of the monastery showing Venetian influence, is the primitive isolation of its situation. The monastery is also noted for its hospitality to strangers and wayfarers. Indeed, it is reputed to be one of the richest monasteries in Greece as it owns much land in the region.

From Toplou a dirt track leads overland north-eastwards towards the sea and after about 8 km. joins the road from Palaikastro to Itanos and Vai (see below).

[19 km.] Having returned to the main road from Sitia, however, from the Toplou fork you proceed another 4 km. eastwards to arrive at the village of **Palaikastro**. Some 2½ km. down a dirt road leading to the sea is a pleasant beach. In this area were found the remains of a Minoan settlement, and also minor settlements from the Geometric period to Hellenistic times. Excavations have shown that Palaikastro must have been an important commercial settlement somewhere in the late Minoan period. It was larger than Gournia, but because it was more spread out the natives have carried off the stone over the centuries and the remains do not offer much to the amateur. The town lay close to the shore, at the foot of the hills; with its acropolis rising above it, the curving bay and lofty headlands, it must have been an imposing place. Excavations revealed a well-paved main street, lined by houses and shops; in one were found weights, jars, a sink and a drain. There was a many-roomed palace of large stones, the seat of some local prince. Palaikastro was one of the few places on Crete to be rebuilt after the great disaster of 1400 B.C. Minoan cemeteries were also found, dotted over the plain, and a Minoan sanctuary discovered in a rock shelter in the near-by hill of Petsofa.

Among the most important finds of the later periods were remains of an Archaic-Hellenic temple, with a fragment of a frieze, and a *stele* – memorial column – inscribed with a hymn to Dhiktaian Zeus (now in the Archaic Room (XIX) of the Iraklion museum). The carving on the *stele* only dates from the third century A.D., but the hymn itself is centuries older and reveals the religious sentiments of an earlier age. Other valuable finds were bronze tripods, shields, terracotta figurines, ivory plaques, and a great quantity of pottery and vases.

[27 km.] Having taken a dirt road to the north from the village of Palaikastro you come in 8 km. to a fork in the road. The right branch brings you in about 1½ km., passing through the spectacular palm grove of *Vai*, to a fine tropical-looking beach, itself ringed with palm trees. There is a café that serves simple meals in the summer.

If instead you take the left branch, you will proceed north to reach, again in about 1½ km., the ancient site of *Itanos* – known to the local people as Erimoupolis, 'the deserted city'. Originally a Minoan site, it remained inhabited into Roman and Byzantine times. Only a few fragmentary remains are now to be seen – the wall of an Hellenistic acropolis, the base of a Roman statue, and parts of an early Christian church. As so often on Crete, it is the setting of the site that justifies the trip: the near-by sea, the black headland, Cape Sidheros to the north.

Praisos

This post-Minoan site, and a few other places en route, might make a day's excursion from Sitia, but would be of interest mainly to specialists.

Route
Follow the road south from Sitia for Khandras; after 13 km. turn left at Epano Episkopi for Nea Praisos [17 km.].
Bus
There is a bus service from Sitia as far as Maronia, which would leave a walk of some 7 km. overland to Praisos.

As you leave Sitia you pass near some remains of a Minoan 'farm' of about 1600 B.C.

[3 km.] Arriving at the village of **Piskokephalo** (where were found many votive statuettes in a sacred cave), you could turn off to the left for Zou, near where there are remains of a Minoan 'farm' of about the same period as the one on the edge of Sitia. Taking this turning, you proceed for about 1 km. to **Kato Episkopi**, where you turn right at a fork and continue for roughly another 2 km. to **Zou**. Little of interest has survived, although tools were found here.

[4 km.] Having kept on to the south past Piskokephalo, after about 1 km. there is a right turn that would bring you in about 5 km. to *Akhlada*, a small Minoan settlement. A good specimen of a domed tomb was excavated here.

Incidentally, though few will care to make such a trip, it is possible to go on from Akhlada west and south through the Sitia Range, heading for Stavrokhorion and going down to the south coast at Koutsouras, and then along the south coast to Ierapetra (p. 256). It is a scenic ride of about 65 km., but the road is not good; a map and confidence are required.

[10 km.] Continuing on the main road south from Sitia, you arrive at **Maronia**.

[13 km.] At **Epano Episkopi** there is a track to the left which winds its way up in about 4 km. to **Nea Praisos**, the location of the site of Praisos (also known as Vaveloi).

Praisos

The ancient city of Praisos, located on the summit of a conical hill, is considered to be one of the chief post-Minoan settlements; as such, it was the centre of the so-called Eteocretans – Minoans who retreated from the Dorians. Only jumbled stones remain: a Minoan farm, tombs, the Hellenistic acropolis and a late Hellenistic house of some size hint at the fairly continuous settlement and prosperity of the site from Minoan through Hellenistic times. Here also were found three inscriptions with Greek characters but recording a non-Hellenic language. The inscriptions date from somewhere between 600 and 300 B.C. and have been attributed to the Eteocretans. The American scholar Cyrus Gordon has proposed that the language is of the Semitic family – and, what is more, a direct descendant of the Semitic language that he claims to have deciphered as the language of Linear A. Not all scholars accept such claims.

SELECTED BIBLIOGRAPHY

This is only the cream of the books about Crete. The latest editions (often revised and enlarged) are listed; several have also been published in paperback and some are once more available in facsimile hard-cover editions.

GENERAL

Raymond Matton, *La Crète au cours des siècles* (Institut Français d'Athènes, 1957): the best survey of Crete's complete history.

R. W. Hutchinson, *Prehistoric Crete* (Penguin, 1962): a handy survey of the island to the coming of the Romans.

Michael Smith, *The Great Island* (Longmans, 1965): an interesting mixture of personal travel, folklore and history of the last 2,000 years.

Robert Graves, *The Greek Myths* (Penguin, 1957): a vital source for understanding the essence of Crete.

Mary Renault, *The King Must Die* (Longmans, 1958; Pantheon, 1958; Four Square; Pocket Books) and *The Bull From The Sea* (Longmans, 1962; Pantheon, 1962; Four Square; Pocket Books): imaginative reconstructions of the Theseus legend and Minoan Crete.

Nikos Kazantzakis, *Zorba the Greek* (Simon & Schuster, 1952; Cassirer, 1959; Faber Paperback, 1961; Ballantine), *Freedom and Death* (Simon & Schuster, 1956; Cassirer, 1966; Faber Paperback, 1966; Ballantine), *The Odyssey: A Modern Sequel* (Secker & Warburg, 1959; Simon & Schuster, 1962) and *Christ Recrucified* (Cassirer, 1960; Faber Paperback, 1962): four striking works by perhaps the strongest modern Cretan 'voice'. *Report to Greco* (Cassirer; Faber, 1965) is Kazantzakis's autobiography.

Leland Allbaugh, *Crete: A Case Study of an Underdeveloped Area* (Princeton University Press, 1953): a slightly dated, but still valid, glimpse into the way many modern Cretans live.

MINOAN CRETE: HISTORY AND ARCHAEOLOGY

Arthur Evans, *The Palace of Minos* (Macmillan, 1921–36; Biblo & Tannen): despite all that has happened since, still the seminal work; fascinating to browse through.

—— —— *Knossos Fresco Atlas* (Gregg, 1968).

J. D. S. Pendlebury, *The Archaeology of Crete* (Methuen, 1939; Biblo & Tannen; Norton 1965): a good objective survey of sites and finds up through the Roman period.

—— —— *Handbook to the Palace of Minos* (Parrish, 1954; Dufour).

James W. Graham, *The Palaces of Crete* (Princeton University Press, 1962): a solid analysis of the Minoan palaces.

John Chadwick, *The Decipherment of Linear B* (Cambridge University Press, 1958; Vintage): an excellent account of Michael Ventris's work on the Minoan script, by one who worked with him.

L. P. Palmer, *Mycenaeans and Minoans* (Knopf, 1964; Faber): controversial, but one of several recent reappraisals of the Minoan materials.

—— —— (with John Boardman), *On the Knossos Tablets* (Oxford University Press, 1963).

Nicholas Platon, *Crete* (World, 1966; Frederick Muller, 1966): especially valuable for its account of the new Kato Zakros site by the discoverer and excavator.

Leonard Cottrell, *The Bull of Minos* (Evans, 1953; Holt, Rinehart, 1958; Pan; Grosset): a readable account of the lives, work, and worlds of Schliemann and Evans.

—— —— *Crete: Island of Mystery* (Prentice-Hall, 1965).

CRETE SINCE THE MINOANS

R. F. Willetts, *Ancient Crete: A Social History* (Routledge, 1965; University of Toronto, 1965): Post-Minoan to Roman Crete by the authority on the period.

A. A. Vasiliev, *History of the Byzantine Empire* (University of Wisconsin Press, 1952; Peter Smith): Crete has several mentions in this standard work.

William Miller, *Essays on the Latin Orient* (Cambridge University Press, 1921): some curious sidelights on medieval Crete.

Deno J. Geanakoplos, *Greek Scholars in Venice* (Oxford University Press, 1962; Harvard University Press, 1962): still more curious sidelights on late-medieval and Renaissance Crete.

Edward S. Forster, *A Short History of Modern Greece* (Methuen, 1958): Crete plays its part in this standard work.

Prince George of Greece, *The Cretan Drama* (Speller, 1959): events at the turn of the century narrated by one of the major participants.

Alan Clark, *The Fall of Crete* (Anthony Blond, 1962; Morrow, 1962): an interesting account of the battle of Crete in the Second World War.

George Psychoundakis, *The Cretan Runner* (Murray, 1955; Transatlantic, 1955): a fine account of the Cretan–British resistance operations by one of the participants.

CRETE AND THE ARTS

Marinatos and Hirmer, *Crete and Mycenae* (Thames & Hudson, 1960; Abrams, 1960).

Reverdin and Hoegler, *Crete and Its Treasures* (Viking, 1961).

Friedrich Matz, *Crete and Early Greece* (Methuen, 1962; Crown, 1965).

S. Alexiou, N. Platon, H. Guanella, and Von Matt, *Ancient Crete* (Thames & Hudson, 1967; Praeger, 1968).

These are four of the most splendid illustrated accounts, mainly focused on Minoan Crete.

Romilly J. H. Jenkins, *Dedalica* (Cambridge University Press, 1936): Crete plays a crucial role in this analysis of Archaic sculpture.

Constantine Kalokiris, 'La peinture murale byzantine de l'île de Crète' in *Cretica Chronica* (1954): an introduction to the Byzantine frescoes on Crete.

Giuseppe Gerola, *Monumenti veneti nell'isola di Creta* (Venice, 1905–32): the definitive work on the Venetian structures on Crete.

M. J. Manoussakas, 'La littérature crétoise a l'époque vénitienne' in *L'Hellénisme Contemporain* (mars–juin 1955): the most complete survey of Cretan literature under the Venetians.

F. H. Marshall, *Three Cretan Plays* (Oxford University Press, 1929): translations of three of the Cretan–Venetian dramas.

James A. Notopoulos, 'Homer and Cretan Dramatic Poetry: A Study in Comparative Oral Poetry' in *American Journal of Philology* (July 1952): a glimpse into the oral folk culture of Crete.

CRETE AND RELIGION

Martin Nilsson, *The Minoan–Mycenaean Religion and Its Survival in Greek Religion* (Gleerup, 1950): the standard work on the subject.

—— —— *Greek Folk Religion* (Harper, 1961; Torchbooks).

R. F. Willetts, *Cretan Cults and Festivals* (Barnes and Noble, 1962; Routledge, 1962): a complete survey of mainly post-Minoan religious world before Christianity.

John C. Lawson, *Modern Greek Folklore and Ancient Greek Religion* (Cambridge University Press, 1910; University Books): a minor classic that traces the relationships between the two traditions.

A. Megas, *Greek Calendar Customs* (Athens, 1958): a handy guide to the holy days and traditions.

TRAVELS ON CRETE

Joseph de Tournefort, *A Voyage into the Levant* (London, 1718): the English translation of the French (Paris, 1717) classic.

Robert Pashley, *Travels in Crete* (Murray, 1837): still the one that travels best.

Capt. T. A. B. Spratt, *Travels and Researches in Crete* (J. van Voorst, 1865): another good encounter with nineteenth-century Crete.

Aubyn Trevor-Battye, *Camping in Crete* (Witherby & Co., 1913): a naturalist's adventures on Crete.

Ralph Brewster, *The Island of Zeus; Wanderings in Crete* (1939).

Henry Miller, *The Colossus of Maroussi* (Heinemann, 1960; Penguin; New Directions): strange as it may seem, Miller and Crete make a great match.

Xan Fielding, *The Stronghold* (Secker & Warburg, 1953): an ex-resistance fighter returns to live on Crete.

Claude Dervenn, *La Crète vivante* (Horizons de France, 1957): a sensitive traveller explores Crete.

PRACTICAL

Travellers' Greek Phrase-Book (Jonathan Cape, 1965; Bobbs Merrill).

Map of Crete (1 : 300,000) (Mathioulakis Publications, Athens).

INDEX

SEA OF CRETE

DIA IS.

CAPE STAVROS

AYIA PELAGHIA

△ Melidhoni Cave

FODHELE

AKHLADA

Savarhiana Conv.

GENI GHAVE

DHAMASTA

ROGDHIA

LIMIN KHERSONISON

GULF OF MALLIA

Ma

NIDHA PLAIN

MARATHOS

IRAKLION

Amnisos

GOURNES

STALIS

MALLIA

Axos

ANOYIA

Tylisos

Knossos

Eileithyia

Cave

Nirou

Khani

KALO KHORIO

MOKHOS

MTS.

△ MT.

PSILORITIS

2456 m

Idha Cave

KROUSSENAS

PATSIDES

MT.

IOUKTAS

△

Phourni

ARKHANES

KOUNAVOI

PEZA

AVDOU

POTAMIES

GONIES

KRASI

Kera M

Ion.

RFOURAS

Kamares

Cave

APODHOULOU

VORIZA

Vrondisi Mon.

ZAROS

AYIA VARVARA

PRINIAS

AVYENIKI

Vathypetro

AYII PARASKIE

VONI

KASTELLI-

PEDHIADHOS

PIGI

ASKI

XIDAS

LASITHI PLAIN

PSYKHRO

AV

Valsamonero Ch.

YERYERI

ARKALOKHORION

I

Dhiktaian Cave

AVRA

SOS

VOROI

Gortyna

PANAYIA

N

TIMBAKI

Phaestos

MOIRES

AYII DHEKA

MIROPOLIS

KOUSTOULIANA

VAGIONIA

KHARAKAS

PYRGOS

MTS.

ANO VIANNOS

Ayia Moni Mon.

DHIKT

PEFKO

Ayia Triadha

PLATANOS

PLORA

LOUKIA

Keratokambos

ARVI

PITSIDIA

POMBIA

MESSARA PLAIN

MATALA

PIGAIDAKIA

MIAMOU

VASILIKI

ASTEROUSIA

ANTISKARION

LENDAS

Leben

Kaloi Limenes

Koumasa

MEDITERRANEAN SEA